Cover illustrations: the gathering of Hungarian pilgrims at Csíksomlyó,
Transylvania, Romania, 26 May 2007. Photographs by Zsófia Erdei.

Nándor Dreisziger

Hungarians from ancient times to 1956

biographical and historical essays

ACILE
PEGE
ET
LE
GE

LEGAS

New York   Ottawa   Toronto

Library and Archives Canada Cataloguing in Publication

Dreisziger, N. F. (Nándor F.), 1940-

Hungarians from ancient times to 1956: biographical and historical essays/ by Nándor Dreisziger

Includes bibliographical references
ISBN 978-1-894508-96-4

1. Hungary — Biography. 2. Hungary – History. I. Title

DB906.D74 2007   943.9'0099   C2007-904887-0

The author would like to thank the Hungarian Helicon Society of Toronto for their support of the publication of this volume.

For further information and for orders:

http://www.legaspublishing.com

LEGAS
P. O. Box 040328   3 Wood Aster Bay   2908 Dufferin Street
Brooklyn, New York Ottawa, Ontario   Toronto, Ontario
USA 11204   K2R 1B3   M6B 3S8

Printed and bound in Canada

For Zsóka

Contents

Preface

The idea for this book was born after I published a series of popular history articles in the Toronto Hungarian newspaper *Magyar Élet* and its periodic English-language supplement *Hungarian Life*. In fact, originally I wanted to call the book "Hungarian Life" but discarded the idea as very few of the studies dealt with life in Hungary—although some of the papers touch on the experiences of Hungarian communities in the New World. I am currently doing research on life in some of Hungary's villages but the results of that research will have to wait at least a few years before they will be ready for publication. In addition to the studies that appeared in *Magyar Élet* this volume includes several articles that are based on papers that I had given at conferences or published in little-known or only locally-known periodicals. The provenance of each essay is usually indicated in the footnotes.

I have been involved in Hungarian studies ever since the mid-1960s. In one of my graduate courses at the University of Toronto, in the history of international relations that I took from the late Harold I. Nelson, I had to find a topic for a year-long essay project. In looking through the holdings of the U. of T.'s library, I came across the then newly published diplomatic papers dealing with Hungarian international relations on the eve of the Second World War.[1] I used some of the early volumes of this series to research an oversized essay.

Having been bitten by the "Hungarian bug" I continued my exploration of mid-twentieth century Hungarian history in graduate courses I took with historian Peter Brock who had joined the U. of T.'s History Department not long before I started my graduate studies, and political scientist H. Gordon Skilling. Eventually I completed the then newly-established diploma program in Russian and East European Studies.[2] I was the first history student to do so. The year was 1967. For my diploma thesis I expanded my above-mentioned essay on Hungarian diplomacy.

---

[1] The series *Diplomáciai iratok Magyarország külpolitikájához, 1936-1945*) [Diplomatic documents on Hungary's foreign policy, 1936-1945], general ed. L. Zsigmond (Budapest: Akadémiai Kiadó, 1962f).

[2] On this see H. Gordon Skilling, *The Education of a Canadian: My Life as a Scholar and Activist* (Montreal: McGill-Queen's Press, 2000), chapter 10.

It was at this time that Toronto's Hungarian Helicon Society announced an essay competition. In response to this I produced still another version of my study and sent it to the Society's special committee struck for the adjudication of the works submitted. I won the competition. Next I learned that the Society decided to publish my work in book form. The result was the volume *Hungary's Way to World War II*. I recall Gordon Skilling telling me at the time that I should convince the Society to publish my book through the University of Toronto Press. Knowing that the Society wanted to see the book published through the printing establishment of one of its long-standing members, I didn't take up Skilling's advice. In this way the book was printed rather than published and I never got any editorial advice beyond the few comments that I had received as a student from Professors Nelson and Skilling, and the members of the Helicon Society's prize committee. The latter were knowledgeable and helpful but had no experience in scholarly publishing. Years later I realized that the book was a "premature publication"—something from which I have been trying to save young scholars in recent years.

One Hungarian project spawned another. In the early 1970s a member of the Helicon Society, the late Ferenc Harcsár who was a scientist but had a keen interest in Hungarian studies, decided to launch a journal dealing with Hungary on the pattern of the revived *Hungarian Quarterly* and some other ephemeral journals that had appeared in the Hungarian Diaspora in the post-World War II period. To help edit this journal he approached me. By then I was a member of the Royal Military College's Department of History, surviving on one-year appointments. I accepted with the proviso that as soon as a more experienced editor could be found, I would resign. Some three-and-a-half decades later I am still editing the *Hungarian Studies Review*. Work on this journal exposed me to Hungarian studies in a manner that could not have been equalled unless I moved to the United States—to Bloomington Indiana (Indiana University) or to New York City (Columbia University)—to undertake still another doctoral program, this time in Hungarian history. Such a move would have cost me a lot of time and money and would have probably reduced my chances of finding an academic position in Canada.

In the mid-1970s still another Hungarian studies venture came my way. At that time the newly established Multiculturalism Directorate of the Government of Canada was recruiting authors for the writing of histories of Canada's immigrant groups. With a small team of other Hungarian specialists I applied to undertake the project of writing the volume on Canada's Hungarians. I was to write the chapters on Hungarian immigrant life in Central and Eastern Canada, while Professor Kovacs of the University of Regina those on Hungarians in the Canadian West. Professors Paul Bődy and Bennett Kovrig were to write introductory chapters on Hungarian history and emigration from Hungary respectively. The contract was awarded to us and the result was, nearly a decade later, the volume *Struggle and Hope: The Hungarian-Canadian Experience*.[3] In the end, Professor Kovacs's chapter covered his original subject only until 1918 and I told the story of the entire Hungarian-Canadian community since the First World War. The chapters and conclusions I wrote for this book constitute some of my best research and writing efforts. Most of this monograph's knowledgeable reviewers had only praise for it. The book was followed by numerous papers that I wrote in part from the research I had done for this book, and in part from subsequent researches.

Other Hungarian projects I undertook in the ensuing years stemmed mainly from my work connected to my role as editor—and for a while co-editor, with Professor George Bisztray of the U. of T.'s Hungarian program—of the *Hungarian Studies Review*. One of these was a collection of papers that appeared in 1998 under the title *Hungary in the Age of Total War, 1938-1948*. Another was the 2001 volume of the journal, a special issue entitled *Hungary, 1001-2001: A Millennial Retrospection*.

The collection of articles in this volume covers a great variety of subjects. I do not have expertise based on primary research in all of these fields. Nevertheless, I believe that my decades of exposure to the study of Hungarian history allows me to venture into fields not entirely my own.

Through my involvement in various Hungarian projects over the years I have become indebted to people who gave me information, advice and encouragement. Mentioning them all would probably fill several pages. Accordingly, I will list, in an eclectic manner, only a few.

In my researches concerning Hungarians in Canada at what used to

---

[3] Published by McClelland and Stewart for the Multicultural Directorate, in the series *The History of Canada's Peoples*. The book is available in French as well: *Lutte et Espoir L'expérience des Canadiens hongrois* (Ottawa, [1983]).

be the National Archives of Canada had been helped by archivists including Myron Momryk and Arthur Grenke. Over the decades many scholars acted as knowledgeable "resource persons" for me in my Hungarian projects as well as other ones, especially those related to "ethnic" studies. It is too late to thank some of them personally as they had passed away, yet I do so for the record: Howard Palmer of the University of Calgary, Robert Blumstock of McMaster University, Robert Harney of the University of Toronto, Thomas Szendrey of Gannon University, György Litván of the 1956 Institute in Budapest, among others.

Still others are alive fortunately: in Canada the already-mentioned George (Gyuri) Bisztray, Olivér Botár (University of Manitoba), Andor Tari (late of the University of Guelph), and Judy Drache (formerly Judy Young of the Multiculturalism Directorate in Ottawa); in the United States S. Béla Várdy (Duqesne University), István Deák (Columbia University), Peter Pastor (Montclair State University), Thomas Sakmyster (University of Cincinnati), Susan Glanz (St. John's University); in the United Kingdom Mark Pittaway (Open University); and many in Hungary only a few of whom can be mentioned: János Barta, Zoltán Fejős, Tibor Frank, Géza Jeszenszky, Mária Palasik, Géza Pálffy, Ignác Romsics and László Veszprémy. In recent years a few young (and some not so young) scholars and editors have joined this group, among them Béla Bodó, Deborah Cornelius, Éva Kossuth, Jason Kovacs, Kenneth McRobbie, Ágnes Somorjai, Judith Szapor, and in Hungary Tibor Glant, Krisztian Ungváry, Balázs Ablonzy, and the list could go on.

I owe much to people who had helped with the editing and/or managing the *Hungarian Studies Review* at various times in its history: Susan Papp-Aykler, Éva Tömöry, Margit Lovrics, Agotha Schwartz, Marlene Kadar, and especially Oliver Botar and George Bisztray. Denis Szabo of the Université de Montréal had been at times a great benefactor of the *HSR* — although he is probably unaware of the fact. Among the organizations that had at times supported the journal financially had been, at various times, the University of Toronto, cultural programs of both the Government of Ontario and the Government of Canada, the Széchenyi Society of Calgary, the Hungarian Studies Association of Canada and, of late, the Hungarian Studies Association (USA). In Hungary, the journal has been receiving support from the country's National Széchényi Library and the printing establishment of the Hungarian Academy of Sciences.

I also wish to acknowledge the financial help I received, in particular for the publication of this book, from the Helicon Society of Toronto.

Along with this support came the encouragement from several of the Society's members, above all from Margit Lovrics. It is perhaps befitting that the Helicon Society has helped in this undertaking as it had helped with the publication of my first monograph on a Hungarian subject.

Throughout the years and especially during the last two decades I also had help (and moral support) in my writing, editorial and other undertakings from my family. From my daughter Jessica since the late 1990s when she began honing her writing skills in English, and my wife Zsóka mainly when it came to corresponding with people in Hungarian—my formal training in the Magyar language ended when I left Hungary at the age of sixteen. Members of my family also put up with my frequent absences from family activities especially when one or another of my Hungarian projects crowded in on my otherwise also busy academic life. For their patience and understanding in these situations I have to express my appreciation.

Nándor Dreisziger
Kingston, Ontario, Canada
20 August 2007

Introduction

The first essay in this volume deals with a great Hungarian, the composer, ethnomusicologist and concert pianist Béla Bartók. Whether he is the greatest Hungarian of the modern age can be debated. If we are to judge greatness by the number of works that deal with the individual and are to be found in some North American university libraries, Bartók would probably win the prize. I have seen such libraries, they had more works by and about Bartók than they had books about Hungarian history.

The nineteenth century produced several candidates for the title "greatest Hungarian" of modern times. One of these was Lajos (Louis) Kossuth, the charismatic leader of the 1848-49 War of Independence against the House of Habsburg.[1] Kossuth was indeed a great leader, outstanding orator, an indefatigable worker and an inspirer of his countrymen. There seems to be evidence, however, that on occasion he didn't understand reality, that he didn't always realize that politics was the art of the possible. His contemporary, István Széchenyi, was more realistic in his assessment of Hungary's economic and international situation and was more enthusiastic about the idea of Hungary becoming a modernized country and playing an important role in a reorganized Habsburg monarchy. Perhaps the greatest Hungarian of the century was Ferenc Deák who was the principal author of the 1867 Compromise with Austria that gave Hungarians a prominent place within the reorganized Dual Monarchy and initiated an age of unprecedented economic development in the country.

In the realm of culture, probably the best-known Hungarian of the time was Franz or Ferenc Liszt, the composer and virtuoso pianist.[2] Liszt's ethnic German background, Austrian family name (originally spelled List), lack of knowledge of Hungarian, and devotion to music

---

[1] For the most comprehensive English-language political biography of Kossuth see István Deak, *The Lawful Revolution: Louis Kossuth and the Hungarians 1848-1849* (New York: Columbia University Press, 1979; paperback edition: London: Phoenix Press, 2001).

[2] On Liszt see the multi-volume biography by Alan Walker, *Franz Liszt* (New York: Alfred A. Knopf, 1983f). On Liszt's ethnic origin see the chapter in Vol. 1, entitled "Liszt's Family Background," (pp. 30-49). Franz Liszt always proclaimed himself Hungarian.

that was more international than authentically Hungarian, makes him more of a great figure in European rather than Magyar cultural history. In this respect Bartók can be considered much more of a representative of Hungary, even though he too was of ethnic German background on his mother's side.

Twentieth century Hungary is more devoid of great men. István Tisza, Hungary's Prime Minister for the first two years of World War I, was no doubt a statesman but his attachment to the old order and his support for a war that threatened the existence of his country, as well as that of the whole of Europe, makes him an unattractive a candidate for true greatness.[3] Some people, especially political militants (both the moderate and extremist kind), might point to Hungary's post-World War I revolutionary leaders, in particular Mihály (Michael) Károlyi or Béla Kun, as "great" men. History, however, judged the two otherwise. Today neither of them is seen as an effective politician, capable of judging the political situation, in Hungary and in Central Europe, with acumen. Both were out of touch with the country's masses.

The next leader Hungary had is equally controversial, both with the general public and with historians. He is Miklós (Nicholas) Horthy, the man who stood at the helm of Hungary's ship-of-state from 1920 to 1944. The admirers of this last admiral of the Austro-Hungarian Navy would point to the fact that he had brought stability to Hungary after a year of chaos, presided over the country's reconstruction after war and revolutions, curbed (after many delays) the influence of the right-radicals in the early 1920s and kept them from gaining control over the country in the 1930s. After the outbreak of the Second World War he helped to guide the country toward neutrality for nearly two years, restrained the influence of Nazi Germany even after Hungary's involvement in the war, made Hungary a relatively safe heaven for Jews and some refugees from Nazi-occupied countries, and, after the *Wehrmacht*

---

[3] Initially, in July of 1914 Tisza had opposed the idea of an Austro-Hungarian declaration of war on Serbia, believing that it was too risky and contrary to the interests of Hungary within the Dual Monarchy. Once the imperial government in Vienna decided on war, however, Tisza supported it. On Hungary of the times see Peter Pastor, "Hungary in World War I: The End of Historic Hungary," *Hungarian Studies Review*, 28, 1-2 (2001): 163-184; and in the same journal, Gabor Vermes, "Count István Tisza and the Preservation of the Old Order" 2, 1 (Spring, 1975): 33-42. See also Vermes's biography of Tisza: *István Tisza: the liberal vision and conservative statecraft of a Magyar nationalist* (New York: Columbia University Press, 1985).

occupied the country in March of 1944, at one point he used loyal elements of the military to stop the deportation of Jews. After an unsuccessful coup to defect from the Axis in October of the same year, Horthy and his family were themselves deported to a prison camp in Germany.

Horthy's detractors argue otherwise. They claim that rather than being a benevolent statesman he was a "bloody dictator" who in 1919-1920 orchestrated (rather than just tolerated) the terror inflicted on alleged and real participants (many of them Jews) of the 1919 revolutions by "White" officers' detachments.[4] They point to the reactionary nature of Hungary's interwar society; the introduction of anti-Semitic legislation both in the 1920's and, in a more comprehensive manner, starting with the late 1930s; the enthusiasm Horthy had shown at times for Hungary's increasing alignment with Nazi Germany; the aid Hungary provided for the Nazi war effort; his failure to resign when Hitler had Hungary occupied in 1944; and so on.

In this war of words it is difficult to see the real Horthy. His detractors had a great head-start because during the interwar years and especially after 1941 anti-Horthy propaganda was pervasive throughout Western Europe and the New World. The numerous intellectuals who fled Hungary in the interwar years had a lot to do with this situation. As we'll see in my article on Oscar Jaszi, they devoted much of their energies — and, in Jaszi's case, his considerable polemical skills — to denouncing the Horthy Regime. Particularly vocal was in this respect the Hungarian-language communist press in North America.[5] During the war itself, "Hungary bashing" became a favourite occupation of many Western intellectuals also.

Horthy has been judged very differently by historians as well. His biographers have been less disparaging of him than many of his contemporary critics.[6] Still they find much that is unattractive about him and the

---

[4] On the story of these detachments see Béla Bodó, "Militia Violence and State Power in Hungary, 1919-1922," *Hungarian Studies Review*, 33, 1-2 (2006): 121-56. Bodó argues that the White militia units were rogue elements of the military with an agenda of their own. They were eventually put out of action by the Hungarian government when their usefulness ended and their actions became an embarrassment to the country's elite.

[5] On this subject see Thomas L. Sakmyster, "A Communist Newspaper for Hungarian-Americans: The Strange World of the *Új Előre*," *Hungarian Studies Review*, 32, 1-2 (2005): 41-70. The Canadian equivalent of the *Új Előre*, was the *Kanadai Magyar Munkás*.

[6] Thomas Sakmyster, *Hungary's Admiral on Horseback: Miklós Horthy, 1918-*

regime he headed. To some extent the exception is that great British friend of Hungary, C.A. Macartney, who concluded about the Hungary of the Horthy Era that what happened to the country before and during the war was very much beyond the control of her leaders,[7] and in the mael-storm of the Second World War, the country Horthy presided over was more the drifting ship than one in command of her destiny.

If Horthy cannot be called a "great Hungarian" it might be asked if any of his contemporaries, the other members of Hungary's elite, can. There would be historians who would probably say yes and point to Count István Bethlen, Hungary's prime minister throughout much of the 1920s, and an advisor to Horthy right up to 1944. Bethlen was more of a polished speaker, writer and diplomat than Horthy. Yet he too, ended up a refugee from the Gestapo in his own country in 1944, only to end his life in a Soviet prison after the war.[8]

We might wonder at this point if post-1945 Hungary had any individuals who might be considered truly great. The man who ruled Hungary for much of the second half of the twentieth century, in fact for a few years longer than the era that has been named after Horthy, was János Kádár. He had his enthusiasts, and there are probably still some people in Hungary who recall the "Kádár Era" with fondness.[9] But, for

1944 (Boulder, CO: Eastern European Monographs; dist., New York: Columbia University Press, 1994); and Peter Gosztony (Péter Gosztonyi), *Miklós von Horthy: Admiral und Reichsverweser* (Göttingen: Musterschmidt, 1973), with a Hungarian edition: Péter Gosztonyi, *A Kormányzó, Horthy Miklós* [The Regent, Miklós Horthy] (Budapest: Téka, 1990). See also my writing on the subject in the book *Hungary in the Age of Total War, 1938-1948*, N.F. Dreisziger, ed. (New York: East European Monographs/Columbia University Press, 1998).

7 On the subject see C.A. Macartney, *October Fifteenth: A History of Modern Hungary, 1929-1944* (Edinburgh: Edinburgh University Press, 1957, 2nd edition, 1961), 2 vols. Published in the United States as *A History of Hungary, 1929-1944* (New York: Praeger, 1957).

8 On Bethlen see Ignác Romsics, *Bethlen István: Politikai Életrajz* [István Bethlen: A Political Biography] (Budapest: Magyarságkutató Intézet, 1991). A similarly tragic figure of contemporary Hungary is Count Pál Teleki, the Prime Minister who committed suicide when he realized that he wouldn't be able to prevent Hungary becoming involved headlong in Hitler's invasion of Yugoslavia in April of 1941. On Teleki see Balázs Ablonczy, *Teleki Pál* (Budapest: Osiris, 2005).

9 He had his admirers among ex-patriate Hungarians as well, even though the vast majority of them regarded him as a bloody dictator and traitor. One for-

most Hungarians, too much Magyar blood had soaked Kádár's hands for him to be ever considered a "great Magyar statesman." Many Hungarians would be much more willing to consider Imre Nagy, Kádár's 1956 nemesis, as a great man. However, Nagy's communist past and the fact that he never had a chance to preside over an independent Hungary for more than a few hours, prevent him from being a viable candidate for this honour, no matter how heroic his choice of death rather than compromise in the wake of the 1956 Revolution had been.[10]

Having not found a politician to fit the title "modern Hungary's greatest son" we are left with considering an artist, and Béla Bartók is probably the best candidate. I make my case for my choice in the rather long article which can be read in this volume.

The next article in the collection deals with Oscar Jaszi. He is attractive for me above all for his life-long advocacy of peace and co-operation among the peoples of central Eastern Europe. Actually, in this Jaszi shared sentiments with Bartók. Furthermore, Jaszi was an early advocate first of a Danubian confederation, to be followed by the federation of the whole of Europe. He was also a prophet. During the mid-1930s he prognosticated the coming of another world war. "And after the war" he continued, "will come the revolution" that will bring the "kolkhozes..." to East Central Europe, as well as the "dictatorship of the proletariat." "Not Europe but Asia will then rule in this part of the world..."[11]

After the Second World War Jaszi contemplated returning to Hungary. The communist takeover there dashed any such plans. In the

---

mer Arrow Cross supporter (the Arrow Cross was a party of right-radicals in pre-1945 Hungary) told me, after his visit to the Hungary of János Kádár, that Kádár had brought great prosperity to Hungary's villages and that he (as an Arrow Cross man) regretted only that Ferenc Szálasi (the one-time leader of the Arrow Cross) never got a chance to do the same. We know now that much of the prosperity Kádár had brought to Hungary was financed by western loans.

[10] On Nagy see János M. Rainer, János M. Rainer, *Nagy Imre: Politikai életrajz* [Imre Nagy: A Political Biography] (Budapest: 1956-os Intézet, 1996f), 2 vols. See also the same author's "1956—The Other Side of the Story, Five Documents from the Yeltsin File," *The Hungarian Quarterly*, 34 (Spring 1993): 100-114.

[11] In the 1934 Dec. 12 and 26 issues of the periodical *The Nation*. The article is entitled "War Germs in the Danube Basin." It is reprinted in Oscar Jászi, *Homage to Danubia*, ed. György Litván (Lanham, Maryland: Rowman & Littlefield, 1995), pp. 77-86. The quotation is from p. 85.

interwar period he could not go back to Hungary because he was seen by Hungary's ruling elite as a leftist radical, after 1948 he could not go back because Hungary's communist leaders saw in him an agent of American imperialism. He did go back for a visit in the late 1940s but he died in exile without being able to pay still another visit to Hungary. After the collapse of communism in 1989 his remains were re-patriated to his homeland, as he had requested in his will in the mid-1950s.

What Jaszi and Bartók shared, beyond their concern for Hungary's ordinary people as well as her nationalities, was this fate of homelessness. Both of them had left Hungary in part because the political atmosphere there became incompatible with their beliefs. A great many other Hungarians would have liked to follow them but did not have the qualifications that enabled these two to obtain contracts for employment in the United States. Both often toyed with the idea of returning to Hungary but political developments stood in the way of their re-patriation. As a result they both remained in exile. They both became Hungarian Americans. In fact, both of them participated in the organized political life of the Hungarian-American community. That Jaszi did so is common knowledge. Bartók's dallying with emigre politics is less well known.[12]

While Jaszi and Bartók belong also to the study of Hungarian-American history, the next two individuals that are dealt with in this volume, Amrosius Czakó and Sándor (Alexander) Bölöni Farkas, might better be discussed in a Canadian context. The former was probably the first intellectual refugee to have come to Canada from Hungary. He had an interesting career. In order to get an education that he otherwise would not have been able to get as the child of poor parents, he joined the Cistercian Order at age 15. After a promising start, which saw him getting his doctorate and doing post-doctoral studies abroad, he broke with is church after his theological writings, well-received by liberal clerics, were condemned by conservative church authorities. He next trained as a Calvinist minister. During the revolutionary regime of Mihály Károlyi, Czakó took a government position. He also translated into Hungarian theological works that were not appreciated in conservative circles. Worse still, in a journal he started Czakó criticised

---

12 I have written about the subject: "A Hungarian Patriot in American Exile: Béla Bartók and Émigré Politics," *Journal of the Royal Musical Association* (Oxford University Press), 130, 2 (Dec. 2005), pp. 283-301. My other publications dealing with Hungarian-American politics are listed in the various bibliographies printed in this volume.

Hungary's establishment. Soon his periodical was suppressed and he left Hungary for Vienna with the aim of emigrating to the United States. His entry into the American Republic was denied but, in time, people who respected his work convinced the United Church of Canada to bring him to this country. He arrived in 1928 and soon he was appointed minister of the United Church's Hungarian congregation in Toronto. He saw himself not so much a theologian but as a teacher who would educate his countrymen who had been denied a decent education in their native country. Helping in this task was the journal *Tárogató* that he launched in 1938 with the help of a subsidy from his church.[13]

Unlike Czakó, Sándor Bölöni Farkas never settled in Canada. One reason I have for including an essay about him in this volume is that very few people know about his "Canadian" connection. But he did spend some time touring Central Canada (what in his time were the British North American colonies of Upper Canada and Lower Canada). What is even more important that what he saw here — and heard from Canadian anti-British radicals including the future rebel leader William Lyon Mackenzie—helped to confirm Farkas's belief that the monarchical system of government was contrary to the interests of the general public everywhere. His book about his tour, *Journey in North America* (1831), was so imbued with republican ideals that the Austrian censors of the times felt they had to ban it.

Of course many other temporary or long-term Hungarian visitors to or settlers in Canada would also deserve being included in a volume of readings about Hungarians who had come to North America. About a few of these people, including some very early ones, books have been written. These early visitors include Stephen Parmenius of Buda who came to Newfoundland in 1584.[14] Another is Márk Szalatnay, a veteran of the Hungarian War of Independence of 1848-49. He was an advocate of socialism and a lobbyist for workingmen's causes. In the late

---

[13] In old age Czakó returned to the Catholic Church and the teaching of art history. See my article "Social Progress and Ethnic Solidarity: Ambrosius Czakó's *Tárogató*," in *Tárogató: the Journal of the Hungarian Cultural Society of Vancouver*, 27, 9 (Sept. 2000): 55-56. (The two journals are unrelated.)

[14] On Parmenius see David B. Quinn and N. M. Cheshire, eds. & transl., *The New Found Land of Stephen Parmenius: The Life and Writings of a Hungarian Poet Drowned on a Voyage from Newfoundland, 1583* (Toronto: University of Toronto Press, 1972); and, for a short entry on Parmenius, the *Dictionary of Canadian Biography*, vol. 1, pp. 333-35.

1860s he showed up in Montreal and got involved in trade union activities. Later he moved to Toronto where in 1869 led a strike of workers employed in cigar factories. Szalatnay, however, was soon deported to the United States and ended up fighting for workers' rights there. In fact, he became a martyr of the struggle.[15]

Two other veterans of the War of Independence who could be the subject of articles or even biographies are Paul Oscar Esterhazy and Géza de Döry. Of the two the former is better known. He was the founder of the first viable Hungarian pioneer settlements on the newly-opened prairies in the mid-1880s. The Saskatchewan town of Esterhaz is named after him, and his work is often commemorated.[16] Esterhazy never settled in Canada. De Döry did, yet he is lesser known. He established what was for some time was known as Hun's Valley, the very first Hungarian settlement in the country. But, De Döry died prematurely and his Hungarian settlers scattered to other places.

Still another colourful Hungarian on the Canadian prairies was one of Ambró Czakó's contemporaries, Ferenc Hoffmann. The son of a Calvinist minister, Hoffmann studied agriculture. He visited Canada before the First World War in connection with his work in this field. During the war he served in the Austro-Hungarian army and was captured by the Russians. He fled from the camp he had been taken to in Siberia and managed to get to Vladivostok where, with the help of Allied soldiers, he got onto a troop ship heading for Canada. Once here he finished theological school and became a United Church missionary. He served seventeen scattered Hungarian (as well as other) settlements in rural Saskatchewan. He made his way from one congregation to the next on horseback, and was known as the "lovas pap" (minister on horseback) to his people.

There have been other interesting Hungarian-Canadians since the age of pioneer settlers who would deserve attention, and some of them have been written on,[17] but the few discussed in this volume will have to do for the time being.

---

[15] On Szalatnay see Stanley B. Ryerson's entry in the *Dictionary of Canadian Biography*, vol. X (1871-1880) (Toronto: U. of T. Press, 1972), pp. 670-71.

[16] For example in Martin L. Kovacs, *Esterhazy and Early Hungarian Immigration to Canada* (Regina, Sask.: Canadian Plains Studies, 1974).

[17] Among others by Magda Zalan, in her collection of biographical essays, *Stubborn People* (Toronto: Canadian Stage and Arts Publications, 1985).

* * *

The next part of this collection deals with Hungarian paleo-history. Here I describe the findings of other scholars, including academics whose work is not known to the Hungarian-Canadian or even the Hungarian reading public.

My writings on Hungarian paleo history had been in part prompted by people who keep proclaiming that Hungarians are "not Europeans." Of course this is true. Human beings, in particular Homo Sapiens, originated in Africa. They began appearing in Europe, after their journey through the Middle East, some forty or fifty thousand years ago. The early arrivals were then supplemented by new waves of migrants, for example during the so-called Neolithic Revolution.The original dwellers of Europe had been repeatedly supplanted, swamped or supplemented by the newcomers. The most prominent of these migrations has been the coming of Indo-European-speaking populations, starting about 7,000 years ago and continuing into our age. We could suggest that the migration of the Indo Europeans had lasted to the Middle Ages and beyond, with the coming of the Roma people. Other peoples came as well, for example the Jews who had been scattered from the Holy Land and often ended up in Europe. That is, Hungarians were not the last peoples to have gone to that continent. In fact, they had been in Europe for thousands of years, unless we consider the lands of South-Eastern European Russia not a part of Europe. And, perhaps, Hungarians had been in Europe even before that time. So, the statements that Hungarians are "from Asia" are true, but are often made by people whose European credentials are far more recent.

Much of Hungarian proto- or paleo-history has been based on the findings of paleo-linguists. But linguistics may not be a reliable, or the most reliable guide to the ancestry of peoples. A better guide might be the science that is just emerging, genomics. The science of establishing relationships between human groups is in its infancy, but it is making great progress as we speak. Once the Genographic Project of America's National Geographic Society,[18] as well as others like it, will be completed we might know a lot more about the origins of Europe's—and the world's—populations.

The following articles in the part of this volume entitled Hungary and the World contain information on the attitude to Hungary and

---

[18] On this project see Spencer Wells, *Deep Ancestry: Inside the Genographic Project* (Washington, D.C.: National Geographic, 2006).

Hungarians by outsiders: among them Frenchmen, English-speakers, and during the events of 1956, Americans, Russians and others. This part of the collection might well be read in conjunction with the 2006 special volume of the *Hungarian Studies Review* (volume 33) which is entitled *The Image of Hungary and Hungarians From the Fifteenth to the Twenty-First Century,* and contains articles, among others by George Bisztray, Foltán Fejős, Kenneth McRobbie, Dany Deschênes, and Béla Bodó. Not all their papers deal directly with the image of Hungary, but they all describe developments and situations that had major implications for it.

In the following part (Part IV) of the collection the readers will find examples of my writings on Hungarian communities in the New World. The first study here is a detailed treatment of Canada's earliest Hungarian colonies as they existed a century ago, the second one is an overview of the evolution of Brazil's Hungarian community during the first half of the twentieth century, the third one deals with the decline of Hungarian linguistic presence in North America in recent times, while the last one examines the historiography of these communities.

The volume's appendix contains a list of my publications on Hungarian (as well as non-Hungarian) subjects.[19] These articles, papers, pamphlets and books (mostly edited volumes) might be of interest to the readers of this book.

------

[19] My publications are under various versions of my name: Nándor Dreisziger, N. F. Dreisziger, N. A. F. Dreisziger, N. Fred Dreisziger, and so on. I still have copies or offprints of many of them.

Part I

Remarkable Hungarians

Essays about:

Béla Bartók

Oscar Jaszi

Ambrosius Czakó

Alexander Bölöni Farkas

Béla Bartók.
Commemorative medal designed by artist Dóra de Pédery-Hunt.
Photographed by Elizabeth Frey.
Reproduced here with the permission of Mrs. Pédery-Hunt.

Béla Bartók:
Modern Hungary's Greatest Son

Béla Bartók, ethnomusicologist, concert pianist, and composer of modern music, was born a century and a quarter ago in a provincial town of southern Hungary. He is easily the best known and most respected Hungarian of the twentieth century. I have visited university libraries where there were more works by or about Bartók than there were books about Hungarian history. Fans of Hollywood melodramas and aficionados of international soccer respectively might say that Zsa Zsa Gabor or Ferenc Puskás were more famous Hungarians, but for cultured individuals—and, especially, lovers of music—Béla Bartók stands out as the predominant Hungarian figure of the twentieth century.[1]

Musicologists today list Bartók among the "great five" of modern music. They remark though that while the other four: Stravinsky, Schoenberg, Berg, and Webern—produced mostly work that had a cosmopolitan flavour, Bartók's compositions were "decidedly Hungarian and yet European...." Furthermore, unlike the music of the other great modern masters, from his early days as a composer to his death, and in the decades since, Bartók and his music have always been identified with Hungary and Hungarian culture.[2]

There can be little doubt that Bartók, from his childhood to his last days, had been an ardent Hungarian patriot. The evolution of his homeland can be divided into two highly contrasting halves for the years of Bartók's life. The first half, from 1881 to 1914, was a time of peace, prosperity and hope for Hungary and the Hungarian nation. The second half, lasting from 1914 to 1945, was filled with turmoil, great national calamities and general despair. Since Bartók's life and work can only be

---

[1] An earlier, shorter version of this study on Béla Bartók appeared in serialized form in the weekly periodical *Magyar Élet / Hungarian Life* (Toronto) between 17 December 2005 and 21 January 2006.

[2] Leon Botstein, "Out of Hungary: Batrók, Modernism, and the Cultural Politics of Twentieth Century Music," in *Bartók and His World*, ed. Peter Laki (Princeton, New Jersey: Princeton University Press, 1995), 3-63 (p. 4).

understood in the context of the history of his nation during his lifetime this study will dwell as much on Hungary's evolution from the 1880s to the 1940s as on Bartók's activities and career.

The Hungary of Béla Bartók before 1914

The autonomy which Hungary received through the Compromise with Austria in 1867, along with the fact that she remained an integral part of a large Central European economic unit, benefitted Hungary a great deal and paved the way for her rapid though sometimes uneven economic development in the following decades. This age witnessed one of the most remarkable expansions of the Hungarian economy. "From a backward agrarian state,..." writes historian Ignác Romsics, "Hungary had developed into [a country] with an advanced food-processing industry... [one which was] actively involved in exports."[3] Manufacturing also expanded swiftly. Economic historians Iván Berend and György Ránki have pointed out that between 1898 and 1913, the number of factories in Hungary grew from 2,474 to 5,521. Similarly impressive was the increase in the country's gross national product (GNP). Hungary's GNP in this period grew faster than that of the Habsburg Empire's Austrian and Czech provinces. Because the entire Empire's GNP grew about as fast as those of Great Britain, Italy and Holland, it can be assumed that Hungary's expanded even faster. On the basis of such calculations we can conclude that Hungary's economic progress between 1867 and 1914 was extraordinary, though not unsurpassed by contemporary European standards.[4]

Especially important was the expansion of banking, transportation, and communications. Between 1867 and 1913 the number of Hungarian banking institutions (banks, credit unions, etc.) grew from 107 to nearly 6,000. The length of railways doubled between 1890 and 1913, to 22,000 kilometres. In terms of the length of railways per inhabitants in the country, by 1913 the figures for Hungary were exceeded only by those for France. Hungary's water-borne transportation also expanded,

---

[3] Ignác Romsics, *Magyarország története a XX. században* [The History of Hungary in the 20th Century] (Budapest: Osiris, 1999), 23.

[4] Iván T. Berend and György Ránki, *Economic Development in East-Central Europe in the 19th & 20th Centuries* (New York and London: Columbia University Press, 1974), 122-38, in particular p. 128. Also, Romsics, *Magyarország*, 23f.

especially on the Danube, but also from the sea-port of Fiume on the Adriatic (today's Rijeka in Croatia). The length of telegraph lines increased in the country tenfold between 1867 and 1914, from 17,000 to 170,000 km. Telephone services were introduced in 1881—only two years after they had made their appearance in Paris. By 1914 Hungary possessed 500,000 km. of telephone lines, and some 20,000 telephones were in use in Budapest alone. The Hungarian post office that year handled 800 million pieces of mail, up from 51 million pieces in 1873.[5]

Economic growth was accompanied by rapid advances in other facets of national life. The improvement in public education was both a by-product of and an important contributing factor to the country's economic progress. Many authors have pointed out that the excellence of some of Hungary's turn-of-the-century schools has been illustrated by the fact that half-a-dozen of this educational system's products went on to become Nobel laureates, while several others also gained international acclaim. Of course, these men attended the best schools, while the vast majority of their compatriots, especially those in rural districts, had to be satisfied with spending a few years in one-room, one-teacher schools that offered only the rudiments of an education. Nevertheless, the increased availability of education resulted in the growth of the country's intelligentsia, the back-bone of the Hungarian middle-class. According to historian János Mazsu, between 1890 and 1910, the number of professionals in Hungary increased from 172,000 to more than 311,000.[6]

Increasing economic prosperity, the enlargement of the middle class, and the rapid development of urban centres such as Budapest, filled Hungarians with confidence and pride. In such an atmosphere many of the nation's problems, including those that were created by the country's uneven growth—such as poverty and overpopulation in districts and underdevelopment in sectors of the economy by-passed by the new prosperity—tended to be ignored. The nation was in an optimistic, even truculent, mood.

It was under these circumstances that Hungarians undertook to celebrate the millennium of their arrival in the Carpathian Basin. The festivities accompanying this occasion encouraged the nation to focus too much on the progress it had made, at the expense of the many tasks that

---

[5] Romsics, *Magyarország,* 25-26; for further information on Hungary's economic growth see pages 23-39.

[6] János Mazsu, "The Intelligentsia in Hungary prior to World War I," *Hungarian Studies Review,* 24, 1-2 (1997): 81-96 (p. 89).

lay ahead in the quest for making Hungary a truly advanced society, one
more in line with the norms prevalent in Western Europe. Not surprisingly, Hungary's millennial celebrations were characterized by the over-
bearing patriotism of a people with excessive pride and a false sense of
national security.[7]

The majority of Hungary's Magyars were probably pleased with the
way the millennial commemorations turned out — as were the tens of
thousands of visitors who came to Budapest for the occasion. Not so
satisfied were many of the citizens of the historic Kingdom of Hungary
who felt that the celebrations had left them out: the impoverished masses of many regions of the Hungarian countryside, as well as the country's numerous non-Magyar minorities. Indeed, the years that followed
the festivities were filled with increased tension between the rich and
poor, and between the nation-forming Magyar majority and the country's hardly less numerous national minorities.

Of the two problems, that of the national minorities was probably
the more menacing from the point of view of historic Hungary's survival. The chauvinistic tone of the millennial celebrations, and the
Magyarization that the Budapest government had embarked on at the
end of the 1890s, contributed greatly to the deterioration of relations
between the country's dominant Magyar ethnic group and the national
minorities. The rising mutual distrust and ill-feelings would help to prevent attempts at a solution of the country's nationalities problem in the
years before World War I, and would result in the problem exploding in
the face of the Hungarian nation during the war.

Hungarians of the times, like "most nations," observed historian
Géza Jeszenszky not long before he became a member of Hungary's
first post-communist government after the collapse of communism,
"...believed themselves politically chosen, with a special talent and a
'manifest destiny'... [but] it was a foolish luxury for [them] in their
politically and geographically exposed position, to alienate the people

---

[7] These paragraphs are based on my essay "Thousand Years of Hungarian
Survival," in *Hungary: 1001-2001: A Millennial Retrospection*, ed. George
Bisztray and N. F. Dreisziger (Toronto: a special volume of the *Hungarian
Studies Review* 28, 1-2 [2001]): 1-71 (pp. 27-31).

[8] Géza Jeszenszky, "Hungary Through World War I and the End of the Dual
Monarchy," in *A History of Hungary* ed. Peter F. Sugar, Péter Hanák and
Tibor Frank (Bloomington, Indiana; Indiana University Press, 1990), p. 270.
One of the consequences of Hungary's "impatient nationalism," to use the
words of Jeszenszky, was the diminution of the country's prestige aboard. On

with whom they had lived for centuries..."[8]
Unfortunately, from the point of view of the survival of a vibrant
and potentially powerful Hungarian state, very few Hungarians at the
time realized or even remotely suspected that their impatient nationalism was a foolish luxury. It should be added here that militant nationalism was not a unique Hungarian phenomenon at the time: it could be
observed throughout contemporary Europe and even in the New World.

Béla Bartók as a Child and a Young Man, 1881–1914

Bartók was born into this increasingly prosperous, ebullient Hungarian
society in 1881. His father, Béla Bartók Sr. (1855–1888) was the head-
master of the agricultural school in Nagyszentmiklós (today's Sinni-
colau Mare, Romania), in the southern Hungarian county of Torontál.
His mother, Paula Voit (1857–1939) was a school teacher. Torontál was
an ethnically mixed region of Hungary and the Bartók family was bilin-
gual, Mrs. Bartók being of Transylvanian German (Saxon) background.
As an adult, Béla Bartók Jr., would pride himself of having command
of at least half dozen languages. The family was also a musical one and
Bartók was encouraged to develop his musical talents at a very early
age. His piano lessons started at age 5 and he soon tried his hand at composing.[9]
    Despite the loving and culturally rich environment, Bartók's child-
hood was full of difficulties. He was often ill and was sometimes kept
in prolonged isolation from other children. Some authors speculate that
these episodes contributed to Bartók's difficulty of interacting with others in social situations, as well as at public appearances, as an adult.
Further grief came to the young Bartók—he was only seven—when his
father died. During the next six years his mother moved from one
provincial centre to the next in search of a stable employment and suit-
able educational environment for Béla Jr. and his sister Elza (1885-

that subject see Jeszenszky's book, *Az elvesztett presztízs: Magyarország
megítélésének meg változása Nagy-Britanniában (1894-1918)* [The lost prestige: the transformation of Hungary's image in Great Britain (1894-1918)]
(Budapest: Magvető, 1986).

[9] Biographical works relating to Bartók are numerous (see the bibliography
below.) One succinct yet comprehensive overview is by Malcolm Gillies,
"Bartók, Béla," *The New Grove Dictionary of Music and Musicians* 2nd ed.
(London: Grove/Macmillan, 2001), vol. 2. pp. 787-818.

1955). For a time they lived in Nagyszöllős (today's Vinogradov, Ukraine) and then in Nagyvárad (today's Oradea, Rumania), where Béla was enrolled in a German-language school. In 1894 the family managed to settle in a major cultural centre, Pozsony (today's Bratislava, Slovakia). Here Béla could concentrate on his musical education. He would soon be the organist of his school, succeeding another student who would be a famous musician later: Ernő Dohnányi. He also studied with the noted music teachers László Erkel and Anton Hyrtl. During the second half of the 1890s he produced one composition after another. Had it not been for his persistent health problems, he would have no doubt produced even more.

When Pozsony could no longer provide musical schooling for him, Bartók applied to both the Vienna Conservatory of Music and the Budapest Academy of Music. Though Vienna was close to Bartók's home, had a fine reputation among music lovers, and the Conservatory was eager to admit him, Bartók chose to study in Budapest.

Early influences on Bartók's compositional works came mainly from German composers: Robert Schumann, Johannes Brahms, and especially, Richard Strauss. His views on art and life were influenced by the German philosopher Frederick Nietzsche. This reliance on German artists and writers was ironic in view of the fact that the young Bartók was an intensely patriotic individual. It is a well-known fact that he sometimes reprimanded even his mother and sister for speaking German at home instead of Magyar.

Bartók's nationalism manifested itself mainly in anti-Habsburg sentiments that were common among Hungarian youth at the time. These feelings found their most prominent expression in his *Kossuth Symphony* that he composed in the spring and summer of 1903. Just about this time Bartók's career as a concert pianist also began to flourish with performances in several European cities including Vienna, Berlin, Paris, Manchester and Budapest. Just when his career as a pianist began to wane because of a decrease in the number of invitations, he was appointed to teach piano at the Academy of Music in Budapest. He would teach piano there until 1934.

Bartók as an Ethnomusicologist

In 1904 Bartók began developing an interest in peasant music. He also began experimenting in adopting such music for his compositions. His quest for a compositional style that was based on indigenous peasant music would be realized only later. First had to come a systematic effort at the collection of Hungarian folk music. In this enterprise Bartók found an ally and friend in a fellow student at the academy, Zoltán Kodály. In 1906 the two embarked on a great project of collecting the folksongs of their homeland. They felt that the undertaking was urgent as the growing appeal of artificial or imitation folk songs threatened to condemn true Hungarian peasant songs and music to oblivion. As a first step in the preservation of Hungary's authentic musical legacy, in 1906 Bartók and Kodály adopted to voice and piano and published 20 folksongs that they and others had collected. The appearance of the collection made few headlines in Hungary as the country's middle-class and urban public was much more interested in contemporary Western European music as well as the music provided by Gypsy bands.

Despite the cool reception of his first venture into a new musical idiom, Bartók never returned to his previous style. There would be no more compositions such as the immensely popular *Kossuth Symphony*, and Bartók would continue to explore Hungarian peasant music. Soon he would also start collecting the music of other peasant folks living in the Kingdom of Hungary: the Slovak, Rumanian, Ruthenian and South Slav. Later, he would visit, for the purposes of collecting village songs, regions where the Hungarians had lived before their settlement in the Carpathian Basin. These visits took him to northeastern Rumania, and to the lands inhabited by the Chuvash and Tatar peoples of the middle Volga Valley of Imperial Russia.

The most interesting and most useful of his visits in these years were to the Székely counties of Transylvania (what is nowadays central Rumania). In the summer of 1907 he was collecting songs from the old people of the region known as Csík. Here he came upon songs of pentatonic tunes (anhemitonic or lacking semi-tones) that convinced him that what he found belonged to the oldest types of Magyar folk songs. The discovery had profound impact on the evolution of Bartók's compositions. He became convinced that he could strike out on a new style of his own, based upon the folk music he had collected, music that provided him with new and unique models of melody and even rhythm. The next few years were full with experimentation for him and sometimes resulted in compositions that one of his publishers refused to publish on the ground that they were "too difficult" and "too modern" for contemporary audiences.

In the fall of 1909 Bartók married Márta Ziegler who during the next decade-and-a-half served as his companion and assistant in many of his professional undertakings. She also bore him a son, Béla Jr., in

1910. About the same time commenced Bartók's career as a sought-after concert pianist. His March 1910 performance in Paris evoked the comment "young barbarian" from a music critic. In response to this he composed one of his famous piano pieces, the really "barbarian," quite atonal, loud and demanding *Allegro Barbaro*. In 1911 followed the opera *Bluebeard's Castle,* patterned to some extent on French composer Claude Debussy's *Pelléas et Mélisande*, but based on the inflections of old Hungarian folksongs.

Bartók submitted *Bluebeard's Castle* in two opera competitions in Budapest, but the judges were not impressed and deemed the work unperformable. Gone was the age when Bartók would produce compositions similar to his *Kossuth symphony* and continue to receive the adulation of the mainstream music-loving public in Hungary. By 1912 so negative was the reception of his work that he discontinued performing in public. For several years thereafter he focused almost entirely on ethnomusicological work: folk-song collecting and writing about folk-music.

At first, his new collecting trips were confined to the Carpathian basin, especially the Hungarian and Rumanian district of Mármaros (Maramures), but in 1913 he ventured far afield, to North Africa, in particular to the oasis settlement of Biskra with its Berber inhabitants. After the outbreak of war in the summer of 1914, however, folk-music collecting abroad, and even in Hungary, especially in Transylvania, became difficult if not impossible. On more than one occasion in 1915-16 the Russians were on the verge of breaching Hungary's Carpathian defences. As if this was not enough, in the summer of 1916 Romania declared war on Austria-Hungary and for a brief period occupied parts of Transylvania – until Austro-Hungarian and German forces threw the invaders back into the Wallachian plain and beyond. Despite this development, or probably largely as a consequence of it, conditions in Transylvania continued to be tension-filled, a fact that discouraged Bartók from doing ethnomusicological work there. He must have been distressed by this turn of events and even more by the rising tensions among the various nations inhabiting the Hungary of the times.

While the war brought dislocations and despair for Bartók, it—and, especially, its turbulent aftermath—brought tragic changes in the evolution of Hungary.

The First World War and After

The war that broke out in Europe in the summer of 1914 brought great changes in Bartók's life. It wrought even greater changes in the evolution of Hungary. Bartók lived the first 33 years of his life in an increasingly prosperous nation, in a Hungary that was at peace with its neighbours. After 1914 he lived in a country plagued by national and international crises. In fact, in the early 1920s he was so discouraged by the situation in his homeland that he contemplated leaving Hungary and settling in a neighbouring country—but he stayed. Two decades later, in the autumn of 1940, he finally decided to leave Hungary and even Europe. He moved to the United States. During the next five years of his short life, he watched in agony the sufferings of his beloved homeland and its people. Rather than turning his back on his nation, even in his American exile his thoughts would be with his compatriots in wartorn Central Europe.

The First World War brought an end to the Habsburg Empire, known after 1867 as the Dual Monarchy of Austria-Hungary. The war also brought an end to the historic Kingdom of Hungary that had occupied the Carpathian Basin for much of the previous thousand years. One could go so far as to say that the war was an unmitigated calamity for Austria-Hungary collectively and both Austria and Hungary individually. It started in a series of disasters right from the start. Instead of becoming what the Viennese leadership expected to be a short, victorious campaign against Serbia, the war developed into a world war soon after its outbreak. In this struggle Austria-Hungary faced not only a small Balkan country as enemy, but the Russian Empire as well.

As the result of the decision of the Russian Imperial Court to get involved in the war, the bulk of the Austro-Hungarian forces sent against Serbia had to be diverted to the north to protect the Habsburg Empire's Polish provinces against the mighty Russian military. What was left of the Austro-Hungarian army in the south, was no match for Serbia's battle-hardened forces. It must be kept in mind that while Austria-Hungary had not been involved a war for decades, the Serbs had fought two (the First and Second Balkan wars) in 1912 and 1913.

In the north, in Galicia, the Habsburg Imperial Army began the war by suffering heavy losses (350,000 casualties) in fighting numerically superior Russian forces. The losses continued during the fall and winter. In 1915, when Italy decided to join the war on the Entente side, Austria-Hungary was confronted by the spectre of having to fight a war on three fronts.

In 1916 the Russians mounted a massive offensive mainly against the Austro-Hungarian forces on the Eastern front. With German help, the offensive was stopped, at a cost of more than a million casualties for the Austro-Hungarian Empire. Soon thereafter Romania ended its neutrality by declaring war on the Dual Monarchy. Though the Romanian advance into Transylvania was halted, the Monarchy from this time on had to fight a war on four fronts.

By the end of the war, the Kingdom of Hungary had lost 530,000 of its soldiers. In addition, 1.4 million were wounded, and 833,000 were taken prisoners of war. Many of these POWs returned only years later, some of them with their health impaired, while tens of thousands never returned at all, having succumbed to malnutrition and disease in the POW camps.

The severe losses of men and material on the fronts, the demands made by the war on Hungary's economy, the deteriorating relations between Hungarians and the country's Rumanian and Slav minorities, and the incursions of the enemy into Hungarian territory, placed a heavy toll on Hungarian society.

The damage caused to the country's economy was pervasive. First of all, the war meant that production and investment were diverted from peaceful pursuits. Government interference in all aspects of economic life resulted in shortages of goods, inflation, and a steep decline in the standard of living. The result was labour unrest and other tensions. 1917 witnessed the beginning of hunger riots. With Hungary's cities going hungry, food shipments to Vienna were curtailed. Soon the Austrians accused Hungarians of boycotting of the common war effort.

Even before the onset of tension between Hungary and Austria, friction developed between Hungary's authorities and the country's non-Magyar nationalities. A large part of the problem was the fact that the former suspected the latter of sympathizing and even cooperating with Hungary's enemies. Measures taken against the leaders of these minority groups only reinforced the determination of the masses of these nationalities to separate from Hungary.

By the fall of 1918 social and ethnic tensions in Hungary had reached a boiling point. Neither disciplinary actions nor government concessions could diffuse the situation. Not surprisingly, the thousand-year-old historic Kingdom of Hungary began disintegrating. In the Hungarian heartland this process manifested itself in political revolution, and on the periphery, in ethnic strife and the triumph of separatism.

In Budapest power was gained first by supporters of radical democracy and independence from Austria, and then in March of 1919, by a small group of left-wing socialists and their communist allies. What ensued was a series of parallel conflicts, motivated by greatly diverging ethnic, ideological and social agendas.

While the Hungarian heartland lived through the Red Terror, foreign (Romanian) occupation, and then the White Terror, the geographic fringes of the Carpathian Basin witnessed the coming of foreign troops—Czechs, Rumanians, or South Slavs—whom some of the local inhabitants greeted as liberators while others regarded as enemy occupiers. By the time the military conflicts subsided, the historic Kingdom of Hungary was no more. What remained of Hungary was in the hands of the country's new counter-revolutionary masters. This country was a pale shadow (93,000 km^2) of the great kingdom Hungary had been when the war had begun in 1914 (282,000 km^2). The dismemberment of the Kingdom of Hungary was enacted into international law by the post-war peace settlement, particularly by the Treaty of Trianon of June 1920.

The Trianon peace settlement was patterned on the Versailles Peace Treaty between the Entente (Great Britain and France) and associated powers (above all the United States) had made with Germany. In fact, the vast majority of its clauses were the same or very similar. Hungary's armed forces (like Germany's), for example, were restricted to a tiny fraction of what they had been before 1914. But it was the treaty's territorial provisions that were the harshest.

The territorial settlement imposed on Hungary and its consequences for the Hungarian nation have been outlined many times. We might want to begin with a description provided by Professor S. B. Várdy: "The terms of this treaty were so harsh and punitive that one looks in vain for parallels in modern European history. On the basis of this treaty Hungary lost 71.4 per cent of her territory and 63.6 per cent of her population. Of the four beneficiary states Rumania alone received a larger share... of the country's former territory than that which was left to Hungary...."

The excuse for this territorial settlement was the principle of national self-determination, but in the application of this principle the rights of millions of Hungarians to self-determination were disregarded. Furthermore, Hungarian calls for plebiscites in the territories concerned were ignored, with one minor exception. The irony of the act of dismembering the multinational Kingdom of Hungary was underscored by the fact that the states that benefitted most from this process, were themselves multi-national, in some cases even more mixed ethnically than Hungary had been before 1918.

Added to the territorial losses was the loss of resources and infrastructure. As a result of the Hungary's dismemberment, the country lost 89 percent of its iron-production capacity, 84 percent of its forests, and 62 percent of its railway lines. Although Hungary retained most of its food producing capacity, it had to depend on greatly disrupted export markets to yield any income from exported produce—to pay for the imports that became essential for the economy. Especially hard hit were Hungary's food producers. Poverty became worse in the country's already impoverished villages.

The Trianon treaty also disrupted Hungary's transportation and communication systems. As has been mentioned, most of Hungary's railway lines found themselves in detached territories. Even lines in the Hungarian heartland ended up with parts of them passing through foreign territory. The same happened to some roads and telegraph lines. Water transportation systems were also disrupted. Some navigable rivers that previously were entirely under Hungarian jurisdiction, became either boundary waters or international waterways controlled by four different countries.

A further disruptive impact of the Treaty of Trianon had been the mass migrations that it caused. Even though living standards in Hungary had plummeted as a result of the war, the post-war revolutions, and the economic disruptions caused by the country's dismemberment, Trianon Hungary was still a more attractive place than its neighbour states for many Hungarians whose native communities the peace settlement had left in foreign-controlled lands. As a result some 426,000 refugees left the successors states and settled in Hungary, often swelling the ranks of the unemployed. In the interwar years there would be a further out-migration of Hungarians from the successor states, this time mainly overseas, as many ordinary Magyars found life in these countries—and, especially, service in their armed forces—unpleasant and readily exchanged it for the relative economic and political security of a country such as Canada.

By far the most dangerous long-term consequences of the Trianon Treaty, according to a few researchers, were the impact they had on the Hungarian national psyche. The post-1920 generations of Hungarians, especially the upper and middle classes as well as the vast majority of refugees from the "lost lands," were intensely preoccupied with the "tragedy of Trianon" and with schemes for reversing it. Another negative consequence of this type of intense preoccupation with "treaty revision" particularly in the immediate post-Trianon era was the tendency for Hungarians to blame all their country's problems on the peace settlement, instead of looking for other possible causes and finding solutions to them. The problems inflicted on Hungary by the war, the post-war revolutions, and the dismemberment of the historic Kingdom of Hungary, were felt by everyone in the country, including Béla Bartók.

After the outbreak of war in 1914 he continued his efforts to collect folk-songs, but had to restrict his activities to parts of the country not threatened by foreign incursions. He also continued to compose. Because of his frail health, Bartók was found unfit for military service. But, since he was a good patriot, he tried to do his share in the warding off the evils that his countrymen experienced throughout 1914-1920. Toward the end of the war he gave a concert in Vienna featuring some of the folk songs he had collected from soldiers. Other developments during the war was a performance, at long last, of his opera *Bluebeard's Castle*, as well of his recently composed one-act ballet *The Wooden Prince*. The latter was a success. He also found a publisher for all his compositions in Universal Editions of Vienna.

The war's end and the immediate post-war period brought further problems and stress for Bartók. He lived outside of Budapest in the village of Rákoskeresztúr where, by 1918 food and coal had become scarce. Unrelated to the war was the arrival of the Spanish influenza pandemic in October of 1918. Bartók caught the virus but overcame it.

Hungary was soon enveloped by revolution. First came the assumption of power by the supporters of Count Mihály Károlyi. Under their rule Hungary became a republic. The country separated from Austria, hoping that an independent Hungary would be spared of the punishment that was expected to be inflicted upon the countries that, in the eyes of the Entente Powers, had initiated the war.

The Károlyi regime took no steps to stop the disintegration of the armed forces of the former Austro-Hungarian Monarchy. Károlyi's friend and minister in charges of nationalities affairs, Oszkár Jászi, tried to negotiate with Hungary's minorities the creation of a federated Hungary. By this time however, most of Hungary's ethnic groups were bent on attaining their sovereignty outside of the Hungarian state.

The Károlyi regime also initiated limited land and other reforms in Hungary. Before any of these could be implemented, the regime collapsed and, in March of 1919, power passed into the hands of Marxists, led eventually by Béla Kun and a group of his Bolshevik followers who had been converted to Leninist ideals in Russian prisoner-of-war camps. They soon embarked on the building of communism in Hungary—but faster than in Soviet Russia.

Bartók reacted to these events at first with enthusiasm and later with disapproval. He had high hopes for the reforms promised by Károlyi's liberals and socialists. He hoped that reforms under their regime might reach Hungary's artistic and musical life and would result in the modernization of musical education in the country. Hungarian orchestras might soon be able to play modern music—he hoped.

But it was not too be. Some steps were taken in that direction. During the winter of 1918-19, Bartók even accepted membership in the Board of Directors of his school, the Academy of Music—while his friend Kodály took on even more important responsibilities. Before they had time to implement any substantive reforms, the Károlyi regime collapsed. During the ascendancy of Béla Kun, the Academy's directors were appointed "advisors" to the Soviet Government in the sphere of cultural policies. This development has prompted some historians to argue that Bartók had assumed a political role in 1919, but this is far from the truth. Bartók, and more importantly Kodály, were just caught in the political whirlwind sweeping through Hungary at the time. Bartók would never voluntarily accept a public let alone political role, until he toyed with the idea very late in life, in his American exile during World War II. Some time after the events of 1919 he confessed that he was much relieved when the communist experiment in Hungary came to an end.

Unfortunately for Bartók and especially for Kodály, the demise of the Béla Kun regime was followed by a stressful incident. After the establishment of the counter-revolutionary regime in Hungary in the late summer of 1919, Kodály became the victim of a political witch-hunt. Some of his detractors alleged that at the time of the collapse of the Kun's regime, the Academy was slow to hoist the Hungarian national flag. He was dismissed from the Academy. Next, a tribunal was appointed to investigate Kodály's activities during the spring and summer of 1919. Bartók was among those who came to his friend's aid and testified on his behalf. Fortunately for Kodály and the world of Hungarian music, no ground was found for charging him with any crimes against the Hungarian state and he was soon reinstated as a member of the Academy's faculty.

Nevertheless, in the chauvinistic pubic atmosphere of post-1919 Hungary, neither Kodály or Bartók could go about their professional work without encountering public criticism. They published some of their music in Bucharest. Soon they would be berated in Hungary's nationalist press for what some of their enemies considered an unpatriotic act. More attacks followed when Kodály and Bartók suggested that some of the roots of the Magyar peasantry's music could be traced back to times before the Carpathian Basin's conquest by Prince Árpád and his Hungarians. As if criticism in Hungary wasn't enough, Bartók was censured also by nationalists in Romania who perceived in him a Hungarian chauvinist.

For much of the 1920s Bartók composed, often works that were perceived as too modern and even atonal by the music-loving public of his country. One of these works was the opera *The Miraculous Mandarin*. Although Bartók considered it one of his finest works, it was not staged at the time, probably because its plot appeared rather sordid to Hungary's musical elite. In the 1920s he also wrote a great number of popular as well as scholarly essays on subjects ranging from ethnomusicology to modern music. There were also important developments in his personal life. He suddenly divorced his wife Márta Ziegler and married his student Ditta Pásztory. In July of 1924 a son, named Péter, was born to Béla and Ditta. As has been mentioned, Bartók already had a son from his first marriage, Béla Jr.

In the 1920s furthermore, Bartók's performing career resumed with both international and Hungarian invitations. His concert tours took him to most of Europe's musical centres where he usually performed his own works. In 1929 he was invited to tour the Soviet Union. From the point of view of his development as a musician the tour was of little consequence; however, the tour served to solidify the dislike of leftist radicalism that Bartók already developed during the 1919 communist experiment in Hungary.

Bartók had no illusions as to what he would find in Soviet Russia or that he would be able to learn much about the conditions that Russian musicians lived under. "I was aware," he wrote on returning from his trip, "that a foreigner... can hardly see anything of real life in Russia." On most of his stops he had no chance to talk to the musicians of the orchestras he played with. In a few places he did. "Nobody" he reported later, can speak openly in front of anyone else." Despite this, Bartók had a chance to get a few glimpses of the Soviet musical world, as a result of which he could feel the miseries of the "old middle class," and the "terrifying" housing conditions that most Russians had to endure. For concerts, he learned, "program content is selected according to... governmental intentions." Religious content was restricted. Concert life in Russia, he concluded, was characterized by "confusion and chaos...." The negative impressions he gained of life in the Soviet Union on this tour reinforced the disdain he had felt towards the communists in 1919 and accompanied him throughout the rest of his life. Accordingly, during his American exile some fifteen years later he refused to have anything to do with the organizations of leftists émigrés.

The Background to Bartók's Decision to Leave Hungary, 1933-1940

While Bartók's experiences in Russia were short-lived, his professional ties to Germany were plentiful. He first performed there when he was twenty-three and his last recital there took place early in 1933, only a short time before Adolf Hitler's appointment as Chancellor. Throughout this time and even for a few years thereafter, Bartók's compositions were often played in German concert halls. German audiences appreciated his novel approach to music.

1933 ushered in a dramatic change in German history. Early that year Adolf Hitler, the leader of the National Socialist Party, became the country's Chancellor, after elections that gave his party the largest number of seats in the German Parliament. In the course of the next three years Hitler's Nazis eliminated all opposition to their rule and began a program of dismantling the Versailles Peace Settlement that had been imposed on Germany by the victorious Entente Powers in 1919. In 1936 German troops entered the Rhineland, a part of Germany that was supposed to be off limits to the Wehrmacht. With the Rhineland re-occupied, France was no longer able to launch a preventive war against Germany to dislodge the Nazi regime that was no longer complying with the terms of the peace settlement.

With his regime secure from attack from both within and the outside, Hitler embarked on rearming Germany at a break-neck speed. In the spring of 1938 he occupied Austria. In the fall of the same year he forced Czechoslovakia to surrender the mainly German-inhabited Sudetenland to his Third Reich. In the spring of the following years he occupied what was left of the lands of the Czechs while in the eastern half of what used to be Czechoslovakia he allowed the establishment of a nominally independent Slovak Republic—Nazi Germany's first satellite in East-Central Europe.

These developments had grave consequences for musical life in Germany and eventually in all of Central Europe. As early as 1933 started the gradual politicisation of everything related to the world of music in Germany. The process began with the removal of outstanding Jewish musicians, including some of Bartók's acquaintances, from prominent positions in musical institutions. Next the Nazi regime subordinated these institutions, as well as associations of musicians and even publishers of music, to Nazi control. The Nazis did not ban modern music, but their dislike of it became well-known and gave a free hand to pro-Nazi music critics to assail all modern compositions as well as composers.

1938 brought the Nazi threat closer to home for Bartók. The annexation of Austria that year established a common border between Hungary and the Third *Reich*. Soon after it happened, Bartók's Viennese publisher sent him a questionnaire inquiring about his Aryan status. But, anti-Semitic measures were by this time not confined to the territories of the Third Reich. The fact is that at about this time, Hungary's parliament enacted the first of a series of "Jewish laws" restricting the participation of Jews in Hungarian economic and cultural life.

These events aroused concern and indignation in Bartók. He refused to answer the questionnaire from Vienna regarding his "Aryan" or "non-Aryan" status. He made a new will in which he specified that, as long as public places were named in Hungary after Hitler, no places should bear his name. Further, when a group of prominent Gentile intellectuals formally protested Hungary's "Jewish laws," Bartók signed their petition. He was especially bitter about these developments in his private correspondence. He complained about his Christian countrymen approving Nazi ideas. Bartók was ashamed of his own compatriots.

It was not only the Gentile middle class of Hungary that found some Nazi ideas attractive. Hungary's leaders, while disdainful of certain Nazi behaviour and methods, also found some elements of Nazi foreign policy to their liking. In particular, they hoped that the Third Reich would help to destroy the peace settlement that was imposed on East Central Europe after World War I. In this process Hungary could hope to regain some of the territories that had been taken from her in 1919-1920.

Indeed, the first revision of the borders created by the Treaty of Trianon took place in the fall of 1938 when, as a result of the so-called First Vienna Award, the southern part of Czechoslovakia was returned to Hungary. The Award came as a result of arbitration by Germany and Italy and followed the pattern of the arbitration handed down by Britain, France, Germany and Italy at Munich somewhat earlier in which a part of western Czechoslovakia, the so-called Sudetenland, was transferred to the Third Reich. Sudetenland was predominantly German, just as the land returned to Hungary by the Vienna Award was predominantly Hungarian. Hungarians rejoiced as a result, not realizing that through these changes Nazi influence in Central Europe became greatly enhanced.

In the spring of 1939, at the time of the disintegration of what was left of Czechoslovakia, Hungary regained the Carpatho-Ukraine, and in the summer of 1940, through another arbitration by Germany and Italy, half of Transylvania was returned to Hungary by the Second Vienna Award. Almost a third of the territories and at least a half of the Hungarian population that had been taken away from the country by the Treaty of Trianon some twenty years earlier had now been regained. The price was not immediately evident to most Hungarians: German influence in the region, and especially in Hungary, had increased.

Still, Hungary managed to remain neutral in the war that had broken out when Nazi Germany (and soon thereafter, its ally the Soviet Union) invaded Poland in September, 1939. Unfortunately it was questionable if Hungary could retain its neutrality should the war spread and envelop even more of Eastern Europe. The prospect of Hungary becoming involved in the war did not escape the attention of many of her citizens, including Béla Bartók.

Bartók had good reasons to fear the spread of the war to his country. His son from his second marriage, Péter, was about to reach military age. Should the war come to Hungary, Péter would no doubt be drafted and would probably end up fighting on the front. Nearly twenty-five years ago Bartók himself faced this situation, but his frail health kept him from being conscripted. There was no such reason to save his young son from the dangers of military life. At the same time, Bartók assumed that his son from his first marriage, Béla Jr., would not be drafted as he was past the age when men were called up for service.

Under these circumstances Bartók and his wife Ditta began considering leaving Hungary, at least for the duration of the war. They hoped that they could take Péter with them or that he could follow them and join them in their temporary exile. Béla Sr.'s situation was made easier by the fact that his mother had died and he didn't have to worry about leaving an elderly parent behind if he left his homeland.

The opportunity to leave Hungary came in the late summer of 1940 when Bartók got an offer from the United States to do work in the field of ethnomusicology. The offer came from Columbia University and involved the finishing of a project that had been started by ethnomusicologist Millman Parry of Harvard University. Parry and his team of researchers had collected epic folk-songs in Yugoslavia. Parry had planned to transcribe these into musical notes but died before he had made much headway with this project. His publishers, Columbia University Press, asked Bartók to complete this demanding and time-consuming task. They offered him a stipend of $3,000—a substantial sum in those days. Bartók decided to accept the offer and he and Ditta left for the United States. Because Yugoslavia, Italy, Spain and Portugal were still neutral countries, the Bartóks had no trouble in leaving Central Europe. They embarked on the trans-Atlantic voyage in Lisbon and arrived in New York City in October of 1940.

Bartók's American Years 1940-1945

After settling in America, Bartók's time and energies were devoted to working on the Parry collection of Serb and Croat epic songs. Whenever he could find time, he also continued his work on his project, started long before his arrival to the United States, involving the Romanian songs he had collected many years earlier. He also prepared a volume of Turkish melodies. These projects would not result in publication until after his death.

In addition to his work in the field of ethnomusicology, Bartók and his wife went on concert tours of the United States on two separate occasions. During this time Bartók was offered teaching positions by the music faculties of more than one American university. Although his contract with Columbia to work on the Parry material was for only two years, he declined all such offers. Privately, he did accept to teach a few students piano or composition.

Bartók's life in America was not without irritations. His luggage disappeared for a while during the transatlantic voyage. The first apartment he rented was noisy for a man who was used to a quiet place and found it difficult to work in a noisy environment. Soon the Bartóks moved to a quieter part of the city. Furthermore, the concerts they gave, especially the two-piano performances he and his wife undertook, got less than enthusiastic reception. There were incipient health problems also. Bartók had had occasional pain in his shoulder already before his departure from Europe, and such episodes became more frequent in America. It may have been bursitis, or it was the first symptom of the disease that would increasingly plague him and which was eventually diagnosed to be leukaemia.

A further irritant during much of the first two years of the Bartóks' stay in America was the fact that getting a visa for their son Péter proved to be more time-consuming than they had expected. Eventually they succeeded and Péter left Europe. Because he was unable to inform his parents of his arrival date, he disembarked from his ship in New York not knowing how to meet his parents. Miraculously, father and son soon stumbled upon each other accidentally.

Bartók's battles with American bureaucracy would not end however. Because he had to apply for an extension of his visa every year, he had to leave the United States annually and return with the permission of the immigration authorities a day later. This is how Bartók ended up visiting Montreal occasionally. His financial concerns, his difficulties in handling the "culture shock" of adjusting to life in a new country, his unending battles with American bureaucracy, more than once prompted Bartók to contemplate returning to Hungary.

In the meantime his homeland became involved in Hitler's campaign against Yugoslavia in the spring of 1941. This was followed by Hungary's involvement, at the end of June, in Hitler's invasion of Soviet Russia. What Bartók had feared had happened. He could take satisfaction in his decision to leave Europe, and his craving to see his homeland again abated, at least for a while. Nevertheless, the fate of his country and its people continued to preoccupy him. It was under these circumstances that he became involved in the politics of the Hungarian community of America.

During the Bartóks' first year of stay in the United States they had few contacts with professional emigres and politicians. Their friends and acquaintances were from New York's artistic community. Late in 1941 this situation began to change. During the late summer of that year Tibor Eckhardt, a prominent Hungarian politician arrived in the United States. He came on a secret mission: to prepare the ground for the establishment of a Hungarian government-in-exile should Nazi Germany occupy Hungary or turn the country into a satellite of the Third Reich by other means. To accomplish this Eckhardt and his Hungarian-American supporters had to launch a political movement among North America's sizable Hungarian immigrant community. Their organization became known as the Movement for an Independent Hungary (MIH).

Viktor Bátor, a friend of Bartók who had helped him with immigration matters, became associated with MIH. Through him Eckhardt and his associates invited Bartók to participate in their movement. Bartók accepted and at first became the chairman of MIH's so-called Artistic and Scientific Committee. As head of this committee Bartók began approaching by mail prominent Hungarian-American intellectuals and asked them to support the aims of the movement.

From the day of his arrival in America, Eckhardt was denounced by leftist Hungarian-American emigres, as well as representatives of the Czechoslovak and Yugoslav governments-in-exile, as a right-winger and "agent" of Hungary's conservative and "pro-German" government. Eckhardt's political situation further deteriorated when Hungary's government, following the example of Nazi Germany, declared war on the United States in December of 1941. Six months later Eckhardt realized that, in order to keep his "Movement" alive, he would have to step aside as its leader. The Movement's executive asked Bartók to take over. Surprisingly, Bartók, who had never assumed a political role before, agreed.

Bartók's promise to take over didn't save MIH from failure. Although for some time he did try to lobby famous American Hungarians to work for a democratic post-war Hungary, his limited efforts were not enough to keep MIH alive. Bartók abandoned emigre politicking by the winter of 1942-43.

By that time Bartók's personal situation and health had deteriorated. His employment with Columbia University was coming to an end. He did get a short-term visiting fellowship at Harvard University but that employment did not solve his financial problems and did not put his mind at ease about his family's financial future. Invitations for concerts and concert tours became fewer and fewer. In any case, he was often unable to accept these as his health kept deteriorating. His bouts with what he took to be bursitis became more frequent. There also came episodes of fatigue and low-grade fever.

In May 1943 came an event that caused Bartók to see hope and to rally again in spirit. That month he received a commission from the Russian-American conductor Serge Koussevitzky to compose a major orchestral piece. The result was, after several months' of effort, the *Concerto for Orchestra*. It premiered in Boston in December of 1944 and met favourable reception. In early 1944 Bartók also produced a sonata for solo violin, on the suggestion of violinist Yehudi Menuhin.

Throughout 1944 Bartók's health continued to deteriorate. The cost of his treatment was covered by the American Society of Composers, Authors and Publishers, since Bartók's income was insufficient to pay for his medical expenses. Now the symptoms pointed clearly toward leukaemia. Nevertheless, through blood transfusions and drug therapy the illness was kept under control for more than a year. Bartók also received penicillin injections. He was one of the first civilians in American history to have had such treatment. During periods of relative freedom from his symptoms, Bartók resumed performing his works at recitals.

Bartók spent the last three summers of his life at a cottage on Lake Saranac in New York State. Here, away from the distractions of city life, he would spend much of his time composing. Among his last compositions were his *Third Piano Concerto* and his *Viola Concerto*. The latter was completed by a composer acquaintance of Bartók after his death.

In the spring of 1945, post-war Hungary's provisional National Assembly elected a handful of distinguished Hungarians living in exile as its members. Bartók was among them. On hearing the news, his first reaction was to go home. Soon this by then quite frail and ill man had second thoughts and postponed the return to his homeland. Yet, as late as the summer of 1945, he is known to have urged wealthy Hungarian-Americans to give to charities that were aiding victims of the war in Hungary.

At the end of the summer Bartók's condition deteriorated. He died in September. He was at the prime of his powers as an artist, especially as a composer. His illness and death prevented him from bequeathing to posterity more outstanding compositions. They also prevented him from doing more for his compatriots, both in exile and in Hungary, as a distinguished public figure.

How much Bartók would have been able to do as a spokesman for Hungary or, possibly even as a Hungarian statesman, is difficult to estimate. He was respected by Hungarians everywhere and he had no record of partizan politics that could have been used against him. But Bartók was an extraordinarily shy man who most likely wouldn't have been able to function as a political figure. There can be no doubt that, had it not been for his illness, he would have returned to Hungary after the war. We can also suspect that life in increasingly communist-dominated Hungary would have been repugnant to him. Undoubtedly too, the Soviet leaders and their Hungarian allies would not have tolerated an honest man and a true democrat in any important position.

Although death had prevented Bartók from continuing his contributions to the world of music, and possibly also from working to benefit of his compatriots, what he had accomplished in his lifetime helped to improve the image of Hungarian culture in particular and the Hungarian nation in general. His compositions continued to be performed after his death world-wide; in fact, the popularity of his music increased, especially with lovers of modern music, as the decades passed.

Bartók was not a man without faults or limitations. In particular, he often had problems managing interpersonal relationships. Though an outstanding musician, a good writer and a fine linguist, his talents did not extend to relating to the wider public. To put it briefly, he did not have a charismatic personality, even though some of his students, especially a few young ladies, found him quite attractive. His failings and shortcomings notwithstanding, he was a great man.

Bartók is the best-known modern composer Hungary has produced. If anyone doubts his stature, he or she should look up the catalogue of any major American, British or Canadian university library. He or she will no doubt find more references to Bartók's music and to books discussing his work than to any other figure in Hungarian artistic life — or political history. Some musicologists go so far as to predict that for future generations of musicians, Bartók's legacy as an ethnomusicologist will be even more important than his contributions to modern music as a composer. The magnitude of his contributions to the world of music, however, should not obscure the fact that Bartók was a decent citizen of Hungary and of the world community. Though a Hungarian patriot all his life, he appreciated and valued the contributions to culture of other nations, in particular, of all ethnic groups living in the Carpathian Basin. In an age of racial and national intolerance, he was a tolerant man; in an era dominated by totalitarian ideologies, he was a moderate and a democrat; and, in an epoch of great conflicts, he believed in peace among all nations and nationalities. Hungarians should be proud of him.

A Selected Bibliography of Works Related to the Life and Art of Béla Bartók

Bartók, Béla Jr. *Apám életének krónikája* [The Chronicle of My Father's Life]. Budapest: Zeneműkiadó, 1981.

Bartók, Peter. *My Father*. Homosassa, Florida: Bartók Records, 2002.

Bayley, Amanda ed. *The Cambridge Companion to Bartók*. Cambridge, Cambridge University Press, 2001.

Botstein, Leon. "Out of Hungary: Batrók, Modernism, and the Cultural Politics of Twentieth Century Music," in *Bartók and His World*, ed. Peter Laki. Princeton, New Jersey: Princeton University Press, 1995.

Breuer, János. "Kodály and the Powers That Be." *Hungarian Quarterly*, 34 (Spring 1993): 156-61.

Chalmers, Kenneth. *Béla Bartók*. London: Phaidon Press, 1995.

Crow, Todd ed. *Bartók Studies*. Detroit, Michigan: Information Coordinators, 1976, reprints from the *Hungarian Quarterly*.

Demény, János ed. *Béla Bartók Letters*, trnsl. Péter Balabán and István Farkas. London: Faber and Faber, 1971.

Dreisziger, N. F. "A Hungarian Patriot in American Exile: Béla Bartók and Émigré Politics." *Journal of the Royal Musical Association* 130, 2 (Dec. 2005): 283-301.

Durbeck, Edward. "Béla Bartók: A Selected Discography of his Opera *Bluebeard's Casle*." *Music and Society in Eastern Europe* I, 1 (2006): 185-194.

Eősze, László. *Kodály Zoltán életének kronikája* [The chronicle of Zoltán Kodály's life]. Budapest: Zeneműkiadó, 1977.

Fasett, Agatha. *Béla Bartók—The American Years*. New York: Dover, 1970.

Originally published under the title *The Naked Face of Genuis* in 1958.

Frigyesi, Judit. "Béla Bartók and the Concept of Nation and Volk in Modern Hungary." *The Musical Quarterly* 78, 2 (1994): 255-87.

——, *Béla Bartók and Turn-of-the-Century Budapest*. Berkerly, Los Angeles, London: U. of California Press, 1998.

Gillies, Malcolm. *Bartók Remembered*. Boston: Faber & Faber, 1990.

——, "Bartok in America." In *The Cambridge Companion to Bartók* ed. Amanda Bayley (Cambridge, Cambridge University Press, 2001), 177-201.

——, "Bartók, Béla," *The New Grove Dictionary of Music and Musicians* 2nd ed. (London: Grove/Macmillan, 2001), v. 2. pp. 787-818.

Gluck, Mary. "The Intellectual and Cultural Background of Bartók's Work," in *Bartók and Kodály Revisited*, ed. György Ránki (Budapest: Akadémiai Kiadó, 1987), 9-23.

Griffiths, Paul. *Bartók*. London & Melbourne: Dent, 1984.

Helm, Everett. *Bartók*. London: Faber and Faber, 1971.

Juhász, Vilmos. *Bartók's Years in America*. Washington D.C.: Occidental Press, 1981. (A useful collection of interviews with people who knew Bartók).

Laki, Peter, ed. *Bartók and His World,*. Princeton, New Jersey: Princeton University Press, 1995.

Kenneson, Claude. *Székely and Bartók: The Story of a Friendship*. Portland, Oregon: Amadeus Press, 1994.

László, Ferenc ed. and comp. *99 Bartók levél* [99 Bartók letters]. Bucharest: Kriterion, 1974.

Molnár, Antal. "Az új magyar zene kibontakozása" [The development of the new Hungarian music], in Antal Molnár, *Eszmények, értékek, emlékek* [Ideals, values and memories], comp. Ferenc Bónis (Budapest: Zeneműkiadó, 1981), 85-135.

Pethő, Bertalan. *Bartók Rejtekútja* [The Secret Path of Bartók]. Budapest: Gondolat, 1984.

Ránki, György ed. *Bartók and Kodály Revisitied*. Budapest: Akadémiai Kiadó, 1987.

Satory, Stephen. "Bartók and Kodály: A Parting of the Ways." *Hungarian Studies Review*, 19 (Spring-Fall 1992): 59-68.

Schlacks, Charles. "The First Recordings of the 1920s, 1930s, 1940s, and 1950s Published on Piano Rolls and 78 R.P.M. Records." *Music and Society in Eastern Europe* I, 1 (2006): 141-148.

——, "Long Playing Béla Bartók: A Selected Discography." *Music and Society in Eastern Europe* I, 1 (2006): 149-168.

——, "High End Béla Bartók: The Stereo Anolog Recordings of the 1950s,

1960s and 1970s." *Music and Society in Eastern Europe* I, 1 (2006): 169-184.

Schneider, David E. "Hungarian nationalism and the reception of Bartók's music, 1904-1940," in *The Cambridge Companion to Bartók*, ed. Amanda Bayley (Cambridge, Cambridge University Press, 2001).

Somfai, László. "Batók and France: Aspects of a Relationship," *Hungarian Quarterly* 35 (Spring 1994): 174-79.

Suchoff, Benjamin ed. *Béla Bartók Essays,*. Lincoln, Nebrasca: U. of Nebrasca Press; published in London by Faber & Faber, 1976; Bison Book ed., 1992.

Suchoff, Benjamin. *Bartók: Concerto for Orchestra: Understanding Bartók's World*. New York: Prentice Hall, 1995.

Stevens, Halsey. *The Life and Music of Béla Bartók*, 3rd edition, prepared by Malcom Gillies. Oxford: Clarendon Press, 1993.

Szántó, Tibor ed., *Bartók Béla köszöntése* [Honouring Béla Bartók]. Budapest: Láng, 1988.

Szigeti, Joseph. *With Strings Attached: Reminiscences and Reflections* 2nd, revised and enlarged ed. New York: Alfred A. Knopf, 1967.

Szöllösy, András ed. and comp. *Bartók Béla öszegyüjtött írásai* [The collected writings of Béla Bartók]. Budapest: Zeneműkiadó, 1966.

Tallián, Tibor. *Bartók fogadtatása Amerikában, 1940-1945* [Bartók's Reception in America, 1940-1945]. Budapest: Zeneműkiadó, 1988.

Ujfalussy, József ed. *Bartók brevárium: Levelek, írások, dokumentumok* [A Bartók breviary: letters, writings and documents]. Budapest: Zenem_kiadó, 1974.

Ujfalussy, József. *Bartók Béla*. Budapest: Gondolat, 1976, 3rd, revised edition. Also published in English (Budapest: Corvina Press, 1971).

Oscar Jaszi as a Prophet: His Early American Years, 1925-1937*

When **Béla Bartók** arrived in the United States in October of 1940, the most prominent Hungarian émigré living there was Oscar Jaszi (in Hungarian Jászi Oszkár, 1875-1957). He is known to historians above all as a life-long advocate of the confederation of the peoples of the Danube Valley. In fact, as an adult Jaszi had always maintained that the ultimate solution to the problems of the whole of Europe was union in a federation. Jaszi was also a strong believer in progress in human affairs: the advancement of the technical and social sciences, of democracy, education and human rights. As far as political convictions are concerned, he can be best described as liberal—this in an age when many of his contemporaries gravitated not to liberalism but to either left- or right-wing radicalism. For all the years he lived in exile, he remained loyal to his native land—though certainly not to the leaders and regimes that ruled it. Besides being a scholar, teacher, social critic, Jaszi also engaged in political prognostication—never more so than during the first decade of his American exile when he kept warning the world, especially America, of the dangerous situation that existed in Central Europe. This period of Jaszi's life and this aspect of his work that are little known, and it is these that will be explored in this essay.

There were few periods of peace and tranquility in Jaszi's life. In the years leading up to 1914, and especially during World War I, he was involved in acrimonious intellectual and political debates in his native land.[1] In the immediate post-war period he, as a prominent member of

---

* Most of this study is based on papers I gave at conferences at Concordia University in Montreal and at Charleston College in Charleston N.C. in 2003 and 2004 respectively. The last few paragraphs are based on my review article "A Hungarian Liberal in American Exile: The Life of Oscar Jaszi," that appeared first in the *Hungarian Studies Review*, 32, 1-2 (2005): 127-36.
1 The most complete biography of Jaszi is György Litván, *Jászi Oszkár* (Budapest: Osiris, 2003). Its English version appeared two years later: *A*

his country's first post-war government, tried in vain to put into effect a plan for the decentralization of the multinational Kingdom of Hungary—all in the midst of the paralyzing chaos that descended on the country in the wake of the war. The years from 1919 to 1925 saw him involved in intense political lobbying as one of his country's most prominent political exiles, while the Second World War years brought new turmoil for him by re-opening—if only for a brief time—the prospect of a wholesale revamping of the international order in East Central Europe.

Compared to the political turmoil of these periods in Jaszi's life, the first dozen years of his American exile, from 1925 to about 1937, was a rather tranquil age for him, or it should have been. It should have been partly because this was an era of relative political stability both in his adopted land and in his native Carpathian Basin, and partly because this

---

Tentieth-Century Prophet: Oscar Jászi 1875-1957 (Budapest: Central European Press, 2005). An earlier biographical work is still useful: Péter Hanák, *Jászi Oszkár dunai patriotizmusa* [The Danubian patriotism of Oscar Jaszi] (Budapest: Magvető, 1985). There are also collections of Jaszi's speeches and writings, including *Jászi Oszkár publicisztikája* [The writings of Oscar Jaszi], ed. György Litván and János F. Varga (Budapest: Magvető, 1982); and, Oscar Jászi, *Homage to Danubia*, ed. György Litván (Lanham, Maryland: Rowman & Littlefield, 1995). There are also a great many articles dealing with Jaszi. See for example Péter Hanák, "Oscar Jaszi's Danuibian Patriotism," *Hungarian Studies Review,* 18, 1-2 (1991): 11-16; György Litván, "Jaszi's Viennese Years: Building Contacts with the Democratic Left in the Successor States," *ibid.,* 43-58; also by György Litván, "Egy barátság dokumentumai: Károlyi Mihály és Jászi Oszkár levelezéséből" [The documents of a friendship: from the correspondence of Mihály Károlyi and Oszkár Jászi] *Történelmi Szemle,* 18, 2-3, (1975): 175-209. While most such articles are from the pens of Litván and Hanák, others have written on Jaszi as well. See for example, Thomas Szendrey, "Some Reflections on Oscar Jaszi and his Philosophy of History," *Hungarian Studies Review,* 18, 1-2 (1991): 51-58; and Attila Pók, "Jaszi as the Organizational Leader of a Reform Movement," *ibid.,* 17-25. Articles by still others will be listed below. My own publications on Jaszi include: "The Evolution of Oscar Jaszi's Political Ideas during the First World War," in *Király Béla emlékkönyv* [Béla Király Festschrift] ed. P. Jonas, P. Pastor, P.P. Toth (Budapest, 1992), 159-67; "Between Nationalism and Internationalism: Oscar Jaszi's Path to Danubian Federalism, 1905-1918," *Canadian Review of Studies in Nationalism,* 19, 1-2 (1992): 19-29; and, "Oscar Jaszi and the 'Hungarian Problem:' Activities and Writings during World War II," *Hungarian Studies Review* 18, 1-2 (1991): 59-91.

was a time of economic security in his life, facilitated by the fact that he had long-term employment as a teacher at Ohio's Oberlin College.[2]

That these years were not exactly years of tranquility in Jaszi's life was more the consequence of his character than of political or economic circumstances. During these years Jaszi continued his struggle for his ideals: democracy, modernization, the protection of minorities, and above all, a federal solution to the ills of East Central Europe. He also began to battle what he saw as a new scourge of his age: the growing influence of intolerant nationalism and fascist ideas in Central Europe.

It should be noted that Jaszi was not, strictly speaking, a refugee from fascism. He left Hungary during the so-called Republic of Councils of Béla Kun and his associates. Accordingly, he was a refugee from communism or its Hungarian Bolshevist variety. In reality, Jaszi the exile American academic was a refugee from right-wing politics, as there can be little doubt that, if the Béla Kun regime in Hungary had been followed not by a counter-revolutionary regime but a liberal or socialist one, Jaszi would have returned to Hungary and played a prominent role in her intellectual and even probably her political life. But, return to interwar Hungary, even for a brief visit, was not possible for someone who had been an ardent critic of the Hungarian right before his departure, and who became a tireless castigator of the regime of Admiral Miklós Horthy ever since its rise to power in Hungary in the fall of 1919. Furthermore, in the eyes of the counter revolutionaries, Jaszi was a "Jew" even though his parents had converted to Christianity.[3]

While Jaszi was not a typical interwar refugee to the United States in that, nominally at least, he fled his native country because of communism rather than fascism, he was not a typical Hungarian ex-patriot in the USA because he was admitted under the Rumanian quota for immigrants. This was possible because his home town had been assigned to Rumania in the Peace Treaty of Trianon that the Allies

---

[2] There was also a new start and stability in his personal life: he had come to the US with his new wife, the young and beautiful Recha Wollmann, with whom he had fallen in love during his Viennese exile. Péter Hanák, writing in his introduction to the Hungarian edition of Jaszi's *The Dissolution...* cit. p. 7.

[3] Jaszi did not receive religious upbringing of any kind. See his memoirs: *Emlékeimből: Szülőföldemen* [From my memories: In the land of my birth]. These are printed in *Jászi Oszkár publicisztikája*, pp. 539-91. The references to his early childhood are on pp. 541-45. See also Litván, *Jászi*, pp. 19-22.

signed with Hungary in June of 1920. This fact also made little impact on Jaszi's attitudes and activities as he would, throughout his American exile, associate himself mainly with other Hungarian emigres and his writings would focus mainly on the affairs of Hungary and Hungary's relations with its neighbours.

* * *

Jaszi's childhood experiences predisposed him to an interest in the lives of different ethnic groups. He grew up in Szatmár country (today's Satu-Mare, in Northwestern Rumania), a region with a mixed Hungarian-German-Rumanian population of different (Catholic, Orthodox, Protestant and Jewish) faiths. His father had a medical practice in the county seat, Nagykároly (today's Carei, Rumania), from where he looked after patients of various faiths and ethnicities in the surrounding countryside. The young Oszkár often accompanied his father on his visits to the villages of Szatmár.[4]

Despite this early exposure to the realities of life in the multi-ethnic Kingdom of Hungary, in the first three decades of his life Jaszi did not develop a keen interest in the nationalities problem of his native land. His attention as young man was devoted to active intellectual life and the promotion of reformist ideas. By about 1900, he had become one of the up-and-coming radical intellectuals of his county. Together with other, similarly motivated young men, they launched the sociological journal *Huszadik Század* [Twentieth Century] in 1900, and the Társadalomtudományi Társaság or TT (Society for Social Studies) in the following year. It was only in 1905 that Jaszi turned his attention to the nationality problem.

The "nationalities question" had been the historic Kingdom of Hungary's most intractable and in the end, unsolvable problems. It had its roots in the days of Ottoman rule in Hungary and the early period of the subsequent Habsburg imperium. What happened was that during the wars of the Ottoman-Habsburg conflict in the sixteenth and seventeenth centuries, large portions of the Kingdom of Hungary became depopulated. These regions were then re-settled by refugees from the Balkans or, during the early decades of Habsburg rule, by immigrants from the South-Slav lands, Wallachia, or from the Germanic states of the Holy Roman Empire. In some parts of formerly Ottoman-occupied Hungary,

---

[4] Jaszi, *Emlékeimből*, p. 545.

Magyar settlers were banned by Habsburg authorities—they preferred to augment their Empire's population by immigrants from other than Habsburg lands.[5] The long-term result of these processes was that the Kingdom of Hungary, which in the 15th century had a solid Hungarian majority, became much more multi-ethnic in character, in fact a country in which Magyars made up barely half of the population.

While this fact caused few problems and little concern for the country's Habsburg rulers in the eighteenth and early nineteenth centuries, the "nationalities problem" blossomed into a major political conundrum in the age of nationalism, that is by the mid- and, especially, towards the end of the 19th and in the early part of the 20th centuries. The problem was insolvable. As the author of a recent English-language overview of thousand years of Hungarian history has put it: "The problem that ultimately proved insoluble may well have been insoluble indeed: even the maximum of concessions... [by the Hungarians]... would have been less than satisfactory for the national minorities...."[6]

The insoluble nature of the nationality question was certainly not evident in 1905, but it appeared serious enough to many, including Jaszi, who turned his attention to it no doubt for that very reason. Once he realized the importance of the nationalities issue, Jaszi undertook a systematic study of it. He researched the nationalities policies of Hungary's revolutionary regime of 1848-49. He familiarized himself with the writings on the problem of some of Austria's leading reform-minded thinkers. In the years following he took great pains to visit many of his country's non-Magyar inhabited regions and to establish contacts with minority intellectuals.[7]

By early 1906 he could claim to have achieved an understanding of the relationship between the national state and socialism. Yet much work stood ahead of him in the unravelling of the complexities of the nationality problem in Hungary and elsewhere. Undaunted, he set out to master the subject and began lecturing and writing on it. In late 1908 he

5 Géza Pálffy, "The Impact of the Ottoman Rule on Hungary," *Hungarian Studies Review*, 28, 1-2 (2001): 109-32; and János Barta, "Habsburg Rule in Hungary in the Eighteenth Century," in the same volume, pp. 133-61. Also: Franz A. J. Szabo, *Kaunitz and Enlightened Absolutism 1753-1780* (Cambridge: Cambridge U. Press, 1994), especially chapter 8 "The Problem of Hungary."

6 László Kontler, *Millennium in Central Europe: A History of Hungary* (Budapest: Atlantisz Publishing House, 1999), 263.

7 Hanák, *Jászi Oszkár dunai patriotizmusa*, pp. 36-40.

published his first major article on the subject, in *Huszadik Század*.[8] The following year appeared his pamphlet, *A nemzetiségi kérdés és Magyarország jövője* [The nationality question and Hungary's future].[9] He had also started working on a major book on the subject. The basic premise that Jaszi had arrived at already was the belief that nationality groups should have the right to express their cultures their own way. Attempts at the forceful assimilation of ethnic groups were wrong and could be counter-productive. The giving of equal rights to members of the nationalities as individuals, something that some of the more liberal of Jaszi's countrymen were willing to concede, was not sufficient. Nationality groups were entitled to collective rights, which included the right to have their own schools, courts, and access to government services in their own language.[10]

The major work that Jaszi had been working on throughout these years appeared in 1912. *A nemzeti államok kialakulása és a nemzetiségi kérdés* [The development of nation states and the nationality question] has been the earliest and most significant Hungarian contribution to the theoretical literature on nation states and national minorities.[11] While in researching this book Jaszi had relied on the works of some prominent Austrian socialists, including Otto Bauer and Karl Renner, on many

---

[8] Oszkár Jászi, "A nemzetiségi politikánk iránya" [The direction of our nationality policies], *Huszadik Század* (Twentieth Century), Dec. 1908. It is discussed in Hanák, *Jászi Oszkár dunai patriotizmusa*, pp. 41f.

[9] Published in Budapest by the Galilei Kör (Galileo Circle), an association of reform-minded university students. See my paper, "Central European Federalism in the Thought of Oscar Jaszi and His Successors," in *Society in Change: Studies in Honor of Béla K. Kiraly*, ed. S. B. Vardy and A. H. Vardy (Boulder, Colorado: East European Monographs, 1983), pp. 540f.

[10] Hanák, "Oscar Jaszi's Danubian Patriotism," p. 13. Dreisziger, "Between Nationalism and Internationalism," 21. Equal educational rights for the nationalities was the cornerstone of Dualist (i.e. post-*Ausgleich*) Hungarian policies but by the turn of the century these rights had started to erode in the atmosphere of increasingly strident nationalism of the day. On Hungary of the times see two recent monographs: Alice Freifeld, *Nationalism and the Crowd in Liberal Hungary, 1848-1914* (Baltimore and London: Johns Hopkins University Press, 2000), and Judit Frigyesi, *Béla Bartók and Turn-of-the-Century Budapest* (Berkerly, Los Angeles, London: U. of California Press, 1998).

[11] A new, partial edition appeared in 1986 (Budapest, Gondolat). It was edited and introduced by György Litván.

issues he presented his own conclusions and offered his own solutions. The book's basic ideas can be summed up as follows: the awakening of an ethnic identity, a feeling of belonging to a cultural group, is a natural part of the historical development for all peoples. The process leads to the emergence of nation states, but the ultimate result of this process is not the nation state itself but the creation of large federation of states. Nationalism then, is a constructive force in human evolution which leads to internationalism. The process of evolution from nationalism to internationalism can be derailed when nationalistic emotions are exploited and are used to foster the oppression of one ethnic group (usually a minority) by another (usually the majority). This, according to Jaszi, often happens in backward, economically underdeveloped countries, where unenlightened leaders implement policies designed to thwart the aspiration of minorities for cultural emancipation. The result is ethnic conflict.

Such conflicts, according to Jaszi, did not need to develop into life-and-death struggles, as they could be solved; and the recipe for a solution was progress, especially industrialization and democratization, as well as the establishment of large federations of democratic nations — he specifically mentioned a federation of the states of Europe. The immediate solution, which he wished to call to the attention of his countrymen in particular, was what he had advocated earlier: schools, courts and government services for the minorities, in their own languages.[12]

Not surprisingly given the existence of strident nationalism in Hungary of the times, Jaszi's recommendations were rejected by a large majority of Hungary's intelligentsia. Undaunted, Jaszi continued his work and by early 1914 he was ready with another study, an examination of the writings on the nationality issue of the nineteenth century Hungarian thinker and statesman Baron József Eötvös.[13] Though Jaszi had high praise for many of Eötvös's ideas, especially his opposition to

---

[12] For those who read Hungarian, detailed overviews of Jaszi's 1912 arguments are available, including György Litván's introduction to the 1986 edition of Jaszi's book (pp. 18-34). A brief summary in English is given in my "Between Nationalism...", pp. 21f.

[13] Eötvös (1813-1871) was the driving force behind post-Compromise Hungary's first nationalities laws. Jaszi's analysis of his ideas, entitled "Báró Eötvös József Állambölcsészete és Politikája" [The statecraft and politics of Baron József Eötvös], first appeared in *Huszadik Század*, 2 (1914). I summarize it in a few paragraphs in my "Between Nationalism...," pp. 22-23. On Eötvös see the works of Paul Bődy, including his *Joseph Eötvös and the*

the notion of the forceful assimilation of minorities, he faulted him for not realizing the full potential that run-away nationalism had for hindering the peaceful coexistence of ethnic groups and nations. Had Eötvös realized this, Jaszi argued, he would have known that nationalism could become a state-destroying instrument "wherever a national minority finds it impossible to satisfy its aspirations for liberty within the political framework, and where it possesses enough power to establish a more favourable state structure."[14]

World War I wrought great changes in Jaszi's political outlook and gave him an opportunity to try to implement his ideas during the conflict's turbulent aftermath. He greeted the outbreak of hostilities in 1914 by withdrawing from public activities. Out of his despair surfaced the hope that the turmoil and destruction would serve some historical purpose, that out of the ashes of war a better world would emerge, a world cleansed of intolerant nationalism. He first put his faith in German liberalism and the hope for the reorganization of Central Europe along Friedrich Neumann's plans for a *Mitteleuropa*. The increasing subordination of German politics to the military during the second half of the war dampened Jaszi's enthusiasm for a post-war world dominated by Germany. Until 1917 he worried about the possible expansion of autocratic Russia and the setbacks that such expansion would mean for progress and democracy in Central Europe. After the February Revolution in Russia, however, Jaszi looked to that country to lead Europe to "a united international organization."[15]

In the meantime, Jaszi maintained his keen interest in the nationalities issues of the Dual Monarchy. He continued to cultivate his contacts with leading minority intellectuals within the Kingdom of Hungary. He went on a fact-finding tour of Galicia, that ethnically highly mixed region of the Dual Monarchy. He also continued to criticize his own country's government for its nationality policies and for the deteriorating relations between Budapest and the nationality regions of Hungary.[16]

Modernization of Hungary, 1840-1870 (Philadelphia, PA: American Philosophical Society, 1972). A brief version of this story can be found in Paul Bődy, ed., *Hungarian Statesmen of Destiny, 1860-1960* (New York and Boulder CO: East European Monographs/Columbia University Press, 1989).

[14] Jaszi, "Báró Eötvös..." my translation, see "Between Nationalism," p. 23.

[15] Jaszi quoted by Hanák, "Oscar Jaszi's Danubian Patriotism," p. 13.

[16] A recent study that offers an overview of these deteriorating relations is Peter Pastor, "Hungary in World War I: The End of Historic Hungary," *Hungarian Studies Review*, 28, 1-2 (2001): 163-84, especially 168-69.

And, he began working on a blueprint for a postwar Central Europe. The plans Jaszi had for the reorganization Middle Danube Valley were outlined in his book *A monrachia jövője, a dualismus bukása, és a dunai egyesült államok* [The future of the Monarchy, the failure of dualism, and the Danubian united states]. The work, completed months before the end of the war, was published only at its end. In it Jaszi outlined his concept of a "Pentarchy," a confederation of the five nations living in the Middle Danube Valley: the Czech, Austrian, Polish, Hungarian and the South Slav nations, which the Rumanians might wish to join at some point in the future. Like the Dual Monarchy it was to replace to a large extent, this state was to be a customs union and was to have a federal army as well as a united foreign policy. Hungary, significantly, was not to be dismembered in the process of creating this federation, although Jaszi acknowledged that Croatia would probably want to belong to the "Illyrian republic," i.e. the South Slav state within the Pentarchy.[17]

When Hungary's wartime government collapsed under the weight of a failed war effort in late October of 1918, a left-of-centre coalition assumed power under the leadership of the opposition politician Count Mihály Károlyi. Soon, Jaszi was placed in charge of nationality policies. His task was to reorganize Hungary before the centrifugal forces of minority nationalism, greatly strengthened by the war, tore the country asunder and resulted in the disintegration of the Middle Danube region of Europe into small nation states.

Jaszi undertook his Herculean assignment with determination. He no doubt looked upon the prospect of the disintegration of Hungary into its component ethnic units with exasperation. Despite what some of his detractors had claimed after 1918, he had never advocated the dissolution of the multi-ethnic historic Kingdom of Hungary—he only wanted to reorganize it by giving collective rights, a certain degree of cultural autonomy, to the nationalities. He had another reason to fear the disintegration of his country. As we have seen, Jaszi had been a firm believer in the organization of the world, in particular Europe, into larger and larger political units or federations. The establishment of small nation states in the heart of Europe would have gone completely counter to

---

[17] For an English-language overview of Jaszi's 1918 plans see Béla K. Király, "The Danubian Problem in Oscar Jaszi's Political Thought," *The Hungarian Quarterly*, 5, 1-2 (1965): 124-30. Jaszi's plan for an East Central European federation had its antecedents in the plans that Lajos Kossuth developed after the failure of the 1848-49 Hungarian War of Independence.

such historical processes. Such a development, which he (already before the war) had disdainfully called the solution of *Kleinstaaterei*, would contradict his predictions and would constitute regression and not progress.[18] Indeed, in an article published in the September-October issue of *Huszadik Század*, he re-stated his belief that history was not the process of the rise and fall of states but "a gigantic process of assimilation, rejuvenation and democratization, whose purpose was the establishment of ever-widening, civilizing and co-operating units [i.e. federations of states]."[19]

By November of 1918 the chances of creating a Pentarchy along the lines of Jaszi's earlier plans had become nonexistent. All Jaszi could hope for was to reorganize Hungary along ethnic lines. His efforts were in vain. Only with the country's small Carpatho-Rusin minority did he reach an agreement which would have involved—had events not intervened—Subcarpathia receiving a large degree of self-government in Hungary on the pattern of the Hungarian-Croatian compromise of 1868. Jaszi's negotiations with Hungary's Slovaks and Rumanians met with failure. Even the leaders of Hungary's German minority rejected Jaszi's attempts to reorganize the country more in line with the ethnic realities and the democratic aspirations of its peoples.[20]

Instead of a democratic "Eastern Switzerland" emerging in the Middle Danube Basin from the ruins of war, there arose an agglomeration of small, independent states. Their existence was sanctioned by the international community through the post-war peace treaties, especially by the Treaty of Trianon of June 1920, which dismembered the historic Kingdom of Hungary and sanctioned the transfer of two-thirds of its territories to the other "Successor States" of Czechoslovakia, Rumania, and the Kingdom of the Serbs, Croats and Slovenes, later known as Yugoslavia. Ironically, these three new states were just as, if not more multi-ethnic, as the old Hungarian Kingdom had been before its collapse in 1918-1919.[21]

---

[18] Hanák, "Oscar Jaszi's Danubian Patriotism," pp. 13-15.

[19] Oszkár Jászi, "A nemzetiségi kérdés" [The nationality question], *Huszadik Század*, 19 (September-October, 1918): 97-99. My translation, see "Between Nationalism...," p. 25.

[20] See Hanák, *Jászi Oszkár...*, pp. 74f. For an account of the reception of these plans by Hungary's large German minority, see Thomas Spira, "The Reaction of Hungary's German Minorities to Oscar Jaszi's Plans for an 'Eastern Switzerland'," *Hungarian Studies Review*, 18 (Spring-Fall, 1991): 27-42.

[21] On the Treaty of Trianon see Ignác Romsics, *The Dismatling of Historic*

In Hungary itself, the regime of Károlyi gave way to the Republic of Councils under the communist leader Béla Kun. Jaszi left the country and began his long exile, from which he never returned to his native land except for a visit.[22] His exile found him first in Austria and then in the United States. Throughout his years of exile he continued to devote his time and energies to the furthering of the cause of the establishment of a Danubian confederation in Central Europe. Having been disappointed in the Western democracies for having imposed a "wrong and short-sighted" peace settlement on Hungary, early during his exile Jaszi put his faith in the governments of the Little Entente countries (Czechoslovakia, Rumanian and Yugoslavia) and strove to build good relations with their leaders. "He conceived this alliance," wrote his biographer György Litván, "not as a mere tactical one, necessary to defeat [Hungary's] Horthy regime, but as a long term necessity in... seeking rapprochement with the Successor States, in the integration of Hungary in a new democratic environment and,... in [bringing about] a Danubian Confederation."[23]

At first Jaszi was encouraged by his successes, especially his visits to Prague, Bucharest, Belgrade and elsewhere. Soon, however, his relations with official circles in the Little Entente states soured, even though his ideas and plans were still well-received in the democratic intellectual circles of all three countries. By 1923 Jaszi had started to realize the

Hungary: The Peace Treaty of Trianon, 1920, transl. Mario D. Fenyo (Boulder, CO and Wayne, N.J.: Social Science Monographs and the Center for Hungarian Studies and Publications, 2002; distributed by Columbia University Press). On some of the after-effects of Trianon see Steven Béla Várdy, "The Impact of Trianon upon Hungary and the Hungarian Mind: The Nature of Interwar Hungarian Irredentism," in *Hungary in the Age of Total War, 1938-1948,* ed. N. F. Dreisziger (Bradenton: East European Monographs, 1998; distributed by Columbia University Press), 27-48. For my own most recent observations on the consequences of the Treaty of Trianon see my article "The Long Shadow of Trianon: Hungarian Alliance Policies during World War II," *Hungarian Studies* (Budapest), 17, 1 (2003): 33-55.

[22] In 1991 Jaszi's remains were transferred from a cemetery in Oberlin, Ohio, to the Jaszi family burial plot in Budapest. To help celebrate the occasion a Festschrift was published: György Litván, ed., *Jászi Oszkár hazatérése* [The homecoming of Oscar Jaszi] (Budapest: Társadalomtudományi Társaság, 1991).

[23] György Litván, "Jaszi's Viennese Years," p. 44.

hopelessness of his policy of expecting help for a democratic reorganization of the Middle Danube Valley from the regimes in Prague,
Belgrade and Bucharest. He perceived, as Litván wrote, that "the policy
of the Little Entente, which was [by then] tolerant towards the Hungarian
regime [of Horthy] and intolerant towards the Hungarian minorities, was
ruining... his own position."[24] Having realised the futility of his
approach, he abandoned emigre political activities for the time being and
emigrated to the United States. He arrived there in September of 1925.[25]

Entering the United States had become problematic for Hungarians
by the mid-1920s. The quotas imposed on East European would-be
immigrants by Congress limited their chances of admission greatly.[26]
Further complicating the situation was the fact that the Hungarian quota
was heavily oversubscribed. Fortunately for Jaszi, as has been mentioned before, he had managed to get in under the Rumanian quota.
Also, as has been mentioned, in sharp contrast to some refugees from
fascism that entered the US many years later, he had steady employment—at Oberlin College, in Ohio. While at Oberlin, Jaszi taught,
worked on his academic publications, and continued his campaign for
reforms of all kinds in Central Europe.

There can be little doubt that the conscientious and hard working
Jaszi was a dedicated teacher. His teaching and related activities have
been described by Curtis L. Kendrick of Oberlin College:

> [After his arrival] ... Jaszi quickly became, and remained, an impor-
> tant member of the faculty community of Oberlin College. He had an
> accurate grasp of Oberlin's problems and potentialities, and a deep
> loyalty to its welfare. He carried conscientiously and effectively the
> large and small responsibilities of a professor and a department chair-
> man. He had an influential voice in the making of college policy, to
> which he brought both practical judgement and clearly thought-out
> principles....[27]

---

[24] *Ibid.*, p. 47.

[25] The late Péter Hanák described the circumstances of Jaszi's arrival in the
United States in his introduction to the Hungarian edition of Jaszi's book, *The
Dissolution of the Habsburg Monarchy* (Chicago: University of Chicago
Press, 1929): *A Habsburg-Monarchia felbomlása* (Budapest: Gondolat,
1983), 5-8.

[26] For a recent discussion of this subject see Tibor Frank, "Patterns of Interwar
Hungarian Immigration to the United States," *Hungarian Studies Review* 30,
1-2 (2003): 3-27, especially 3-8.

[27] Curtis L. Kendrick, speaking at the Oscar Jaszi Memorial Conference,

The major work that Jaszi produced during his early years at Oberlin, was his *The Dissolution of the Habsburg Monarchy*.[28] He was invited to write this book soon after his arrival in America. At first he doubted whether he could combine teaching courses he hadn't taught before—in a language that he was not completely fluent in—with a major writing project; however, his misgivings soon evaporated. He explained to his friend and political ally Károlyi that accepting this task would make sure that it would not be given to some American scholar who knew the subject only second hand, or to some professional Habsburg "expert." If he would write the book, it could serve "our cause."[29]

Jaszi's employer was good to him: he was given half-a-year's leave, with full salary, and even some funds to do research in Vienna.[30] The aid proved a good investment for Oberlin College: Jaszi produced a massive study in a surprisingly short time. Though written more from the perspective of the sociologist and political scientist than that of a historian, over the decades it gained the respect of many historians of East Central Europe. In particular, as one US academic remarked some fifty years later, the book "earned the admiration of American scholars."[31]

Though *The Dissolution* was largely and academic undertaking, it also served political purposes that were close to Jaszi's heart. In this respect, it presumably served his "cause" as Jaszi had explained to Károlyi in 1926. For the book had certain warnings for its audiences. Its message was very much the same that Jaszi had posed before and would repeat many times in his more overtly polemical publications in the years to come. He warned the statesmen of East Central Europe against

---

Oberlin College, in November of 1985. Reprinted in Document 6 of the Appendix of the conference's partial proceedings: *Oscar Jaszi: Visionary, Reformer and Political Activist*, ed. N.F. Dreisziger and A. Ludanyi (Toronto and Budapest: *HSR*, 1991): 103f. Jaszi tells us that he didn't like to fail students. See Oscar Jaszi, "On Becoming an American Citizen," in Oscar Jászi, *Homage to Danubia,* ed. György Litván (Lanham, Maryland: Rowman & Littlefield, 1995), 178-81.

[28] (Chicago: University of Chicago Press, 1929). Re-published in Hungarian translation as *A Habsburg-Monarchia felbomlása*, ed. György Litván (Budapest: Gondolat, 1983).

[29] Jaszi, in a letter to Mihály Károlyi, January, 1926. Paraphrased in Hanák's introduction to the Hungarian edition of *The Dissolution... cit.,* p. 8.

[30] *Ibid.*

[31] Kendrick, p. 103.

policies of undue centralization, bureaucratization and the pursuance of state autarchy. He called for civic education and the fostering of tolerance among peoples. He stressed, as he had concluded long before 1914, that all nationalities had to be assured cultural autonomy. Further in this connection, he counselled the international community that the more blatant injustices of the peace settlement had to be remedied. Some of Jaszi's advice was aimed at all countries in the region, including Hungary, while other counsel of his was aimed at the victors of the peace settlement, the countries of the Little Entente. He specifically warned that if these sates will not heed the lessons of the collapse of the Habsburg Monarchy, they will suffer the same fate.[32]

Beginning with the early 1930s, Jaszi would produce a stream of articles whose subject and message would be more overtly political than those of his *The Dissolution*. These essays were prompted by political trends in Central Europe. The phenomena that distressed Jaszi more and more was the persistence and in fact strengthening of right-wing movements in that part of the world. Jaszi's knowledge of politics was not confined to Hungary, or even the Carpathian Basin. He was a keen observer of the situation in Germany also. In this connection what concerned Jaszi especially was the rise of Nazism. Demonstrating his extensive familiarity with German history and the situation in that country at the time, he gave an explanation for the rise of Hitler that would impress many specialists of Nazi history even today. It might be worth while to summarize the conditions and factors he listed.[33]

The foremost cause for Hitler's success, Jaszi argued in early 1934, were the injustices of the Treaty of Versailles. Germany was truncated, impossible demands were made on her in the name of reparations, and the country was ostracised from the community of nations, all under the false claim that "Germany alone was responsible" for the outbreak of the war.[34] Another fundamental cause, according to Jaszi, was the fact that the German people had gone bankrupt economically and morally. These two factors accounted for "fifty percent" of Germany's descent to a Nazi state. A somewhat less important cause was the counter-revolutionary effort by the aristocracy, the officer corps, and the industrialists, to regain the power and influence that had been taken from them by the

---

[32] Jaszi, *A Habsburg-Monarchia* [The Dissolution...], 560-61.

[33] Oszkár Jászi, "A hiterizmus gyökerei" [The roots of Hitlerism] *Új Kelet*, February 1934, reprinted in *Jászi Oszkár publicisztikája*, pp. 434-38.

[34] *Ibid.*, p. 436.

Weimar constitution.[35]

Next, Jaszi listed seven more factors that, in his opinion, also contributed to the rise of Hitler: 1. the anti-liberal and anti-democratic atmosphere so characteristic of German (and, especially, Prussian) history; 2. the bankruptcy of democracy and socialism, a regime that had been imposed on Germany, and one that tolerated the rise of illegal armed groups established for the purpose of its destruction; 3. the fear of bolshevism; 4. the weaknesses of the German constitution (proportional representation, too much power in the hands of the President,...); 5. The sprit of "state capitalism," in which the free market had been supplanted by monopolies and special privileges; 6. the "disproportionate influence of Jews in public administration and in intellectual life."[36] And, 7. The putative "success" of Mussolini, which was proclaimed by German reactionaries an example that had to be emulated.

"We are facing," he concluded, "the tragedy of a great people," one that poses a "mortal danger to Western civilization." Yet he ended on an optimistic note:

> no matter how unfortunate, in fact repugnant, the present situation, and the outlook for the years immediately ahead, [we] should not lose faith in the German people. It is clearly impossible that this great nation, from which issued the spirit of a Kant, a Goethe, a Beethoven, will once and forever abandon their lofty ideals for the sake of the crude and bloody mysticism of a Hitler, a Göring and a Goebbels.[37]

It seems that the very optimism that drove Jaszi never to give up hope for the realization of his goals, influenced his judgement of Hitlerism. While he saw the danger posed by the rise of Nazi power, he was incapable of imagining the depths to which it could carry the German nation.

Unfortunately for Jaszi, and all of Central Europe, political malaise (the growth of intolerance, of authoritarianism, the increasing disregard

---

[35] *Ibid.*

[36] My translation. The original Hungarian reads: "A zsidók aránytalan befolyása a közigazgatásra és a szellemi életre." *Ibid.*, p. 437. Alas, Jaszi did not elaborate, so we are left guessing what he meant. A later comment (on the same page) suggests that what he had in mind was that this "disproportionate influence" was the excuse for anti-Semites to blame the Jews for Germany's problems.

[37] *Ibid.*, p. 438. My translation.

for human rights, the persecution of minorities) was not confined to
Germany of the times. He discovered—more precisely, witnessed in
person—this in the same year on a visit to Danubian Europe. But before
we discuss the events and results of that visit, we might comment on
some of Jaszi's earlier writings on this region.

A recurring theme in these writings was his criticism of the post-
World War I peace settlement. The Peacemakers, he would repeatedly
point out, had disrupted the region's economic unity and created new
irredentas. He admitted that drawing clear-cut ethnic boundaries in
Danubian Europe was not possible without doing injustice to some
minorities, but he insisted that the post-war territorial settlement inflicted "unnecessary cruelties which could have been avoided by a wiser
sprit of justice..."[38]

After chastising the peacemakers, Jaszi usually also censured
Hungary's conservative regime, mainly for not undertaking democratic,
social and economic reforms. He argued that if such reforms were introduced much good could flow from them both for Hungarians and the other
peoples of the Middle Danube Valley. If Hungary could be de-feudalized,
de-militarized, and meaningful agrarian reform could be introduced there
it would be easier to establish good relations between Hungarians and
their neighbours and conditions would become more conducive for the
creation of a democratic confederation in the region, one based on free
trade and meaningful autonomy for all the minorities.[39] Jaszi's 1934 trip
to the region gave him the impression that the chances of achieving this
democratic confederation—and, in particular, free trade and autonomy of
all minorities—had declined considerably in recent years.

In December of 1934 Jaszi reported on his findings among other
places in the liberal weekly *The Nation*.[40] He began by pointing out that,
originally, the situation in this regard had not been hopeless. The peace
treaties had clauses in them for the protection of minorities and, in the
1920s, there had been efforts, particularly in Czechoslovakia and
Rumania, to treat the minorities fairly. Unfortunately, Jaszi admitted,
the provisions of the post-war treaties in this regard had been "extreme-
ly vague" and the policies of conciliation by the victor powers in the
region, were "difficult to carry out." "Impatient nationalism" in many

---

[38] Oscar Jaszi, "Dismembered Hungary and Peace in Central Europe," *Foreign Affairs* 2, 2 (December 1923): 270f.

[39] Jaszi's writings on this theme, including his book *Revolution and Counter-Revolution in Hungary* (London: King, 1924), are commented on in my paper "Central European Federalism," pp. 544-545.

regions demanded revenge against the "former oppressors." There was much animosity between the new states and Budapest. The situation was not made easier by the fact that the former ruling groups in the region, the Germans and the Magyars, represented a "higher stage of culture" than their new masters.[41] Under the circumstances it perhaps should not have come as a surprise to Jaszi on his 1934 visit to the region, that the nationality problem had not been solved and that the efforts then being undertaken to solve it were "inadequate to bring about peaceful cooperation." "Even in Czechoslovakia," he went on, there was "a growing spirit of nationalism."[42]

In Rumania, the situation according to Jaszi was "alarming." He listed myriad complaints by Hungarians (as well as Germans) there, of discrimination and denial of their rights to express their ethnicity. Though Rumanian officials denied these charges, Jaszi came to the conclusion that even if some of the complaints are "exaggerated or untrue" the "residue... fully explains the general despair and indignation" of the minority populations. Still, the situation was not as bad as in Yugoslavia, where under the royal dictatorship, minorities were denied even the opportunity of complaining about their treatment.[43]

Jaszi ascribed the deteriorating situation to four factors. 1. Nationalism was becoming more intense and pervasive. It was now embraced by the whole population rather than just the middle class, as it had been the case before 1914. Even ordinary people aspired to civil service jobs, and expected the government to deliver these to them and not to former "oppressors" and potential "fifth columnists" in a future conflict. 2. The situation of intellectuals had deteriorated after the war and they wanted the jobs held by minority intellectuals. 3. The new bureaucracy obstructed the settlement of the citizenship status of members of minorities. They denied passports to these people on the flimsiest of pretexts. 4. Hungarian irredentism annoyed the officialdom of the Successor States.[44]

Jaszi saw no solution to these problems in the immediate future. He

---

[40] In the Dec. 12 and Dec. 26 issues (pages 669f and 736f respectively). The article is entitled "War Germs in the Danube Basin." It is reprinted in *Homage to Danubia*, pp. 77-86.

[41] *Ibid.*, p. 78.

[42] *Ibid.*, pp. 78-79.

[43] *Ibid.*, pp. 79-80.

[44] *Ibid.*, pp. 80-81.

concluded that Hungary would not be satisfied with minor frontier adjustments. At the same time, Jaszi found on his trip that the leaders of the Successor States, even those who had proclaimed themselves prepared to discuss territorial modifications, were against the idea now. Frontier revision was not possible now. In any case, Jaszi concluded, it was not the fundamental issue. What was more important was the "dissemination of education, the alleviation of the agrarian crisis, and the efficient defence of national minorities," and the latter was impossible under the "present" circumstances. The minorities needed a "system of cultural autonomy," and protection for their schools at every level. Minority institutions should receive "financial support from the state" proportional to what the state gives to other cultural institutions, and minorities should have the right to "a proportional share in the administration and judiciary of the state." This means that 'nationality' and 'citizenship' should be separated and the new states [should] become "nationally federated like Switzerland..."[45] And Jaszi went on:

> ... these things cannot be accomplished under the present... system. Instead of autarchy, the peoples need growing areas of free trade; instead of armed notational sovereignties, they need a federal union; instead of tariffs protecting the wealthy farmers, they need a new technique of agriculture based on an efficient credit and cooperative system. It is only necessary to enumerate these requirements in order to understand the immense obstacles in the way of their realization.[46]

Without "fundamental reforms", Jaszi concluded, a "new war will come. And after the war will come the revolution" that will bring the "*kolkhozes*" and the "soviets of nationalities" and not a "free system of federalism" but the "dictatorship of the proletariat." "Not Europe but Asia will then rule in this part of the world..."[47]

Evidently, Jaszi's 1934 tour of the Little Entente countries dealt a profound blow to his hopes for the solution of Danubian Europe's problems. What he had found were disturbing developments and conditions, especially in Rumania and Yugoslavia. In other articles that he wrote about his trip, this time for the prestigious academic journals *Slavic Review* and the *Journal of Central European Affairs,* he was equally pessimistic. He summed up his experiences by saying that what he had found was hate-

---

45 *Ibid.*, pp. 84-85.
46 *Ibid.*, p. 85.
47 *Ibid.*, p. 86.

mongering and nationalistic mass hysteria in the countries he visited, and
the rule of "unbalanced" intellectuals. The result, according to Jaszi, was
a "hidden *bellum omnium contra omnes*" everywhere.[48]

With this pessimistic assessment ended Jaszi's first-hand reporting
on the situation in interwar Danubian Europe. He would continue to
write, but had to rely on second-hand information for his new accounts.
In 1936 he did have vague plans to return for another fact-finding mission, but by late 1937 he had come to the conclusion that he could not
and should not go. In fact, he feared that he would never see his native
and beloved Carpathian Basin again. For the next few years he would
watch the unfolding of events there often with dismay and would worry
about the future of his friends and acquaintances there, as well as his
wife's German relatives.[49]

* * *

Warning America and the world about the dangers of the situation in
Central Europe, sometimes with uncanny sagacity, was just one of the
contributions Jaszi made to his new homeland during the first decade-
and-a-half of his American exile. He also contributed through his teaching and through performing administrative duties at Oberlin College. It
should be pointed out that he was not alone among Hungarian interwar
emigres to provide valuable service to the USA. By the 1930s there was
a fairly large community of Hungarian ex-patriots who were putting
their energies and talents into endeavour that would benefit not only
themselves but the whole of America.[50] More Hungarian refugees from
right-wing politics would arrive in the USA in the late 1930s and early

---

[48] "Neglected Aspects of the Danubian Drama," *Slavic Review* 14, 1 (July
1935): 54-56; and, "The Future of Danubia," *Journal of Central European
Affairs* 1, 2 (July 1941): 135.

[49] Litván, *Jaszi*, p. 376-77.

[50] An outstanding work that touches on some of these Hungarian emigres is
Lee Congdon, *Seeing Red: Hungarian Intellectuals in Exile and the
Challenge of Communism* (DeKalb, Ill.: Northern Illinois University Press,
2001). The same author's earlier monograph is also relevant as many of the
Hungarian exiles in interwar Germany also ended up in the United States:
*Exile and Social Thought: Hungarian Intellectuals in Germany and Austria,
1919-1933* (Princeton, N.J.,: Princeton University Press, 1991). A volume of
essays that I had edited, *The United States and Hungary in the Twentieth
Century* (Toronto and Budapest: Hungarian Studies Review, 2003) deals with

1940s. These early and later arrivals were all part of that extraordinary wave of immigration whose members had helped to bring about great changes in American cultural and scientific life in the interwar years and thereafter. Many of these people were of Jewish background, even though some, like Jaszi, were neither followers of the Jewish religion nor possessors of a definite Jewish identity.[51]

While Jaszi contributed heavily to the intellectual life of his adopt-ed land after his arrival, he also continued to contribute to that of Central Europe where he had helped to keep alive ideas and ideals that had inspired reform-minded individuals in that part of Europe before his departure from there, and even thereafter—and, in fact, even after his death in 1957.

In 1925 it seemed for a while that this part of Jaszi's life and intel-lectual legacy might come to an end. That year Jaszi seemed to have become determined to leave behind the politics of East Central Europe and start a new life in the USA as an academic. As we know, in this quest he was not entirely successful. His heart and his mind remained anchored in the problems of his native land, the Middle Danube Basin, the territories of the defunct Habsburg Empire. When the new war broke out in 1939, and when the war enveloped the Carpathian Basin in 1941, Jaszi put aside his post-1925 reservations about emigre politics com-

---

or touches on this subject, especially the essays by Tibor Frank and Judith Szapor, but also some of the introductory notes by myself, including "Prominent Hungarian Americans Remembered," pp. 127-28. The particulars of the two essays mentioned above are as follows: Tibor Frank, "Patterns of Interwar Hungarian Immigration to the United States," *Hungarian Studies Review* 30, 1-2 (2003): 3-27; and Judith "From Budapest to New York: The Odyssey of the Polanyis," *ibid.*, pp. 29-60.

[51] In Hungary such people are usually referred to as "assimilated Jews." On the subject of Jaszi's Jewish origins and non-Jewish upbringing see Litván, *Jászi*, pp. 17-19. Another outstanding interwar emigre from Hungary with a similar, "assimilated Jewish" background was the avant-grade artist László Moholy-Nagy. On him see Oliver A. I. Botar, "Connections between the Hungarian and American Avant-gardes in the Early Twenties," *Hungarian Studies Review* 15 (Spring 1988), 38-52; also, in the same volume, Alain J. Findeli, "De la photographie à la peinture: la leçon de László Moholy-Nagy," pp. 53-62; Diane Kirkpatrick, "Time and Space in the Work of László Moholy-Nagy," pp. 63-76; and, Oliver A.I. Botar, ed., "Documents on László Moholy-Nagy," pp. 77-87; also, Lloyd Engelbrecht, "The Formation of a Renaissance Man: László Moholy-Nagy's Secondary Schooling in Hungary," *Hungarian Studies Review,* 31, 1-2 (2004): 1-14.

pletely and flung himself into action—and even headed one of the several political organizations of Hungarian emigres in America. He had hoped for some time during the war that the conflict might lead to favourable changes in the evolution of Danubian Europe and that these changes would include the implementation of his ideas.

The new war, however, brought new disappointments for Jaszi— disappointments that were probably more profound than those he had encountered after 1918. Not only was his hope of a federal reorganization of East Central Europe not implemented after the war, but democratic and other reforms were stifled there with the imposition of Soviet-style communism in the late 1940s. But Jaszi's disappointments went even further. In the jostling for influence among Hungarian emigres during the war, he lost some earlier friends, one might say he was deserted, by among others his former political partner and friend Károlyi.[52]

In the spring of 1919 when Jaszi left Hungary he was a refugee from left-wing extremism. Throughout the period we talked about, he was in fact a refugee from the right wing politics, prevalent first in Hungary and then increasingly throughout all of Central Europe. One of the saddest consequences for Jaszi after the Second World War was that, as the thirtieth anniversary of his departure from Hungary approached, he became a refugee from left-wing politics again, as the imposition of Stalinist rule in Hungary meant that he could no longer contemplate returning to his homeland in old age. As Litván has remarked, in the Horthy era Jaszi was a "revolutionary" in Hungary, during the Rákosi era he became a "counter-revolutionary"—and a "spokesman of American imperialism."[53]

He died in early 1957 (he outlived his nemesis, Admiral Horthy, by

---

[52] For discussions of Hungarian-American emigre politics during World War II in English see my papers "The Atlantic Democracies and the Movements for a 'Free Hungary' during World War II," *20th Century Hungary and the Great Powers*, ed. Ignác Romsics (Boulder, Colorado: Social Science Monographs, distr. Columbia University Press, 1995), 185-205; and also, and to a lesser extent, "Emigre Artists and Wartime Politics: The Hungarian-American Council for Democracy, 1943-45," in *Hungarian Artists in the Americas*, ed. Oliver A. I. Botar (Budapest and Toronto: HSR, 1994), pp. 43-75. For a more up-to-date discussion see Litván, *Jászi*, pp. 394-96.

[53] Litván, *Jászi*, pp. 7-8. Mátyás Rákosi ruled Hungary, with an iron hand, during the last five years of Stalin's life. Jaszi met him during his only visit to Hungary—in 1947, before the Communists took power. The two disagreed

a few days) and was buried in Oberlin. After the end of Communist rule in Hungary, his remains were returned to the family burial plot in Budapest (not very long before Horthy's remains were returned to Hungary). Interestingly enough, his "repatriation" was followed by preparations for Hungary's accession to the European Union. Jaszi's dreams of the people of East Central Europe being united in a democratic federation were disappointed in his lifetime. It seems now that these disappointments were only temporary setbacks and that the cause he had fought for all his adult life might finally triumph.

Jaszi's role then in interwar America, aside from his being a hardworking academic, was warning his American countrymen of the dangers lurking in Central Europe—and the fact that not too many were listening was not his fault. Jaszi saw the dangers both in the Middle Danube Valley and in Germany. He did not venture to say in public which area posed a greater danger to world peace. His stronger focus on the former might have created the impression in his readers that he considered it the more menacing of the two, after all the last war had issued from the ethnic tensions of the Middle Danube region. As we know the new war was unleashed by Nazi Germany, yet the situation in East Central Europe, the national hatreds and rivalries there, greatly facilitated the expansion of Nazi influence in that region from the mid-1930s on. Jaszi's warnings about trouble lurking in the Middle Danube region were not misplaced.

In assessing Nazi Germany he perceived great dangers but he was unable to foresee the depravity that Hitler and his associates would be capable of less than a decade down the road. He was also not able to foresee the process that Hitler biographer Ian Kershaw described as the "cumulative radicalization" of the Nazi State, a process that culminated in total war and genocide.[54]

Aside from such failings—and just who could foresee the Holocaust (and the mass murder of Gypsies, Slavs and even Germans with handicaps) in the mid-1930s when Jaszi wrote his article on the roots of Hitlerism?—Jaszi was often a good prognosticator. In his old age in the mid-1950s, he seemed to have come closest to witnessing the

on what reforms were needed in the country. Litván, *Jászi*, p. 432. For the details of the visit, see *ibid*., pp. 427-40.

[54] "The longer the regime lasted," writes Kershaw in one of his studies, "the more megalomaniac were its aims, the more boundless its destructiveness." Ian Kershaw, "Hitler and the Nazi Dictatorship," in *20th Century Germany*, ed. Mary Fulbrook (New York and Oxford: Oxford University Press, 2001),

realization of his 1934 prediction about the arrival of the *"kolkhozes,"* the "dictatorship of the proletariat" and, in general, the "rule of Asia," in the Middle Danube Valley after a new war. But this was not to be the final verdict of history, nor the final message of Jaszi's life.

His teachings and his struggle for reforms ever since the early years of the 20th century, his repeated refusal to be discouraged on a long-term basis by setbacks, had been predictors of the coming of a federal solution to the problems of Central and East Central Europe. He had started out on this path of advocating—and, in fact, predicting—such a solution in 1905. A century later, his predictions are becoming a reality, even though some parts of the Carpathian Basin have yet to be fully integrated into the European Union. Just when his remains were returned to his native land, his most important ideals started to be implemented. His life's most important contributions were not only to his adopted land, but to his native land as well, in fact, to the whole of Europe.

Jaszi's life and career were in some of their details untypical of those of the many intellectuals that had arrived in the United States in the interwar and early war years (he had fled a communist country originally, he arrived in the USA earlier than many of the refugees from fascism—to recapitulate just two of these details). In engaging in activities that in the long run also benefited the wider human community—including his homeland—he was probably not at all untypical.

* * *

As a postscript to this essay it should be added that Jaszi's contributions to America (and to Europe) have not been adequately recognized either in his native Hungary or in his adopted homeland the United States. A major step toward their recognition has been the publication of a full-fledged biography of him, first in Hungarian and then in English translation. The biography was written by the recently deceased György Litván. Litván was undoubtedly the most qualified scholar to have undertaken such a project. Over the decades he had edited and arranged for re-printing several volumes of Jaszi's writings,[56] and published a

---

99-120. The quotation is on p. 118. To me it seems that every problem the Nazis created required an even more radical solution than the last one, which then created a set of new, more serious problems, calling for even more radical, new solutions.

[55] Litván, *Jászi Oszkár*, *op. cit.*

great number of articles dealing with him, his activities and writings.[57]

Litván's preface to his biography of Jaszi points out that Jaszi's refusal to endorse either the radical (or reactionary) right or the radical left earned him the enmity of the regimes that ruled Hungary most of his lifetime. In pre-1918 Hungary he was seen as a troublesome critic of the establishment and its policies. Throughout most of the interwar years he was regarded as a dangerous progressive, while during Hungary's communist era, he was seen as an agent of American imperialism. From 1920 to 1944 Jaszi couldn't really contemplate a visit to his homeland because he was branded a "leftist radical" by the regime of Admiral Horthy; after 1948 he couldn't visit because the regime of Mátyás Rákosi deemed him an opponent of "true" (i.e. Soviet-style) socialism. Jaszi spent his remaining years in American exile.

Litván's biography portrays Jaszi's youth, his involvement in Hungary's public and political affairs before his departure, his early years in Austrian exile, as well as his early American years. He then goes on to describe in similar detail his activities in the Second World War and post-war periods. A few words ought to be said about this part of Jaszi's life.

The outbreak of World War II caused Jaszi to fling himself into political action—he even headed one of the several political organizations of Hungarian emigres in America. During the early years of the war he had hoped that the conflict might lead to changes in Danubian Europe and that these changes would result in the implementation of his ideas. The war, however, brought new disappointments for Jaszi—setbacks that were probably more profound than those he had encountered after 1918. Not only was his hope of a federal reorganization of East Central Europe not realized after the war, but democratic and other reforms were stifled there with the imposition of Soviet-style communism.[58]

The decade that followed the end of the war brought more disillusionment for Jaszi. He was saddened by the spread of Soviet influence throughout Eastern Europe and the diminishing prospects for democracy and federalism in the region. He was greatly upset by the treatment of minorities by Hungary's neighbours, especially by Czechoslovakia whose leaders expelled hundreds of thousands of the country's minorities. In the nick of time, in the fall of 1947, not long before the assump-

---

[56] Including: *Jászi Oszkár publicisztikája, cit.*; Jászi, *Homage to Danubia, cit.*, and a new, partial edition of Jászi, *A nemzeti államok kialakulása... cit.*

[57] Including the article: "Jaszi's Viennese Years..." *cit.*

[58] Litván, *Jászi*, pp. 394-396.

tion of total power by the communists in Hungary, he managed to pay a visit to his homeland.[59] The trip was the last of the septuagenarian Jaszi's major undertakings. Ageing and ailing, he took a long time to recover from it. His declining levels of energy and advancing age were not the only disappointments in his life. He had marital troubles. Furthermore he lost many of his friends. His friendship with Rusztem Vámbéry suffered in part because of the latter's continued association with the Czech leaders and Hungary's increasingly communist-dominated government. Jaszi's decades of congenial correspondence with Karl Polanyi also came to an end under the strain of ideological differences. And Jaszi once again broke off his friendship with Mihály Károlyi, this time in a more serious manner than during any of their previous misunderstandings. In Jaszi's eyes, as the late 1940s approached, Károlyi appeared to be more and more an opportunist, a Bolshevik fellow-traveller. This decision caused Jaszi much agony. On the other hand, with Michael Polanyi (whom he called Misi), that most astute and unrepentant critic of Marxism,[60] he remained on friendly terms to the very end.

During his long life Jaszi had his share of admirers. The most prominent of these was the poet Endre Ady. Interestingly, Litván points out that some Hungarians have forgiven Ady for his censure of Hungary's establishment but have not forgiven Jaszi for doing the same. Late in his life, the intellectuals who esteemed him clustered around the periodical *Látóhatár* [Horizon] and included Gyula Borbándi, the prolific writer on the affairs of Hungary and the Hungarian diaspora. And there were others, some of them main-stream political and/or intellectual figures, including the respected diplomat Aladár Szegedy-Maszák.

Jaszi's detractors were more numerous: members of Hungary's pre-1918 establishment and supporters of the Horthy regime, as well as the leaders of the 1919 and post-1948 communist regimes in Hungary. To the former two groups he was the revolutionary, to the latter two he was a counter-revolutionary. From 1948 to 1975 in particular, in the People's Republic of Hungary, Jaszi was a non-person or someone whose ideas were seen as misguided. In 1975, the year of the centennial of his birth,

---

[59] The antecedents, events and aftermath of this visit are discussed in great detail in Litván, *Jászi*, pp. 424-444.

[60] On Michael Polanyi see Lee Congdon's article "Polanyi and the Treason of the Intellectuals," *Canadian-American Review of Hungarians Studies*, 2, 2 (Fall, 1975): 79-90. The *CARHS* is the predecessor of the *HSR*.

he was partially rehabilitated, though his critiques of Marxist thought were kept secret.

The regime change of 1989 didn't bring Jaszi greater and wider acceptance in Hungary. Some people still see him as the radical and, in particular, the politician—and later, the would-be politician—who was ready to treat with the "enemies" of the Hungarian nation. Still others call him a self-loathing anti-Semite. To many of his countrymen he is still a "divider" of the nation, though to Litván he appears to be more of a "uniter," a man who was willing to try cooperation with people of a wide range of political views, except the extreme right and the left. And Litván agrees with those who see Jaszi more as a prophet than an ideologue, among other things a prophet of European unity. Regarding Jaszi's unpopularity, Litván admits that Jaszi's criticism of Hungary's establishments before World War I, in the interwar period and during the Cold War, was strident and relentless, a fact that accounts for the many enemies that he made during his lifetime—and continues to make even today. Aside from a few such observations, Litván did not try to evaluate Jaszi's life's work and overall political impact. He left that task to future historians—and to the readers of his book.

The Many Lives of Ambrosius Czakó: Theologian, Art Critic, Educator and Radical Journalist*

Ever since the establishment of Canada's first Hungarian communities at the turn of the last century, there have been attempts at the creation of a Hungarian-Canadian press. These attempts have met various degrees of success. From the appearance of the first Magyar-language newspapers early in the twentieth century, to the establishment of viable press products in the wake of the large-scale influx of Hungarian newcomers to the country in the 1950s, the quest for a Hungarian-Canadian "ethnic press" has been relentless. Less persistent and successful have been the efforts to provide the Hungarian-Canadian community with something more than basic newspapers, i. e. with quality periodicals, especially ones that appealed also to second and third generation Hungarian Canadians, many of whom were more comfortable with reading English than Hungarian.

In the last third of the twentieth century these aspirations were not out of the reach of the by then fairly large and prosperous Hungarian-Canadian community. The 1960s, 1970s, and 1980s were what historians will probably describe as the "golden age" of the Hungarian community of Canada, a time when thousands of fairly young and fairly recent arrivals were involved in Canada's Magyar community life. A great many of these, moreover, were people with a good education. Not surprisingly, this period saw the establishment and flourishing of numerous Hungarian-Canadian press products, including newspapers and periodicals of various types, as well as news-sheets and bulletins. Although by today some of these have ceased publication, while a smaller number have relocated to post-communist Hungary, others still "soldier on," including for example the Vancouver Hungarian Cultural Centre's *Tárogató*.

---

* An earlier, shorter version of this article appeared under the title: "Social Progress and Ethnic Solidarity: Ambrosius Czakó's *Tárogató*," in *Tárogató: the Journal of the Hungarian Cultural Society of Vancouver*, 27, 9 (Sept. 2000): 55-56.

The situation was different during the first half of the twentieth century. There was not much of a market for Hungarian papers and journals. Moreover, intellectuals among Hungarian immigrants were too few to provide their press with qualified editors and writers. What market there was for the Magyar-language press in those days, was often filled by Hungarian-American newspapers and periodicals, which existed in great numbers at the time serving the then very large Hungarian-American reading public. Newspapers and journals were also available from Hungary for those who were willing to read press products published weeks earlier. Under the circumstances it is not surprising that before 1950 only a few attempts were made in Canada to publish high quality Magyar periodicals, especially ones that were at least partly in English and aimed to serve not only Hungarian immigrants but also the second and third generations of Canadians from Hungary.

The first attempt at launching such a press organ came in 1937. It was the *Young Hungarian American* (*YHA*), a monthly paper aimed at second and third-generation Hungarians on this continent. It was the brainchild of Béla Bácskay-Peyerle, the editor of the Winnipeg-based *Kanadai Magyar Újság* (Hungarian Canadian News — hereafter *KMU*), the largest-circulation Magyar newspaper in Canada. The *YHA* featured news from Hungary and elsewhere, and reports about Hungarians and Hungarian organizations in Canada and the United States. The 1930s were not conducive to success for publishing ventures and, after publishing for a few years, the paper ceased to exist. Its publisher-editor, the indefatigable Bácskay-Peyerle, continued to produce the *KMU* and participate in the organizational life of Canada's Hungarian community, but he never tried to launch another English-language paper. A more successful—at least, a longer lasting venture—came about as the result of the efforts of the Reverend Ambrosius (Ambró in Hungarian) Czakó of Toronto.

Czakó was one of the best-educated Hungarians to have entered Canada before the Second World War. It may be recalled, few intellectuals came to Canada from Hungary at the time—in fact, their immigration was not favoured by the authorities in Ottawa.

Czakó was born into a poor Catholic family which meant that if he wanted to go to secondary and post-secondary school, he had to enter a religious order. Accordingly, he joined the Cistercian Order at age 15. After a promising start, which saw him getting his doctorate and doing post-doctoral studies abroad, he broke with is church after his theological writings, well-received by liberal clerics, were condemned by conservative church authorities.

He next trained as a Calvinist minister. During the revolutionary regime of Count Mihály Károlyi, Czakó took a government position. He had also translated into Hungarian theological works that were not appreciated in conservative church and political circles. Worse still, during the early years of the Horthy regime, Czakó associated with opposition elements and edited a journal critical of Hungary's establishment.[1]

Not surprisingly under the circumstances, there was no future for him in the conservative-dominated Hungary of the times. His periodical was suppressed and he was accused of being a subversive. He left Hungary for Vienna with the aim of emigrating to the United States. His entry into the American Republic was denied but, in time, people who respected his work convinced the United Church of Canada to bring him to this country. He arrived in 1928 and soon afterward he was appointed minister of the United Church's Hungarian congregation in Toronto. Czakó undertook his mission with dedication. He saw himself not only, and not so much a theologian, but as a teacher who would educate his poor countrymen who had been denied a decent education in their native country.[2]

Helping in this task of educating and enlightening the Hungarians of Toronto—and, in fact, all of Canada—was to be the journal that he launched in 1938 with the help of a subsidy from his church.

The premier issue of *Tárogató,* dated July-August 1938, described itself as a "monthly periodical for the education and entertainment of Hungarians." It was sixteen pages long, a bulk which would be maintained by most subsequent issues, though by the early 1940s the periodical had become a quarterly. The last four pages were printed in English and featured short reports from the Hungarian and world press. The front cover featured a photograph—later the cover would always present a picture of a man playing the *tárogató*—and the back cover listed the places in Canada that had a functioning United Church congregation for Hungarians.[3]

---

1 Carmela Patrias, *Patriots and Proletarians: Politicizing Hungarian Immigrants in Interwar Canada* (Kingston and Montreal: McGill Queen's University Press, 1994), 114-15.

2 *Ibid.*, p. 119. Czakó described his work in Canada as "I was not a minister (though I had a Protestant minister's diploma) but a teacher,..." Quoted *ibid.* For a short biographical sketch of Czakó see my study: "Hungarians in Canada," *Horizon Canada* (June 1987): 2632.

3 Saskatoon, Willow Brook and Rabbit Lake in Saskatchewan; Niagara Falls, Welland and Port Colbourne in the Niagara Peninsula; Toronto and Sudbury

The readers of *Tárogató* soon discovered that their editor had a certain ideological bent and was not reluctant to voice it. The message of the very first issue was inoffensive enough; it probably disturbed only the most ardently patriotic of Hungarians. A short editorial expressed the view that, for the sake of stability in Central Europe, the Hungarian-populated regions of the Carpathian basin that had been detached from Hungary, should be returned to her. Such a reorganization of the region's borders would allow Hungary to join the Little Entente (the alliance of Czechoslovakia, Rumania and Yugoslavia) which then could effectively oppose Nazi German expansion. Subsequent issues of the journal, however, made it obvious that Czakó's sympathies were with the left.

After the outbreak of the Second World War in September 1939, Czakó kept expressing the hope that Hungary could stay out of the war and that at war's end, Hungary would be able to shake off the dominant influence of the Nazis.

Once Hungary became involved in the war on the Axis side, the *Tárogató's* editorials began denouncing Hungary's leaders with increasing vehemence and made no secret of the fact that Czakó's man for the future leadership of Hungary was the exiled politician Count Mihály Károlyi. In fact, Károlyi's wartime writings were sometimes featured as the *Tórogató's* lead articles. An article in the September 1943 issue of the journal (vol. 4, no. 3) was entitled "Hungarians in the Service of the Future." It claimed that there were many such people but described in detail only three. The selection is significant and speaks of Czakó's ideological orientation.

The first Hungarian described as a man in the "service of the future" was Béla Lugosi, the Hollywood filmstar. Lugosi, the article proclaimed, was a great actor and a progressive Hungarian, a "tireless champion of the Hungarian cause and a loyal soldier of Mihály Károlyi." The next man in service of the future listed in the article was the Hungarian-Canadian artist Miklós Hornyánszky. The article related the story of the artist producing a painting commemorating the siege of Leningrad and then donating it for the purpose of collecting relief funds for the victims of that city's siege by the German army. The third man

---

elsewhere in Ontario; and Montreal in Quebec. It also gave the names of the ministers for most of these places: Ferenc Hoffmann, Zsigmond Balla, and Imre Csendes for Saskatchewan; Károly Fazekas for the entire Niagara area; and Mihály Fehér for Montreal. The Sudbury congregation did not have a minister.

described in the article was Joseph Balogh, the secretary of the Democratic Federation of Canadian Hungarians, the organization of Hungarian communists who, during the war, were afraid to use a name that would betray their true colours.

Though Czakó's *Tárogató* persisted for half-a-decade after the conclusion of World War II, times were less and less favourable to the continuation of a publication that was evidently more left-leaning than Canadian-Hungarian, and in fact, Canadian society at large. The publication's backers, the leaders of the United Church of Canada, no doubt became aware of Czakó' editorial stand. The introduction of communist totalitarianism to Hungary at the end of the 1940s had discredited Mihály Károlyi, who by then was of no use to the communists and was forced once again into exile. Czakó, with his credibility diminished, returned to the Catholic Church. In the end, he resumed his life as a Catholic priest and taught art history at Nova Scotia's St. Mary's College.

Ambrosius Czakó's *Tárogató* had been dedicated to the worthy causes of social progress in Hungary and ethnic solidarity among Hungarians in Canada. It probably contributed little to the achievement of either of these. Half a century later, even memories of this publication have faded away, after its readers had become old and passed away. Even sample issues of this "first" *Tárogató* are hard to come by nowadays.[4]

---

4 Most of the ones I have seen are deposited in the National Library of Hungary (Országos Széchényi Könyvtár) in Budapest.

Alexander Bölöni Farkas:
A Hungarian Critic of
Colonial Canada

The settlement of Hungarians in Canada is usually dated from the 1880's when groups of Magyar colonists were brought to the Canadian prairies by the immigration agent Pál Oszkár Esterházy. Canada, however, was not an unknown land to Hungarians before then. Individual Magyars had come to what was then British North America long before the 1880's, either as prospective immigrants or as visitors. Perhaps the most famous among the latter was Alexander (Sándor) Bölöni Farkas, one of Hungary's most popular authors of the 1830's.

In 1830 and 1831 Bölöni Farkas (1795-1842) accompanied Count Ferenc Béldy, a wealthy aristocrat, on a grand tour of Western Europe and North America. Farkas wrote a memoir of the tour which he published in 1834 under the title *Utazás Észak-Amerikában (Journey in North America)*. The book proved a great success in Hungary. Its first and second editions quickly sold out. In many households, the book was read out loud, so that the entire family could listen. Undoubtedly there could have been more editions and more printings of the book, had Habsburg imperial authorities not taken notice of the book's popularity, and banned it late in 1835.

Béldy and Farkas toured the United States in the late summer and early fall of 1831. Afterwards they entered what was then Lower Canada. Their first destination was Montreal where they boarded a steamer bound for Quebec City. A few days later they began the return voyage, up the St. Lawrence River and on to Lake Ontario.

Obviously, the two Hungarians' travel through British North America was not meant to be a systematic study of that land's political, economic and social conditions. Nevertheless, in his notes on their travels, Farkas did not confine his description of Lower and Upper Canada to comments on scenery, historic sites, and the life of the local population. He wrote much about Canadian public affairs, and what he said was almost always critical.

Bölöni Farkas' first negative impressions of Canadian political and economic life came in St-Jean, a British garrison town south-east of Montreal. Here, Farkas noticed "English soldiers guarding the fort and parading in the city," in great contrast to the United States where, according to Farkas, "not even the President" had a military guard. Because on entering the country Farkas and his companion had been subjected to police questioning, Farkas felt justified in remarking that it was obvious that they had left the "free states" and were once again under "monarchical rule."

Lower Canada, in particular, was an economically "backward" colony. Illustrative of the colony's backwardness, according to Bölöni Farkas, was the fact that the value of land on the Canadian side of the international border was "barely more" than one-tenth of that on the American side.

Aside from the truly "magnificent" St. Lawrence River and a few public buildings, nothing impressed Farkas in either Montreal or Quebec City. His visit to the Governor's residence in the latter place, gave him a chance to comment on Canada's political system. "Both Canadas" were ruled by the governor "as the personal representative of the British crown." There were "legislative bodies," but "constant conflict" existed between the aristocracy, which controlled the "Upper House," and the "democratically inclined Lower House." While there was no direct taxation by Britain, and the mother country bore the cost of defence, England still derived benefit from her colonies because of "commercial reasons."

From Quebec, the Hungarians began their trip to Kingston, stopping several times along the way to change ships or to bypass navigational obstacles by coach. Farkas described the voyage, commenting on sites along the route, on traffic in the St. Lawrence, and on the masses of immigrants that crowded most ships bound for the interior. In Kingston he observed a large party of Indians arriving in canoes to shop for provisions. He had a great deal of sympathy for these "once free" people who were now considered "alien wanderers" in their own land.

From Kingston our visitors first sailed to Oswego, New York, and then to York (today's Toronto), the capital of Upper Canada. Their impressions of this town are interesting: "[York] consists of entirely new buildings. The governor's residence, the colonial legislature, a school named King's College, military barracks, and a few churches are the public buildings. On the streets there are still many thick tree stumps and at barely a half-mile distance primeval forests..."

The visit to York gave Farkas a chance to talk about settlement policy in Upper Canada. He described this as ineffective, as Canadian settlers looked on the American system with "undisguised yearning." Farkas then went on to outline the struggle for constitutional reform in the colony.

From York the Hungarians took a ship to Queenston, in preparation for a sightseeing trip to Niagara Falls. Farkas devoted much space to a description of this scenic spectacle, but made no further comments on public affairs in Canada.

It might be asked why did Farkas, a visitor from a distant corner of the world, paint such a negative picture of Canadian politics? His attitude is all the more difficult to explain as he rendered a very favourable assessment of the United States. The answer to this question lies in part in Farkas' political philosophy. Farkas was not only a liberal, but also a democrat. He had gone beyond those people in contemporary Hungary who advocated constitutional and economic reform, but who did not favour, for the time being at least, a populist democracy. Farkas' ideal of a society was most closely embodied by the young American republic. Because of the Habsburg domination of his own country, he could not write a book describing his ideal of a free and progressive society, but he could publish a travelogue about America. Interspersed among the desriptions of America's scenic wonders, Farkas' book outlined a country that his compatriots could hold up as a model for themselves.

Seen in this light, Farkas' trip to Britain's largest American colonies assumed special significance. Canada was to prove to the author's audience that all that was good and beautiful in American society was not the result simply of a North American environment, but was the product of the political system prevailing in the United States. For Farkas, the Canada of 1831 was living proof that monarchical societies were less free and more backward than constitutional republics.

As a last question we might ask how and from whom Farkas and Count Béldy had obtained their information about political conditions in colonial British North America? The answer to this riddle can be found in Farkas's account of their crossing Lake Ontario from the town of York to Queenston on the lower Niagara River. Here he describes a long and "lively" debate about politics that the two of them had with two "distinguished fellow passengers." Only one of these is named, and is described as a member of the Legislative Assembly at York and a "journalist": a certain "Mr. Mackenzie". This "Mr. Mackenzie" can be no other than William Lyon Mackenzie (1795-1861) the leader of the radical reform movement in Upper Canada of the times and the publisher of the leading opposition newspaper the *Colonial Advocate*. Mackenzie was a strident critic of Upper Canada's establishment. In

1837 he would be the principal figure of what became known as the Rebellion in Upper Canada. Not surprisingly, what the Hungarian visitors learned from him about British North America, and in particular British rule there, was not favourable to the colonial elite.

Suggested Readings and Notes:

Alexander Bölöni Farkas: Journey in North America. Trans. & ed. by Theodore and Helen Schoenmann (Philadelphia, 1977); *Sándor Bölöni Farkas: Journey in North America, 1831.* Trans. & ed. by Arpad Kadarkay (Santa Barbara and Oxford, 1978); N.F. Dreisziger, "The Critical Visitor: Alexander Bölöni Farkas' Tour of Canada in 1831," *The Quarterly of Canadian Studies,* 5 (1982): 145-52.

Bölöni Farkas's book might be compared with that of Ágoston Haraszthy, *Utazás Éjszak-Amerikában* [Journey in North America] (1844). The obvious difference is that Haraszty did not visit British North America. He toured the United States and was impressed by conditions there. He returned to Hungary only to sell his estates and return to the USA as an immigrant. He spent time in Wisconsin but soon departed to California where he became involved in the enhancement of grape growing and wine-making. Many people consider him the "father" of California viticulture. Half-century after Bölöni Farkas's visit, another Hungarian aristocrat, Count Imre Széchényi, toured North America and reported favourably not only about the United States but also the Canadian West. I plan to write a paper about Széchényi's tour in the not too distant future.

It might be mentioned in connection with the story of Bölöni Farkas's meeting with William Lyon Mackenzie that the latter's grandson, William Lyon Mackenzie King, was Canada's Prime Minister in 1941 when the Government of Great Britain, which had just concluded an alliance with the Soviet Union, asked Canada to declare war on the Soviet Union's enemies, including Hungary. With a great deal of reluctance and after some delay, King's government complied with the request. The timing was momentous: December 7. As is well known it was on that date that a massive Soviet counter-offensive was launched that put an end to Hitler's hopes for a quick victory over Russia, and it was later that day that Japan attacked Pearl Harbor, bringing about America's involvement in the Second World War. On the story of the Canadian declarations of war on that day see my article "7 December 1941: A Turning Point in Canadian Wartime Policy Toward Enemy Ethnic Groups?" *Journal of Canadian Studies,* 32, 1 (Spring 1997): 93-111.

Hungarian Biographies:

Nándor Dreisziger's Publications Relating to Remarkable Hungarians (The last 12 years—for a complete list see the Appendix to this volume.)

"Oscar Jászi: Prophet and Danubian Federalist," *Hungarian Quarterly* (Budapest), 47, 1 (Spring, 2006): 159-63.

"A Hungarian Patriot in American Exile: Béla Bartók and Émigré Politics," *Journal of the Royal Musical Association* (Oxford University Press), 130, 2 (Dec. 2005): 283-301.

"A Hungarian Liberal in American Exile: The Life of Oscar Jaszi," a review article in *The United States and Hungary in the Twentieth Century (Part II): Articles and Review Articles,* ed. N.F. Dreisziger, a special vol. of the *Hungarian Studies Review*, 32, 1-2 (2005): 127-36.

"Spying on 'Mr. Bartok' in Wartime America," *Hungarian Quarterly* (Budapest), 46, 3 (Autumn, 2005): 116-24.

"Prominent Hungarian Americans Remembered," an intro. to Part IV of the volume *The United States and Hungary in the Twentieth Century (Part I): Studies, Review Articles, Documentary Articles and Memorial Tributes*, ed. N.F. Dreisziger, a special vol. of the *Hungarian Studies Review*, 30, 1-2 (2003): 127-28.

"Raimondo Montecuccoli, Prince" (1611-80, Field-Marshall & military theorist, commander of the armies of the Habsburg Empire and would-be liberator of Hungary), an entry in *Ground Warfare,* a volume in the new *ABC-Clio Encyclopedia of World Military History* (Santa Barbara, CA: ABC-CLIO, 2002), pp. 586f.

"Bárdossy, László (1890-1946)," and several other entries, in the *Encyclopedia of Eastern Europe,* Richard Frucht, ed. (New York and London: Garland Publishing, 2000), pp. 56, 237, etc.

"Social Progress and Ethnic Solidarity: Ambrosius Czakó's *Tárogató,"* in *Tárogató: the Journal of the Hungarian Cultural Society of Vancouver*, 27, 9 (Sept. 2000): 55-56.

"Péter Gosztonyi, 1931-1999: A Prolific Historian," *Kaleidoscope* (Toronto), 2, 11-12 (Nov.-Dec. 1999): 12-14.

"Francis S. Wagner (1911-1999) and Peter Gostony (1931-1999): Obituaries," *Hungarian Studies Review* 26, 1-2 (1999): 171-74.

"Theodore Roosevelt, Albert Apponyi, and the Fate of Hungary after World War I," *Tárogató,* XXV 12 (Dec. 1998): 39.

"The Tragic Story of Prime Minister Géza Lakatos," in *Habsburg*, Electronic Bulletin, Aug. 1997.

"Miklós Horthy in North American Perspectives," *Tárogató* 24, 12 (Dec. 1997): 46-47.

Regent Miklós Horthy, István Horthy and the Second World War, ed. N.F. Dreisziger (Toronto and Budapest: special volume of the *Hungarian Studies Review*, 23, 1-2, 1996).

"Prime Minister László Bárdossy was Executed 50 Years Age as a 'War Criminal'," in *Tárogató: the Journal of the Hungarian Cultural Society of Vancouver*, 23, 11 (November 1996): 56-57.

"A Dove? A Hawk? Perhaps a Sparrow: Bárdossy Defends his Wartime Record before the Americans, July 1945," in *Hungary Fifty Years Ago*, ed. N.F. Dreisziger (Toronto and Budapest: special issue of the *Hungarian Studies Review*, 22, 1-2, 1995): 71-90.

Part II

Hungarian Proto-History

Essays about:

Hungarian Proto-History

The Linguistic Family Tree

Traditional Views

Alternative Theories

Once More About
Hungarian Pre-History*

"The Hungarians," wrote Peter C. Newman in one of his numerous books, "are not Europeans... they come from Asia."[1] This statement represents one of the myths that people in the West hold about Hungarians. This myth is at once reprehensible and ironic. It is reprehensible because Asians have often been seen as uncouth and barbaric in the West, notwithstanding the fact that more civilizations have arisen in Asia than in Europe, and they tended to last longer.

The myth that Hungarians "came from Asia" is ironic for more than one reason. The first is the fact it can easily be argued that while it is debatable whether or not the ancestors of Hungarians came from Asia, the predecessors of the vast majority of the other Europeans certainly did.

The nations speaking Indo-European languages can trace their ancestry to Asia. Only about seven millennia ago, most of these peoples lived in or near Asia Minor, in particular in Transcaucasia and eastern Anatolia. It is from there that they, in various waves of migrations, spread out throughout much of western Asia (and as far east as India) and, eventually, Europe.[2] Among the earliest groups to come to Europe

---

* A slightly different version of this article had appeared in a Dec. 2004 issue of *Hungarian Life*.

[1] Peter C. Newman, *Titans: How the New Canadian Establishment Seized Power* (Toronto: Penguin/Viking, 1998), p. 129. Newman further describes Hungarians as "wild Asiatic tribes" and worse. He suggests, good-naturedly but also erroneously, that this Asiatic legacy makes some Hungarians successful businessmen.

[2] One widely-accepted theory postulates that, after their migrations to new homelands in the east and then the north-east, some of the proto-Indo-European speaking peoples entered easternmost Europe and spent time in the steppe-lands north-east of the Black Sea, very close to the region inhabited at one point by the ancestors of the Hungarians. Some earlier, now no longer favoured theories had postulated a European homeland for the speakers of the most ancient proto-Indo-European language: also the above-mentioned lands north-east of the Black Sea.

were the Celts, including the ancestors of such peoples as the Welsh and the Scots. Later arrivals were the forebears of the people who speak languages belonging to one of Europe's three main language families: the Germanic, the Romance and the Slavic. Listing the members of each of these would take up much of the page but such a list would include nations such as the English, the German, the French, the Italian, the Spaniard and, to the East, the Russian, Ukrainian, etc.

While Indo-European speakers were involved in their migrations in western Asia, later to southern and eastern Europe, and then eventually to almost every corner of that continent, the ancestors of Hungarians had lived in Europe most of the time. Where exactly in Europe they lived is the subject of debate among Hungarians, and even to some extent, among Hungarian historians.

Of course, if we accept the view of some Europeans that Asia begins at the eastern suburbs of Vienna, than we have to accept Mr. Newman's assessment as truth. And there were such Europeans. We have to remember Prince Metternich of Austria's quip that "Asia begins at the Landstrasse" the Landstrasse being a street in the eastern part of the Austrian capital.

But, to geographers at least, Europe extends to the Ural Mountains of Russia and it is to the West of that land formation that Hungarians had probably lived many millennia ago, though one theory of their migrations accepts the fact that for some time, they ventured to the eastern slopes of the Urals. Still, for most of the past three millennia, Hungarians were inhabitants of Europe.

Where exactly Hungarians lived three, four or five thousand years ago, we have little idea. The peoples of Eastern Europe had no literary traditions at the time, so historians have to derive their information on them from other than written sources. These include the findings of archaeologists and the speculation of linguists, more precisely, of paleolinguists. In the twentieth century medical scientists, and more recently geneticists had joined the teams of scientists who can add information about the study of the past of nations.

To start with the latter, we have to admit that geneticists are not able to reveal much useful about the uniqueness or otherwise of Hungarians. The Magyars' genetic make-up, and even the frequency of certain blood-types in their populations, does not reveal any significant differences between them and their present-day neighbours. This is not surprising of course, since Hungarians have inter-mingled and inter-married with their neighbours—and even with more distant peoples who had come to their land, either as migrants or as invaders—for centuries or even millennia. As a matter of fact, Europeans as whole don't show differences in their blood-types and genetic make-up. Only the Basques, the most obvious of populations in Europe who do not speak an Indo-European language, show some of these differences, in their mitochondrial DNA sequences and in the fact that RH negative blood types in their population are far more frequent than in any other European national group.

Archaeologists have been contributing information about the national pasts of people for a lot longer than medical scientists. But they can contribute only limited amounts of data to the history of peoples who lived thousands of year ago. They are familiar with utensils used by certain peoples at various times of their evolution, as well as with their funerary rites. Once they can be certain about the funerary practices of an ethnic group in the not so distant past, they can extrapolate about these practices generations, even centuries earlier. Through such knowledge they can trace the spacial extent of certain people's settlement in the more distant past as well as about their migrations through space and time. Anthropologists, both physical and cultural, have also made some contributions to the study of the past as well as the study of the relatedness of populations. For the same reasons that geneticists cannot speculate about the inter-relatedness of Hungarians and other peoples, physical anthropologists can not provide much useful information either.

Different type of information is derived from studies conducted by linguists. The science of comparative linguistics is the study of the relationships between and among languages. This field of inquiry is much older than, for example, genetics. Its roots go back about two centuries. Linguists have a relatively easy task when they compare two or more living languages. They have more difficulty in examining extinct tongues, especially if they deal with peoples who didn't have a well developed tradition of writing.

During the past two centuries at least, linguists have dominated speculations about the relationship of Hungarians to other ethnic groups, and even about the evolution of the Hungarian nation through the millennia. They tend to be on fairly firm ground when they compare the Hungarian language to other living languages, but have more difficulty when they try to use the findings of comparative linguistics to extrapolate about the history of the Hungarian nation.

According to some scholars, similarities between languages start to disappear completely after about 6,000 years a separation. The French spoken in Quebec is already different from that spoken in the heartland of France, even though there has been only about three hundred years of separation between the two (and it is not so much the language of the Québécois that changed, but the language of Frenchmen). Accordingly, Hungarian should not be similar to any language spoken by peoples who have not been a part of the Hungarian nation for six millennia. But, according to most comparative linguists, Hungarian is similar to some other languages spoken in Eastern Europe and Western Asia.

Linguists classify Hungarian as part of the very large Uralic-Altaic family of languages, in particular of the Uralic branch of it. Within the Uralic component of this family there is the Finno-Ugric sub-family. There are at the present about 25,000,000 people who speak Finno-Ugric languages. With nearly 15 million speakers, Hungarians constitute the largest nation speaking such a tongue. They belong to the Ugrian half. Other Ugrian languages are spoken by small, isolated groups of peoples in northern Russia, particularly in north-western Siberia. Speakers of Finnic and related languages constitute a larger number of groups, but in total they have fewer speakers. Among the Finnic languages there is Finnish, Estonian, Karelian and Lapp. Somewhat further removed from Finnic but still related are the languages of the Mordvinians, the Cheremis, and the Votyaks or Udmurts. There are about five million Finns, a little over 1.1 million Estonians and about a similar number of Mordvinians.

The affairs of the Finno-Ugric peoples, especially those of the scattered Finnic populations of northern European Russia rarely grab the headlines of the world's mainstream press. Recently however the widely-known journal *The Economist* (Dec. 24, 2005) printed an article about the struggle of the Finno-Ugric peoples of Russia for linguistic and cultural survival, and the resentment of Russian nationalists, including members of the regime of President Vladimir Putin, aimed at the meagre support these peoples receive from outside sources, from Finland and Estonia, as well as from academic institutes of the European Union, for supporting the survival of their languages and culture.[3]

---

[3] The article in *The Economist* can be accessed easily on the internet:
http://www.economist.com/world/europe/dsiplaystory.cfm?story_id=5323735

Hungarian Proto-History:
More on the Linguistic Family Tree*

In a previous essay on Hungarian proto-history I have outlined the contributions of different disciplines to the study of the ancient history in
general. I talked about the role of archeology, anthropology, medical
science and comparative linguistics in the construction of the image of
a nation's past for ages for which there are no written records.

Because anthropology and medical science can provide little information that would allow the reconstruction of the Hungarian past with
any certainty, scholars have relied rather heavily on the findings of comparative linguists.

Linguists can say a lot mainly because there are still peoples in
Eastern Europe and north-western Siberia who speak languages that
show limited similarities to Hungarian. Because, in the case of peoples
who had separated very long time ago, these similarities disappear
almost completely, linguists find only minimal links between Hungarians and their linguistic relatives. In my previous article I mentioned the
fact that, after three centuries of separation, the French spoken in Quebec
has become different from that spoken in France. Or, more precisely, it
probably happened the other way around. That is, in the Quebec of our
days, people speak a dialect that was spoken in France in the seventeenth
century, one that is hardly understandable for Frenchmen today. We can
imagine how different are the languages spoken by two Finno-Ugric
peoples after four or five thousand years of separation.

Fortunately, there are still populations, living mainly in northern
Russia, who speak their ancestral language and these tongues can be
compared to the major Finno-Ugric ones. This situation may not last
very long. Many of European Russia's non-Slavic and non-Turkic languages are dying. Russian nationalists are only too happy to see them
disappear and Finland and Estonia can do very little for them.
Hungary's present-day government cares little, as reported in the
December 24 issue of the journal *The Economist*. Languages such as

---

* A slightly shorter version of this article appeared in *Magyar Élet/ Hungarian
Life* in early 2005.

those of the Mari, Komi and Udmurt are spoken mainly by elderly people. The Russian media and an education system functioning in Russian make sure that the new generations learn Russian, and Russian only.

At the end of the *Economist* article a sentence is given in Estonian, Finnish and Hungarian, supposedly understandable to speakers of all tree. Unfortunately, the sentence is not given in any of the Ugric languages that are more close to Hungarian than to Estonian and Finnish. The sentence is: The living fish swim under the water. In Estonian it is: Elav kala ujub vee all. In Finnish it is: Elävä kala ui veden alla. And in Hungarian: Eleven hal úszkál a víz alatt.

As far as I know, the word "eleven" has changed its meaning in Hungarian during my lifetime. As a child I still learned a prayer that used that word with its old meaning "living", but today that word signifies not "living" to me, but "lively". Languages change, and in today's fast-paced world, they change more rapidly than ever.

With the help of comparative linguistics, supported occasionally by more or less reliable archeological evidence, scholars have reconstructed the Hungarian past for the pre-modern (the age before written records) era in different ways. In future instalments of this study I will outline the traditional interpretations of Hungarian proto-history, as well as some non-traditional ones. But, first, I want to review the findings of modern comparative linguists.

Today's leading experts on paleo-history, including the geneticist Luigi Luca Cavalli-Sforza and the linguist Merritt Ruhlen, classify the world's languages into three main groups (and a few others). The three main groups are: 1. Congo-Saharan, 2. Eurasiatic or Nostratic, and 3. Austric.

The second of these groups, the Eurasiatic or Nostratic, is divided into seven sub-groups. These include the Indo-European family, the Altaic, and the Uralic (as well as four other language families).

I have already talked about the Indo-European group. The second, the Altaic includes such languages as the ones spoken by the Japanese, Koreans, Mongols and Turkic peoples. The Uralic, in sharp contrast to families such as the Indo-European, Altaic and the Sino-Tibetan, does not have many speakers. In fact, Hungarian is its largest component when we count the numbers of speakers. And, relatively speaking, not many people speak Hungarian.

Uralic languages themselves are divided into two major branches. The degree of separation between individual languages within each of these branches is often huge and the distance between a component tongue of one branch and a member of another branch can be greater than for example the difference between English and Russian. This is why so often and by so many people these linguistic affinities are questioned or denied altogether. Yet, some comparative linguists insist on these classifications.

One branch of Uralic linguistic family tree is made up of the Samoyed languages. Little attention has been paid to these languages because of the smallness of the populations involved and their geographic remoteness form the centres of European civilization and learning. According to Finnish experts, most of the Samoyed languages had become extinct by the end of the twentieth century. Five of them are still spoken. One of them, the Selkup, is the easternmost of the Uralic languages — geographically speaking. It is the language of about 1,500 people who live in the middle Yenisey River Valley. The other four are spoken by scattered groups in northernmost European Russia and Northwestern Siberia, north of the treeline. The Nenets have about 30,000 speakers, the Yurats, Enets and the Nganasan have much fewer.

The second branch of the Uralic family tree we want to discuss is more relevant to us. It is the Finno-Ugric family. It is composed of the Finnic language group and the Ugric one. Of the two branches, the Finnic is the more luxuriant, that is it has many more branches than the other. According to certain linguists, it is composed of the Permian group of languages (spoken by the Komi, Permyak and the Udmurt), the Volgaic group of languages (spoken by the Mari and the Mordvins), the Saami language group (composed of languages spoken by among others the people known to outsiders as the Lapps), and the Baltic-Finnic group of languages (spoken by the Finns, Estonians, Karelians and a few other, less numerous, peoples).

Permian languages are spoken by peoples living in northern European Russia, mainly in the Komi Republic. The number of Komi and Permyak speakers is estimated to be about half a million. The Udmurt live further south, mainly in Russia's Udmurt Republic. They number also about half-a-million there, and about 250,000 outside of their Republic, some as far south as Bashkiria. None of these peoples form a majority within their own administrative territories.

Among the speakers of Volgaic languages, the Mordvins are the most numerous. Their numbers are estimated to be between 1,150,000 and 1,192,000. The largest group of them, some 300,000 people, live in the Mordvinian Republic, southeast of Moscow, in the bend of the Volga. The rest of the Mordvins live scattered widely east of their Republic — all the way to the Urals. The Maris (also known as the Cheremis) are also fairly numerous. They speak three very different dialects that some linguists are tempted to classify as different languages. They number about 650,000, half of whom live in the Mari Republic on the north shore of the Middle Volga. The rest are scattered. Over 100,000 can be found in the Bashkir Republic to the east. All of these speakers of the Volgaic languages live among larger populations speaking Russian as well as various Turkic languages.

The Saami language group is the least known to Hungarians, probably because of the limited size of the Saami populations (estimates put their number between 50,000 and 80,000). Yet, affinity between the language spoken by the Lapps and Magyar had been "discovered" by a Hungarian traveller to northern Scandinavia long before linguists began their serious studies of the Finno-Ugric languages. The person in question was János Sajnovics (1733-1785), a Jesuit priest and aspiring astronomer who, during a trip to northern Norway to observe the passage of Venus in front of the sun, did some language "research" and later wrote a book about his linguistic "discovery." Sajnovics is seen by many as the father of the theory that links Hungarian to the Finnic group of languages. His hypothesis was rejected my many of his compatriots at the time, as it is still rejected by some even today.

According to Finnish experts, there are ten Saami languages, spoken from the costal regions of central Norway all the way to the eastern shores of Russia's Kola Peninsula. Of these, the northern Saami is spoken by most speakers. They can be found in northernmost Norway, Sweden and Finland. Further south in Norway and Sweden, southern Saami is spoken. In the Kola peninsula live the speakers of Kildin Saami. The rest of the Saami languages are used by isolated, small groups living mainly in Finland. Many of these tongues are in danger of extinction. Most of these languages are closely related and are understood by neighbouring Saamis. Speakers of the tongues of the easternmost Saami lands, however, have more difficulty in understanding the Saamis from the Westernmost parts of Lappland.

The last of the Finnic languages we have to discuss are those of the Baltic-Finnic group. The two that are spoken by large numbers of people and are not threatened with extinction are Finnish (about 5 million speakers) and Estonian (ca. 1.1 million speakers). These languages are fairly closely related: Finns can easily learn Estonian and vice versa— but not as easily as a Norwegian can learn Danish. The third member of this language branch is Karelian, spoken mainly in Russian Karelia east of the Finnish border by about 140.000 people. Its northern dialects resemble dialects spoken in eastern Finland. Some Karelian speakers, speaking different dialects, live as far east as the Tver region of

European Russia. Other Baltic-Finnic languages are Vepsian, Ludian and Votian, all spoken in a few villages in Northwestern Russia. The article in the *Economist* mentioned earlier, estimates the number of Votian speakers at 20. Another source gives an even lower number. Livonian is spoken by a similarly small number of people in Latvia.

We now come to the Ugrian language branch of the Uralic family of languages. Hungarian or Magyar is spoken by the vast majority of people using the languages of this branch. The Ugrian languages are divided into two groups. One has only a single member: the Hungarian. The other is known as the Ob-Ugrian group, consisting of the languages spoken by the Khanty and the Mansi. These two languages are very far removed from Magyar, as are some of the Samoyed languages from each other. (In contrast, the Veps language in the Finnic branch, for example, very closely resembles Estonian).

The speakers of Khanty and Mansi (also known as Ostyaks and Voguls from the places they mainly inhabit) live east of the Urals—scattered wide in small communities along the Ob River and some of its tributaries. The inhabitants of these settlements number close to 30,000, but the majority of them no longer speak the ancestral language.

It can be safely said that Hungarians speak a unique language. Their supposed "close" linguistic relatives, the Ob Ugrians, speak very different languages. The Volgaic, Permian, Saami and Baltic-Finnic tongues, of course, are even further removed from Magyar. In reality Hungarians are linguistic orphans: they have no close relatives. They are very unlike most Indo-European peoples. In contrast to the Magyars, one might almost say, the speakers of English, French, German and Russian, for example, speak different dialects of the same language, not to speak of the Spaniards, Portuguese and the Italians. Even Welsh and Gaelic speakers have linguistic relatives. Though speaking very different languages, they are part of the Indo-European family.

The only other "orphan" language in Europe is the Basque. And I know of no connection between it and Hungarian, even though both in Hungary and the Basque lands, the sign "*iskola*" can be seen on school buildings. But, of course, the term for school is an Indo-European borrowing and is almost the same word in each of the six Indo-European languages I have tried to learn in my lifetime.

Linguistic affinity offers little help in deciphering the past of any linguistic group. This is especially true for the Hungarians. This fact has not prevented historians from using the findings of linguists to help reconstruct the Hungarian past. In the next instalment of my attempt at delineating the outline of Hungarian paleo-history, I will describe some of the traditional as well as the not-so-traditional interpretations of the Hungarian ancient past.

Descendants of Proto- Uralic Languages

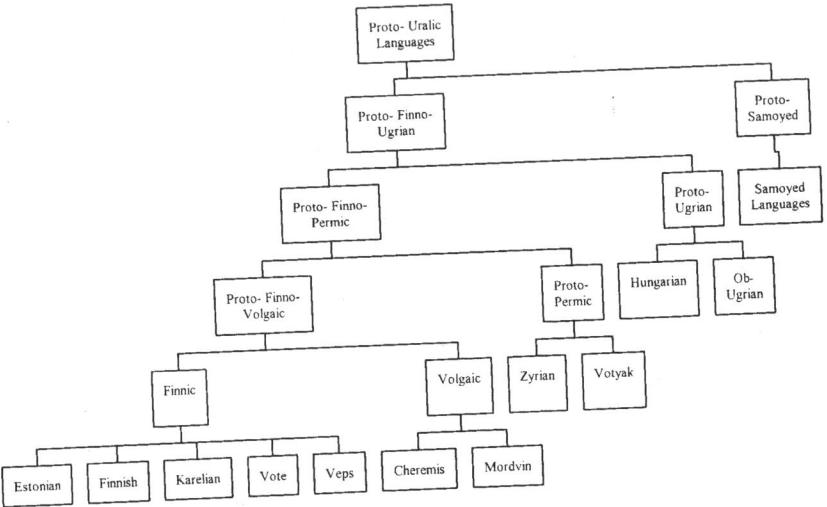

This portrayal of the "family tree" of the Uralic languages is based on the notes to George Bisztray's *Thousand Years of Hungarian Thought,* a special volume of the *Hungarian Studies Review*, 27, 1-2 (spring-fall, 2000): 128. The tree does not include all branches, e.g. the Saami languages.

Hungarian Proto-History:
The Traditional View*

Few aspects of Hungarian history are surrounded by as intense controversy as the Magyar nation's origins. At the same time, the details of the Hungarians' evolution before the seventh century a.d. are shrouded in mystery. Even after that time, which was marked by the beginning of references to them in various European and Near Eastern written sources, some aspects of their national development remain unclear. In this study I will try to sum up the traditional interpretations of Hungarian proto-history, the story of the Magyars before they appeared in the Carpathian Basin of Central Europe.

In an earlier article I had referred to the claim, often made even by professional historians who know very little Hungarian history, that the ancestors of the Magyars had "burst upon" their Central European homeland in the Carpathian Basin from the steppes of Central Asia "only" eleven centuries ago. I am not aware of any interpretation of Hungarian proto-history that would agree with such statements. Some theories of the Magyars' origins question even the very idea that they had come from the steppes of Asia but postulate other places where they had lived before written sources came into being and give historians some tenuous evidence of their whereabouts. The traditionalist interpretations do speak of the Magyars coming from the East, and admit that they had for some time lived on the grass-lands of southern Ukraine and Russia, but not even they place them for any protracted time in Central Asia, not even on the steppe-lands east of the Caspian Sea.

In fact the scholars who uphold the traditional view of the ancient Hungarian past place them firmly much further north at the time of the receding of the ice-sheets of the last glacial period. At the time these regions of what is now the northern forest zone, were probably teeming

---

* An overview of the "traditionalist" view of the history of Hungarians before the ninth century can be found in László Kontler, *Millennium in Central Europe: A History of Hungary* (Budapest: Atlantisz, 1999), 33-39. A much more detailed work is still of interest to those who read Hungarian: István Fodor, *Verecke híres útján* [On the famed path of Verecke] (Budapest: Gondolat, 1975).

with wildlife that followed the receding ice toward the north. This probably was the common ancient homeland of the Uralic peoples. Where its geographic limits were, must be the subject of conjecture. Some place it between the Ural Mountains and the vast basin of the Ob River in Northwestern Siberia, others suggest that it extended much further west, to the Baltic region of northern Europe. The ancestors of both the Finns and the Hungarians, not to speak of the other Uralic groups, lived here and sustained themselves by hunting and fishing. As I had pointed out in one of my earlier articles, words related to fishing are among the few that are shared by latter day Finns, Estonians and Hungarians.

According to the traditional theory of Hungarian origins, the Uralian peoples began breaking up, first into the Finno-Ugric speakers on the one hand and the Samojed speakers on the other, about five thousand years ago. During the next millennium, the Finno-Ugric peoples began breaking up too. Some of them remained in the north while the ancestors of the Ugrian-speaking peoples moved south. There is no agreement whether they did so in the eastern or western foothills and river basins of the Ural Mountains.

In their new homeland they seem to have come in contact with Iranian-speaking peoples. From these neighbours they learned animal husbandry and even the cultivation of land, though hunting remained an important source of sustenance for them as well. They also learned the use of copper and later, bronze. They became acquainted with horses. From this time on for some two millennia, the horse became an ever increasingly important, eventually almost sacred animal for them. In time, the horse was buried along with the warrior when he died, and even ordinary people were interred along with the skull of a horse.

About twelve or thirteen centuries before the birth of Christ, the Ugrian peoples split. Probably as a result of the climate turning dryer, some of them, the ancestors of the Khanti and Mansi (better known as Ostyaks and Voguls from the places they now inhabit), returned to the forests of the more humid north. There they became almost exclusively hunters and fishers again and abandoned any reliance on the horse though that animal remained an important part of their mythology.

At the same time the other Ugrians, the ancestors of the Hungarians, remained in the south. They became true nomads and coexisted in the vast lands south of the Urals with other nomadic peoples such as the Sarmatians and the Scythians from whom they learned the use of iron tools and weapons.

The proto-Hungarians next homeland became the lands east of the bend of the Volga River: today's Bashkiria and what Hungarians later called "Magna Hungaria" or Ancient Hungary. Though most Hungarians moved on from this land after several centuries, there were still Hungarian-speaking peoples there when monks from medieval Hungary, led by the Dominican Brother Julian, visited the region in the early part of the thirteenth century.

At the time when the Roman Empire in the West began declining, the steppe-lands of Westernmost Central Asia and southern Russia were under the domination of Turkic-speaking peoples. They coexisted with the Ugric Magyars and the Iranian-speaking Alans and influenced them in their economic life, culture and even political organization. Many Hungarian words regarding animal husbandry, agriculture, a structured political life, etc. are of Turkic origin, as is the tradition of dual leadership (a spiritual leader and a military commander) that accompanied Hungarians to the time of their conversion to Christianity around the year 1000 a.d. and the acceptance of a single Christian King as both spiritual and military leader.

The middle of the sixth century a.d. finds the Magyar tribes members of a Turkic empire with its centre of power further East in Central Asia. Less than two centuries later, decades after the collapse of that empire, Hungarians become ruled by other Turkish masters within the Khazar Khanate that occupied the lands north of the Caucasus Mountains between the Caspian and Black seas. The Khazars are famous for being the only people in that part of the world to have accepted Judaism as their religion. There is no evidence however that any of their Hungarian subjects had done so as well.

The Khazar Khanate, being composed of an agglomeration of Turkic and non-Turkic tribes and tribal alliances, had a turbulent history. Civil wars within the empire and rebellions against Khazar rule were frequent. After one such crisis in the 670's, a number of tribes, including the ancestors of the Bulgarians and probably some Hungarians, left Khazaria and settled along the Lower Danube. The veracity and especially, the dimensions of this early Hungarian migration to the West are subject to debate among historians.

Khazar rule over the Hungarians who stayed behind lasted for about an additional century-and-a-half. Afterwards these Magyars dominated the steppe-lands of what is now Ukraine for several decades. From here they, often in collaboration with other peoples, launched their military campaigns far and wide, at one time against the Empire of the East Franks, at another against the Bulgarian state in the Lower Danube Valley.

By this time the ancestors of the Magyars were known to outsiders and we have references to them in Byzantine, and to a lesser extent Arab and European sources. To the Byzantines, they were known best of all as "Turks" — their kings would be known as the "Kings of the Turks" down to medieval times. Some Byzantine sources as well as European chroniclers also called them *Ungri* or *Ungari* from the term Onogur, meaning an alliance of ten nomadic tribes the Magyars had been part of ever since Khazari times. From this latter term originated most of the modern Western and Central European names for the Hungarians (Hongrois in French, Ungarisch in German and Hungarian in English). In Arab and other Islamic sources they are referred to as *madzhgir,* a term that might have come from what they probably called themselves, meaning "speakers", and which later became the word *Magyar.*

At the time, the eastern neighbours of the Hungarians were the Turkic-speaking Pechenegs, known to the Eastern Slavs as the Polovetsi. In the last decades of the ninth century the Pechenegs came under increasing pressure from empires in the East and crossed the Don River thereby driving the Hungarians further west. At the end of the ninth century, the Pechenegs struck an alliance with the Bulgarians against the Hungarians and their allies, the Byzantines. Subsequently the Pechenegs launched another campaign into Hungarian-controlled territories, forcing them to look for a new homeland further west. In 895 the Magyars crossed into the Carpathian Basin, the place that became their home for the next eleven centuries.

In this manner the "traditional" interpreters of Hungarian ancient history date the arrival of the Magyars in what later became the Kingdom of Hungary to the end of the ninth century. But, was that the first time Hungarians had come to the Middle Danube Basin of Central Europe? Not all historians give the same answer to this question.

Of course Hungarian warriors had been to the area on their campaigns into Central Europe during the preceding decades. But there is evidence that in the Carpathian Basin, especially in its eastern regions such as Transylvania and the eastern parts of the Hungarian Plain where the 895 arrivals first settled, there had been Magyar settlements already that had their origins generations earlier. As had been mentioned above, in the 670's several tribes escaped Khazar rule and headed for the Lower Danube region. Most of these were the ancestors of the Bulgarians but there might have been many Magyars among them. They may have been the first Hungarians to settle in the Carpathian Basin. They may have been the "late Avars" that some western chroniclers record as having joined the population of the Avar Empire that had existed there at the time.

The speculation that Magyars had been settled in the Carpathian

Basin in appreciable numbers has given rise to the theory of the "double conquest" of the area by the Hungarians. The theory has had its most persevering and articulate spokesman in historian Gyula László who argued that the "late Avars" were indeed Hungarians, and may in fact been the followers of other Magyar-speaking peoples who had come to the area in several waves, some as early as the invasion of the Roman Empire by the Huns in the fifth century. It is common knowledge that the Hungarian-speaking Székely people of southeastern Transylvania firmly believe that they are the descendants of the Huns. Descendants of Attila's people they may not be, but their Magyar ancestors might have been driven to that part of Europe in the demographic upheaval that the arrival of the Huns and their numerous subject and allied nations had caused at the time. It might be worth mentioning here that there is a village named Vissoie, in an isolated valley of Switzerland called Val d'Anniviers, whose inhabitants believe that they too, are the descendants of the Huns, and have myths and traditions differing from their "European" neighbours, including the custom of writing the last name first on their wooden grave-markers—as is done by Hungarians and certain other Eastern peoples. Who really are the ancestors of the people of Val d'Anniviers may never be established from the distance of many centuries.

The theory of the "double conquest" explains a few questions that are difficult to explain in Hungarian history if we reject this theory. One of these is the fact that there are Slavic loan-words in Hungarian that were borrowed most easily by the ancestors of the Hungarians from their South Slav or West Slav neighbours in the eighth or ninth centuries rather than later. Further, Gyula László has found that in many of the conquest era settlements of the Hungarians, that is around the year 900, there is no break in the interment of the dead in cemeteries. This suggests that the newcomers continued to use many of the cemeteries that had existed before, whereas the usual practice of newly arrived conquerors was to bury their dead in newly-established cemeteries. All this suggests that in many parts of the Carpathian Basin the Hungarians who came in 895 settled among their kin-folk who had arrived earlier. Nowadays there are about as many Hungarian historians who accept this theory as there are ones who reject it.

Whether one accepts it or not, one has to question the term "conquest" for what happened in the Carpathian Basin in the late ninth, or the mid-seventh centuries, or even earlier. The coming of the Hungarians even in the ninth century was as much a migration and settlement as it was a conquest, and the earlier influxes (if there had been any) were certainly more the result of in-migration than conquest. In the seventh century especially, the arrival of new peoples, including possibly of Hungarians, must have been with the consent of the remaining Avar population there. Conversely, if such people settled on the western fringes of a nascent Bulgarian state, they probably had the blessing of the Bulgar leaders. Ruling peoples of different ethnicity was never a problem for leaders of empires in those days. All "empires" in the age of the great migrations were agglomerations of peoples brought under one command, often in an ephemeral fashion, by a powerful leader. The best example for such a multi-ethnic empire is probably that of Attila the Hun.

Having occupied much of the eastern third of the Carpathian Basin in 895 and soon thereafter, the Hungarians gradually extended their hold on other parts of what later became the Kingdom of Hungary. Political conditions in Central Europe favoured their territorial expansion. Avar power had declined everywhere even before the Hungarians' arrival at the end of the ninth century: their military had been ground up in conflicts with Charlemagne's Frankish forces in the West and those of the Bulgarians in the East. In the late ninth century much of eastern Hungary was probably a no-man's land between these two powerful states. In the western part of the Basin, the same forces were at work. There the Slavic state that had flourished for over a century, had its power sapped by internal dissention as well as the often simultaneous incursions of the Franks and the Bulgarians. In the year 899 internal dissention arose among the former as well, a fact which made the extension of Hungarian power to Transdanubia, in fact all the way to the foothills of the Alps, possible. In the following years, the Hungarian conquest (and this part of it was a conquest since it was achieved mainly by military means) of most of the Carpathian Basin was completed.

So goes the traditional explanation of the history of the Hungarians before the consummation of their occupation of what would be their homeland for the next millennium and more. As has been mentioned, this historical process, especially the pre-Christian era parts of it, are the subject of intense debate among Hungarians. Some of them deem the theories of the "hunter-gatherer" and "nomadic" origins of the Magyars anti-Hungarian propaganda, first perpetrated by Hungary's Austrian overlords in the days of Habsburg rule in Hungary. Then, according to the proponents of the non-traditional theories of Hungarian origins, the same "Finno-Ugric" theory was upheld by Hungary's communist masters who had similar stake in proclaiming that the Magyars had no distinguished historical lineage. In the next essay in this volume I outline briefly some of these "untraditional" explanations of the Hungarians' historical origins.

Hungarian Proto-History:
Alternative Theories

In my previous essay on Hungarian proto-history, I outlined the reigning, the so-called "Finno-Ugric theory" of the origins of the Magyars. While this theory is widely held in Hungarian academic circles, it is rejected by many Hungarians. The detractors of the Finno-Ugric theory advance various alternative explanations.

The roots of these so-called "alternative" theories of Hungarian pre-history go back in time to the eighteenth century and before. The idea for example, that the Magyars and the Huns were related peoples had been widely accepted in Hungary in pre-modern times. Among Transylvania's Magyar-speaking Székely population, the idea is still very much alive today.

In recent years the study of proto-history has received powerful analytical tools in the emergence of genomics as a means of establishing relationships between populations. The advocates of the Finno-Ugric thesis, as well as its detractors, might have had high expectations that this new tool would reinforce their conclusions. But the limited genetic research that has been done to date has failed to underpin the arguments of either camp. Comparisons of the genetic make-up of Hungarians and Finns has failed to demonstrate any explicit relationship, while studies of the DNA of Hungarians failed to reveal any distinct genetic characteristics or "markers" on their part. It seems that the genetic make-up of Finns resembles that of their Scandinavian neighbours more than that of their Magyar "linguistic cousins". At the same time research on Hungarians concluded that their chromosomal make-up is typically Central European.[1]

---

[1] Only in the region known as Őrség were populations found DNA could be deemed distinct. Interestingly, Őrség is located in south-western Hungary rather than the east, where non-European characteristics might be expected to be more evident. The researchers who came up with these unusual results were C. R. Guglielmino, A. de Silvestri and J. Béres, "Probable ancestors of Hungarian ethnic groups: an admixture analysis," *Annals of Human Genetics*, 64, 2 (March 2000), http://www.blackwell-synergy.com/doi/abs/10.1046/j.1469-1809.2000.6420145.x

All this should not be surprising. After all, for centuries the Finns have intermarried with their neighbours, especially the Swedes, while throughout the last millennium at least, the population of Hungary has been receiving genes from the peoples of Central and Eastern Europe and even from groups living further afield. According to the findings of genetic research, Hungarians, like the vast majority of Europeans, are descendants of a very small group of humans who had lived some twenty millennia ago. Their genetic code is not even as different from their neighbours as is that of the Basques from the rest of the populations of France and Spain.

Lacking the support of the new science of genomics, those who search for alternate theories of the roots of Hungarians resorted to the use of paleo-linguistics. Hungarian fascination with Sumer goes back generations. For those who are not familiar with the history of ancient civilizations, a few words might be said about Sumer.

Sumeria, along with ancient Egypt, is one of humanity's oldest civilizations. It arose in the southern part of what we know as ancient Mesopotamia, the Tigris and Euphrates river valleys, basically the central and eastern regions of modern Iraq. There, by about 3000 B.C. several of long-established agricultural settlements had grown into cities with flourishing commerce. The Sumerians were skilled canal builders and practiced irrigated crop-growing on a large scale. They made use of copper, silver and gold and their artisans made fine pottery, jewellery and weapons. They recorded their commercial transactions, treaties and laws on clay tablets, in what is known as a cuneiform system of writing. The wealth of Sumer enabled its kings to extend periodically their power over neighbouring lands. They both struggled against and interacted peacefully with their neighbours most of whom spoke Semitic languages that were very different from theirs.

Sumer's fortunes waxed and waned until almost 2000 B.C. when their lands became ruled by new masters. Their language, culture and traditions outlasted their political influence by centuries. Sumerian civilization, having existed for a millennium, had made a great impression on people who became familiar with it, especially those among Hungarians who were not enamoured with the idea of being descendants of hunter-gatherers who had turned into nomadic horsemen on the borderlands of Europe and Siberia.

The factors that make it possible to link Hungarian culture with Sumerian have to do mainly with linguistics. Paleo-linguists often have difficulty in placing Sumerian among the ancient world's languages but they usually agree that it was neither a Semitic language (very common in the region today and existing there already at the time), nor an Indo-European one. Furthermore, Sumerian, like Magyar, is an agglutinative language. And, as has been mentioned before, the Sumerians had used a cuneiform system of writing, as did the Hungarians in pre-conquest times. The Hungarian champions of the "Sumerian connection" also point to a great many words and word-roots that, in their opinion, were similar in the two languages. They also contend that such linguistic elements can be found in many of the place names that have existed in the Carpathian basin since time immemorial, long before the supposed arrival there of the Hungarians at the end of the ninth century.

The origin of the Hungarian nation according to the some advocates of the "Sumerian theory" can be loosely summarized as follows.[2] At the end of the third millennium B.C., at the time of the beginning of Sumeria's decline, an out-migration began from Mesopotamia that saw the old empire's peoples migrating to ever more distant places from their ancient and increasingly troubled homeland. The most important route of migration was supposed to have been through the Caucasus and then the lands northeast and north of the Black Sea. In the end scattered elements of these migrants settled in the Carpathian Basin, long before the conquest of that region by the Romans. They came as groups of settlers over a period of time rather than as a conquering warrior class. Their descendants survived Roman rule and the Barbarian invasions of the late- and post Roman period. Their land was occupied or conquered repeatedly by nomadic tribes from the East, by the Indo-European ancestors of both the German and Slav peoples, as well as the Turkic-speaking Huns and Avars. Yet they quietly persisted in their distinct culture and maintained their language that eventually developed into modern-day Magyar. At one point in time, before the spread of Church Slavonic and then Latin towards the end of the first millennium of the Christian era, they even developed a script of their own, distinctly cuneiform. They also survived still another invasion from the West, by the Indo-European speaking Franks of Charlemagne, the ancestors of the French nation. They were subsequently conquered by the warrior nation of Prince Árpád that gave them the name they would be known in history (Magyar), as well as their mythology and military and state-forming traditions. Árpád and his mainly Turkic-speaking warriors

---

2 Books on the subject have appeared in the Hungarian Diaspora, from Argentina to Australia. One that appeared in Canada, in fact in Toronto, is Sándor Nagy, *The Forgotten Cradle of Hungarian Culture,* transl. László and Margaret Botos (Toronto: Patria Publishing, 1973).

would rule their land but would eventually assimilate into the larger Hungarian-speaking population.

This theory fails to explain satisfactorily many aspects of Hungarian proto-history (such as the linguistic similarities between Magyar and other Finno-Ugric languages) but it explains other things. For example, the continuity of some place-names between the pre-conquest and post-conquest eras, the continued use of the same burial grounds between the ninth and tenth centuries, the continuity in the folk traditions (in particular, folk singing) throughout this age that ethnomusicologists Béla Bartók and Zoltán Kodály postulated early during their musicological researches in the Carpathian Basin, and so on. It must be mentioned that the more accepted (by academics) theory of the "Double Conquest" also explains many of these phenomena, or at least much better than the theory of the single conquest (at the end of the 9th century a.d.) postulated by some historians.

The rejection of what many people called the "official" version of Hungarian proto-history with its emphasis on the Finno-Ugric linguistic affinity, often coincided in Hungary with periods when Western values and traditions were questioned. One such period was the aftermath of the 1848-1849 War of Independence when Hungarians felt abandoned by the "West" to the autocracies of Central and Eastern Europe, the Habsburgs and the Romanovs.[3] Another was the post-World War II period when the people of Hungary felt that the Western Allies had sold them out to the Soviets at the war-time (Teheran and Yalta) and post-war conferences (Potsdam and Paris).

---

[3] The Habsburg defeat of the Hungarians was greatly facilitated by the massive army, some 200,000 thousand strong, Russian Tsar Nicholas I sent to aid the young Francis-Joseph in his quest to re-conquer Hungary. Though the Tsarist army did not engage the Hungarian *honvéd* forces in heavy encounters, it forced them to divert precious resources, both manpower and materiel, to the threat posed by this huge army invading Hungary from the east. Interestingly, the Russian-Austrian alliance that was born in 1849, did not last much more than a few years, as during the Crimean War of the mid-1850s, Francis-Joseph did not reciprocate the Russian help he got earlier. But by then Austrian tyranny in Hungary had been re-established and the freedom fighters had been executed, imprisoned or banished to exile. In a few years the situation would change again, as a result of Austria's conflicts with France and later Prussia. And in these, no Russian armies came to Francis-Joseph's aid. Eventually the regime in Vienna had to work out a power-sharing agreement with Hungary. As a result, the Dual Monarchy of Austria-Hungary was born in which Hungarians received a high degree of self-government.

Interestingly, while Hungarian disillusionment with the West tended to reinforce a rejection of the Finno-Ugric theory of the Magyars' origins, it did not necessarily make them turn away from explanation of their Asian origins. They just rejected the idea of links to the mythical "hunter-gatherer" Ugrian people, but not to more glorious and/or warlike Asian ancestors.

The event that had created the greatest disillusionment among Hungarians in "Europe" or "the West", however, was the peace settlement that was imposed on their country by the victors of the First World War. This was the time when the ancient Kingdom of Hungary was carved up by the peacemakers. The disappointment felt by the Magyar people should be no surprise to anyone familiar with the terms of this settlement. The Treaty of Trianon of June 1920 left Hungarians with a fraction of the territories of the historic Kingdom of Hungary (Rumania was awarded more Hungarian lands than was left to Hungary). The excuse for this peace settlement was the self-determination of nations but after it was done, millions of Magyars found themselves living outside their country's borders. Except for a small area, the city of Sopron and its immediate environs, there were no plebiscites to determine the wishes of the populations involved. Moreover, as the settlement separated producers from markets, and industries from resources, and disrupted transportation, its overall effect was to leave Hungary impoverished.

One long-term after-effect of the treaty was to leave Hungarians disillusioned with Western Europe. Hungarians felt that for many centuries they had served as the Christian West's bulwark against the pagan invaders from the East, and their reward was lack of understanding, abandonment, and outright hostility on the part of Western Europe.

This state of mind reinforced in many Hungarians the conviction that the Finno-Ugric theory of their origins that had been favoured by the Austro-Hungarian academic establishment was indeed a theory inspired by foreigners. Under the circumstances disillusionment with the West became extreme. Some Hungarians advocated the abandonment of the Christian religion and return to the pagan values of the 10th century and before.

The reactions of many Hungarians to the post-Second World War peace settlement was similar. Just before and during the early phases of the war Hungary had been able to regain some of the country's former territories, especially those with Hungarian majorities. These were taken away again. Despite the fact that in Western Allied circles there had been extensive discussions of adjusting Hungary's borders more in light of ethnic realities, not much came of frontier rectifications, except in the vicinity of Bratislava (Pozsony/Pressburg) where s few Hungarian villages were transferred—to Czechoslovakia! Worse still, Hungarians felt that, as a result of the wartime Allied conferences, they were assigned to the Soviet sphere of interest.

The disappointment at this outcome of events could not be voiced in Hungary, especially during the communist domination of the country that lasted from the late 1940s to the late 1980s. Therefore it remained the "sacred duty" of the large post-World War II Hungarian emigration to voice these complaints. Not surprisingly, a great many of the emigres rejected the theory of the Finno-Ugric origins of Hungarians that had been accepted by Hungary's communist-dominated academic establishment. It was only after the collapse of communism in Hungary in 1989 that books about the "Sumerian" and other origins of the Hungarians became fashionable in Hungary.

With the questioning of the main-stream version of Hungarian proto-history came the questioning of the main tenets of Hungarian values acquired at the time of the foundations of the medieval Hungarian kingdom, in particular the benefits of the conversion to Christianity. Some Hungarians in Western emigration even proposed a return to the Magyars' old, pre-conversion religion, possibly keeping in mind that the most successful nationalisms are those that combine a unique ethnic identity with a unique religion — as is the case for example with the nation of Israel. Whether this return to the "original" values and religion was to be to the traditions of Prince Árpád's people, or to those of the peoples of pre-conquest Hungary, or to those of the Sumerians, was probably not clear to the champions of the ancient Hungarian faith.

The debate about the Magyars' true origins will probably go on at least until the science of genomics will offer a clear answer to the enigma. But science rarely offers definitive solutions. Even if it will in this case, some people will probably not accept it an the speculation will go on. In fact, there is already conjecture by international scholars, stemming from recent genetic research or "bio-anthropology", to the effect that the proto-Uralic language emerged not in the northern Ural region as held by proponents of the theory of Finno-Ugric linguistic affinity, but further west and over a much larger geographic area among the peoples inhabiting the southern periphery of the continental ice-sheet that extended some 10,000 years ago from the Atlantic Ocean to the Urals.[4]

---

[4] See the essay of Christian Carpelan, "Where do Finns come from?" http://virtual.finland.fi/finfo/english/where_do.htlm

If this new assumption gains more support, the whole theory of "Finno-Ugric ancestry" will have to be re-evaluated.[5] Such re-evaluation will no doubt only fuel the debate over the true origins of the Hungarians.

---

[5] The re-evaluation of the proto-history of Europe in the light of the findings of recent genetic research has already started. See Stephen Oppenheimer, *The Origin of the British: A Genetic Detective Story* (New York: Carroll & Graff, 2006). In the meantime archaeologists have also started to re-write the pre-history of Western Europe. See Colin Burgess, *The Age of Stonehenge* (Edison, NJ.: Castle Books, 2003; earlier editions by Orion Publishing, 2001 and 1980).

Part III

Hungary and the World

Essays about:

France and Hungary

The 1956 Revolution in Hungary

Friends of Hungary in the English-Speaking World

France and Hungary:
A millennium of uneasy relationship

Relations between France and Hungary, between Frenchmen (and women) and Hungarians have been cordial in recent years. In a forthcoming election, the French might even be voting for a man of Hungarian ancestry as their leader: Nicholas Sarkozy. Friendly relations, however, had not always characterized the interactions of France and Hungary in the past. As almost every Hungarian knows, the French leadership had been primarily responsible for the dismemberment of the Historic Kingdom of Hungary in the post-World War I peace settlement. At that time the French considered the Germans of the German Empire, and also the Germans of Austria, as their enemies, and the Slavic peoples of Eastern Europe (the Czechs, Slovaks, the South Slavs, the Poles, etc.), as well as the Rumanians, as their natural allies. For these reasons, the statesmen of France were anxious to create new states (or enlarge others) in Eastern Europe, states that were supposed to become France's allies. Thus were born (or re-born, as in the case of Poland) the countries of Czechoslovakia, Yugoslavia and the enlarged, Greater Romania in the wake of the Paris Peace settlement of 1919-1920.

If we go back even further in the history of relationship between France and Hungary we'll find that mutual hostility was often interrupted by brief periods of friendly relations. Few people remember that on one occasion, French soldiers fought on Hungarian soil in part in aid of the Hungarian struggle against the Ottoman Turks. Part 1 of this paper outlines in broad terms the centuries-old relationship between France and Hungary, and Part 2 will remind us of the time when French soldiers went to Hungary to help in the fight against the Ottomans.

Contacts between the Kingdom of Hungary and the lands that later became France go back in time to the Middle Ages. French missionaries and priests took an active part in the promotion of Christianity in Hungary. Members of French monastic orders were frequent newcomers to Hungary to serve the cause of Christianity in a country that had forsaken paganism only a short time ago. Among those who did this were the canons of the Premonratensian order (also known as Norbertines or White Canons) whose order had its origins in the

Prémontré Valley of France and who, from the 12th century on, had spread throughout much of Europe, including Hungary. Their first centres in that country were in Garab and Jászóvár, but later they took charge of Christian religious and intellectual life in numerous other centres including Hatvan, Zsámbék and Csorna.

While Christianity was one tie that brought Hungarians and Frenchmen together, dynastic ambitions were another. Hungary's rulers, the members of the Árpád dynasty, regularly intermarried with other European royal houses. The most notable of these marriages was contracted by the great Hungarian medieval king Béla III (ruled 1172-96) who, after the death of his first queen, married Margaret Capet, the daughter of King Louis VII of France. As usual, with foreign queens came a retinue of knights and servants who brought outside influences, including French ones, to Hungary.

A little over a century later historic connections between French royal houses and Hungary strengthened when a member of the Neapolitan branch of the French Angevin dynasty, Charles Robert, the grandson of a Hungarian princess who had been married off to Naples, gained the Hungarian throne. Under his son, Louis the Great of Hungary (he was also King of Poland), the late medieval Hungarian kingdom reached its maximum geographic size. Of course, the cultural influence that came to Hungary with Charles Robert and Louis the Great was more Italian than French.

Louis had no male heir and following his death a chaotic interregnum ensued in Hungary. During it some Hungarian oligarchs tried to install Louis of Orleans, the brother of the French king, on the throne of Hungary. Eventually it was Sigismund, a member of the House of Luxemburg, who became first a co-ruler (along with his wife, the daughter of Louis the Great) then King of Hungary. In 1410 Sigismund was elected Holy Roman Emperor, a title his father also held for some time, and thereafter devoted his time and energies increasingly to non-Hungarian affairs.

Later in the same century members of the House of Habsburg began playing an important role in the affairs of Europe, including the region that later became north-eastern France, and by the early part of the 16th century, in the affairs of Northwestern part of Hungary, especially after much of the rest of the kingdom fell under Ottoman Turkish domination. With that development French-Hungarian relations often became intertwined with the relations between the ruling houses of France and Austria. And, more often than not, these relations were not amicable.

The first crisis in the relationship of the Kings of France with the

Habsburgs came in the mid-1470s when the head of the House of Habsburg, Holy Roman Emperor Frederick III, aligned himself with an enemy of Louis XI, the King of France. This "enemy" was Charles the Bold, the Duke of Burgundy who wanted to carve out a kingdom for himself from the territory that today is northeastern France and the Low Countries. Charles even betrothed his daughter Marie to Frederick's son, Maximilian. In supporting the Burgundians against the rulers of France, the Habsburgs made a miscalculation however, for Louis soon eliminated the Burgundian threat to the French throne. However the bitter memory of the Habsburgs befriending an enemy of the French king lingered on.

During the following centuries, French sovereigns including Francis I, Henry IV, Louis XIV, and their ministers—especially Cardinal Richelieu who was obsessed by the idea of France being encircled—often fought the Habsburgs. French hostility against the Habsburgs became pervasive during the War of Spanish Succession between 1701 and 1714. The idea of the House of Habsburg ruling both in Madrid and Vienna was repulsive to the court of Louis XIV and he took on Austria and England to resist this prospect. Louis' appeal to the people of France in 1709 helped to mobilize French public opinion against the Habsburgs.

At the time, anti-Habsburg sentiments at the court in Versailles did not translate into anti-Magyar feelings. In fact, Louis and his ministers were sympathetic to Ferenc Rákóczi and his war of independence against Vienna, but didn't, perhaps couldn't help Rákóczi effectively.

In the middle of the eighteenth century, Chancellor Kaunitz of Austria managed to achieve a rapprochement with the French. As a result, France and Austria, enemies in the War of Spanish Succession and in the War of Austrian Succession (1740-1748), became allies against the Prussia of Frederick the Great and his English backers, in the Seven Years War (1756-1763). This alliance between Bourbon France and the Hapsburg Empire lasted until 1792. The end of the Ancien regime and the French Revolution, however, reactivated Franco-Austrian animosity infusing into it ideological differences between a "revolutionary order" and the "old order" that had been abolished in France but not in the Habsburg Empire.

From the middle of the nineteenth century on, however, the French perception of the space between Germany and Russia became dominated by a fear of a German takeover of most or all of Central Europe. As France's leaders became conscious of the danger of Prussia's German policy, they reassessed the role played by Austria to resist it.

Nonetheless, it was really the shocks of the Austrian and French defeats at the hands of Prussia (at Sadowa and then at Sedan respectively), that gave rise to the vision of an Austria in France that was useful to French interests, without however totally eclipsing the traditional French aversion to anything that was Habsburg. Indeed, from 1867 to 1870, there was a rapprochement between the French and Austro-Hungarian Empires.

The emergence of the Second German Empire gave cause for concern not only among Frenchmen but also among Europe's Slavs. The unity that had been imposed on the German states by Prussian power and Otto von Bismark's astute diplomacy had the effect of fostering feelings of greater solidarity among the Slavic nations of Eastern Europe. These were the halcyon days of the Pan-Slav movement that aimed at uniting all Slavs in one great Slavic federation.

The fear and resentment of ever increasing German power and influence made Frenchmen and Slavs natural allies. The humiliation of France at Sedan resulted in the emergence of pro-Slav sentiments in France and the rise to prominence of Slavic studies in French institutions of higher learning. The most prominent French teachers of Slavic history, languages and literatures also became the most outspoken philo-Slavs in France and, at the same time, critics of the policies not only of the German realm but also of the Habsburg Empire, and after the Austro-Hungarian Compromise of 1867, of the Dual Monarchy of Austria-Hungary.

These friends of the Slavs of Eastern Europe were divided into two camps. The members of one of these called for the outright destruction of Austria-Hungary, the other for its reorganization in a manner which would have given the Empire's Slavs the same privileges as Austrians and Hungarians enjoyed, with extensive self-government for the Czechs, Poles, Croats, Serbs and so on. When war broke out in 1914, increasingly the opinion of these pro-Slav spokesmen, and other enemies of Austria-Hungary, began to favour the complete and immediate destruction of the Dual Monarchy and its replacement by independent nations of the Slavs of Eastern Europe and the Rumanians. Not surprisingly, during the negotiations of the post-war peace settlements, the policy of building powerful Slav nations in Eastern Europe (as well as a Greater Rumania) in triumphed.

In the interwar period, France built up a system of alliances with Poland, Czechoslovakia and Rumania, that was aimed above all to prevent the re-emergence of a powerful Germany. To prevent Habsburg restoration in Austria and/or Hungary, and to keep the Hungarians from re gaining any of the territories they had lost in the Treaty of Trianon of June 1920, the French supported the establishment of the Little Entente, an alliance of Czechoslovakia, Rumania and Yugoslavia designed above all to keep Hungary isolated and weak.

Anti-Hungarian feelings in France were only strengthened when Hungary's leadership managed, during 1938-41, to entangle the country in a Nazi alliance that lasted until the end of the war in the spring of 1945. Not surprisingly after the war the French government supported the policy, advocated above-all by Soviet leader Joseph Stalin but in the end supported by Great Britain and even the United States, of depriving Hungary of all the territories that she had managed to regain, with German and Italian diplomatic backing, during 1938-41.

French opinion, and in fact Western European public opinion, only began to warm toward the Hungarian people during the 1956 anti-Soviet uprising in the country. Of course, members of the French communist party thought otherwise. However, as communist influence in France declined, pro-Hungarian sentiments strengthened. By 1989, when Hungary managed to shake off communist rule, the image of the country in France was no longer that of an enemy nation. Today, it is no shame to be a Hungarian in France, or to have a Hungarian ancestry. In fact, it may well happen that the next leader of the Republic could be such a person.

For most of the past millennium, relations between France and Hungary had been constantly changing and, if we examine them closely, were more often hostile than friendly. Yet, there was a time when soldiers from France risked their lives and gave their blood in fighting on the side of Hungarians against Hungary's enemies. In Part 2 of this article I will tell the story of this largely forgotten incident, the 1664 campaign by a Christian army made up of the units from many of Europe's Christian Kingdoms, including France, that fought an Ottoman horde marching toward Vienna through Hungary and won, scoring the first major Christian victory over the mighty Ottoman war machine in generations.

Part 2: French-Hungarian relations from the Battle of St. Gotthard to the Rákoczi War of Independence (1664-1711)

By the early 1660s the Ottoman Turks, from their original base in western Asia Minor, had been advancing first into southeastern, then central Europe for more than three centuries. Until the beginning of the sixteenth century, their attempts to conquer lands north of the Balkans were usually halted at the southern frontier of the Kingdom of Hungary.

At the end of the fifteenth and the beginning of the sixteenth centuries, a number of developments in the Carpathian Basin and elsewhere began changing this situation. The death of Matthias Corvinus of Hungary in 1490 left the Kingdom without an effective ruler and marked the end of an age of stability and prosperity in the country. A massive peasant uprising under György Dózsa and its bloody repression by the nobility in 1514 further weakened the Kingdom. In the meantime Ottoman power grew. The defeat of Persia in the same year, the conquest of eastern Anatolia, Kurdistan (1515), Damascus (1516), the Holy Places of Arabia and Egypt (1517), elevated the Turkish state of Sultan Selim I to the status of a superpower in the Middle East.

In 1520 Sultan Selim was succeeded by his son Suleiman I, later known as "the Magnificent." With the Near East under his control and its riches at the disposal of the Ottoman treasury, the able and ambitious Suleiman turned his attention to Europe. In 1521 his armies, under the Grand Vizier Ibrahim Pasha, took Belgrade (known to Hungarians at the time as Nándorfehérvár). Five years later, in another campaign, they defeated King Louis II (1506-26) of Hungary and his feudal army in the Battle of Mohács. Louis died in an accident while fleeing the battlefield. In the decades following, Suleiman's armies occupied central Hungary and reduced the eastern part of the country, including Transylvania, to vassalage. The rest of the Kingdom (the so-called Royal Hungary) became ruled by members of the Austrian branch of the Habsburg family. For the next hundred-and-fifty years, Hungary became a battleground between the Habsburg Empire and the Ottomans. Wars were followed by periods of relative inactivity, only to be superseded by renewed military campaigns. One of the periods of protracted conflict was the Long Turkish War which lasted from the early 1593 to 1606. From that time until 1660 a period of low intensity conflict, one might almost say peace, ensued. In 1660, however, large-scale, open warfare resumed.

On the eve of the new Turkish war, power in Istanbul fell into the hands of Grand Vizier Mehmet Körpülü who became the *de facto* ruler of the Empire. An ambitious and able soldier and a ruthless administrator, Mehmet wanted to restore the power and glory that the Ottoman state had enjoyed during the age of Suleiman the Magnificent. As a part of this process, he planned to re-assert tight Turkish control over Transylvania, whose ruler, Prince György II Rákóczi, had often acted contrary to the wishes of the Turkish government in his handling of

Transylvania's external affairs. After a number of campaigns, Mehmet defeated Rákóczi and re-established control over Transylvania.

Mehmet died in 1661 and the position of grand Vizier was entrusted to his twenty-six-year-old son Fazil Ahmet. Probably because of his youth and relative inexperience, Ahmet wished to prove himself worthy of his position and continued his father's policies with boundless determination. In a number of campaigns he tried to expand Turkish control over Hungary and open the door to what previous grand viziers had never been able to achieve: the capture of Vienna.

The re-emergence of the Turkish threat to Central Europe moved Leopold I of Austria and his brother-in-law, King Louis XIV of France, to action. In 1663 French troops arrived in Hungary to help in the war with the Turks. It should be added that in the early 1660s a very unusual situation prevailed in France: Louis XIV was not fighting a war against any country. Accordingly, he could spare a part of his army for a campaign in a distant land.

Unfortunately for Holy Roman Emperor and Austrian ruler Leopold, the forces he had gathered that year were no match for Köprülü's armies. Leopold's commanders lost one fort after another in the Habsburg-controlled part of Hungary. Soon the panic-struck Habsburg court fled Vienna and entrusted the defence of both Austria and Royal Hungary to the Hungarian general Miklós Zrínyi. The campaigning season of the year ended with several victories for Zrínyi. The threat to Vienna was averted and the Habsburg court was given a chance to make better plans for 1664 when Grand Vizier Fazil Ahmet Köprülü was expected to return and resume his quest to conquer more of Royal Hungary and even parts of Austria.

To meet this impending emergency, Leopold I amassed a large force of probably over 70,000 soldiers gathered from various German states, the Austrian provinces, all in addition to the about 5,000 soldiers that had been sent from France. Much to the disappointment of Leopold's Hungarian subjects, the Emperor rejected Zrínyi's campaign plans for 1664 and appointed the Italian general Raimondo Montecuccoli as the Supreme Commander of the imperial and allied forces.

Prince Raimondo Montecuccoli (1609-1680) was a very experienced soldier and a noted theoretician of war. For decades he had commanded the Holy Roman and Austrian-Habsburg forces in campaigns in the Thirty Years Wars and also later in numerous other wars the Habs-burgs fought mainly against their Protestant enemies. Montecuccoli is known to have been a subtle strategist and a keen tactician with excellent skills at manoeuvre. On the matter of conducting war, he often disagreed with

Zrínyi. Montecuccoli favoured cautious use of his armies and was usually reluctant to engage in battle while his Hungarian counterpart preferred bold, lightning strikes at the enemy followed by tactical retreat, a kind of guerilla war fought by light cavalry. Montecuccoli is remembered in the world of popular military history mainly for the saying that three things are needed for waging war: money, money and money.

The year 1664 began with Zrínyi's attacks on the Turks in southern Hungary, and minor victories for Montecuccoli's imperial and allied forces over local Turkish garrisons in northern Hungary. Later, Köprülü's huge army, that had over-wintered in the Southern Balkans, advanced into southwestern Hungary where Zrínyi was unable to stop it with the limited forces available to him.

In the weeks and months following Montecuccoli's main force marched into southwestern Hungary where it was joined by more units, including Louis XIV's French regiment. On August 1, the combined Christian forces met Köprülü's army near Szentgotthárd, in westernmost Hungary not far from the Austrian (i.e. the Styrian) border.

In the days before the two forces made contact, neither side had all the forces gathered for the campaigns of 1664 available for a battle. The Tatar allies of the Turks, who provided the largest contingents of light cavalry for Grand Vizier Köprülü's army, were away, probably terrorizing the population of the Hungarian countryside elsewhere. Köprülü was also missing parts or all of his formidable artillery. On the Christian side, only a fraction of the original army gathered by Emperor Leopold was available to Montecuccoli by the 1st of August. As a result, on that day the Turkish forces far outnumbered the Christian ones in the area.

The Christian forces enjoyed a degree of strategic advantage: to attack them, the Turks had to cross the Rába (Raab) river. Furthermore, there had been heavy rains West of Szentgotthárd the day before the battle and the river's level kept rising throughout the day of the engagement. Thus a river that didn't usually pose a great obstacle to military operations (the Rába is not very deep near Szentgotthárd, but its banks are steep in most places), became a problem for the Turks.

The initiative was taken by the Ottomans who crossed the Rába at the village of Nagyfalu (known to Austrians today as Morgensdorff, and located since the Treaty of Trianon on the Austrian side of the Austro-Hungarian border). After fierce fighting in the morning, they defeated the imperial forces stationed in and near the village, inflicting heavy casualties on them. Other troops under Montecuccoli didn't rush to their comrades' aid just yet, as the Christian command expected the main Turkish attack elsewhere.

Following these events the Christian commanders held a council of war. At first there was no agreement as to what to do. Montecuccoli's forces were outnumbered and were low both on supplies and ammunition. The commander of the French regiment advised retreat. In the end he and the others who had similar ideas were convinced that fleeing the battlefield was not a viable option. The troops would have to retreat in territory where the local population didn't speak their language, and the Turks would be able to give hot pursuit. The only constructive choice was the honourable one: making a stand and fighting to the death.

In the end that is what Montecuccoli's forces did. In the afternoon of the day that had started as a disaster for them they fought a bitter battle against the best of Fazil Ahmet's army, much of it over the dead bodies of their comrades that had fallen only a few hours earlier. And they stood their place and drove the Turks back. In the midst of the battle they became the beneficiaries of a sort of "divine intervention": the bridges the Turks had built over the river collapsed, possibly because of the floodwaters that had arrived at Nagyfalu from the rain that had fallen earlier further upstream. With the bridges gone, the Turks were prevented from reinforcing their troops engaged in the battle. The Ottoman leaders could only watch helplessly as the Christian troops drove the Turkish warriors into the swollen river. The next day Grand Vizier Köprülü aborted his march against Austria and began retreating towards the east, towards the Ottoman military frontier fortress at Buda.

The French troops that had been sent to Hungary had contributed to Montecuccoli's victory. They were prevented from playing a role in a war for the liberation of Hungary in the weeks and months after St. Gotthard because such a war did not take place at the time. Montecuccoli's victory removed any Turkish threat to Vienna and the Austrian provinces, and the Habsburg court saw no need to continue the war. Continuing the campaigning would have been dangerous for Montecuccoli and his imperial and allied forces as they continued to be outnumbered by Köprülü's armies. Nevertheless, the victory at Szentgotthárd foreshadowed the possibility of Christian, European troops defeating the Turks and the liberation of Hungary through the combined action of the Christian rulers of Europe. Indeed, in the next major war with the Turks, between 1683 and 1699, the Ottomans were driven from Hungary.

By the time that happened, Louis XIV's armies were not fighting on the side of the Habsburgs. Three years after the Battle of Szentgotthárd, Louis became involved in a series of wars designed to extend French influence to the northeast of France, eventually all the way into the Low Countries. In these wars France fought the armies of the various

Habsburg possessions and allies in that part of Europe.
Interestingly and in many ways unexpectedly, the Battle of Szent-gotthárd had consequences that would greatly benefit France more than a generation later, in particular during the War of Spanish Succession. The fact is that the battle had significant consequences. These had to do much less with Hungarian-French relations than relations between Hungarians and the Habsburg court in Vienna.

As has been mentioned, after the battle the Habsburg leadership, having averted the danger to its Austrian territories, refused to continue the war. Instead, Vienna sued for peace. It signed the Treaty of Vasvár (Esienburg in German) with the Ottomans. Hungarians, even some of those who had previously supported the Viennese Court, were outraged by the terms of this treaty, which they considered humiliating for Hungary and even for the whole of Christian Europe. They could not understand why, after a victorious battle, the government of Emperor Leopold I had to sue for peace, rather than try to liberate at least those parts of Hungary that had been taken by the Turks in recent times.

This development convinced many Hungarians, especially those who were inclined to think this way in the first place, that the Habsburgs were as bad, if not worse enemies of Hungary, as the Ottomans. The Treaty of Vasvár was soon followed by an anti-Habsburg conspiracy by members of Hungary's elite, headed by Count Ferenc Wesselényi the Palatine (Lieutenant-Governor) of Hungary. The conspiracy was discovered and was crushed by the Habsburg court. It resulted in years of severe repression in Royal Hungary and even beyond, wherever the Viennese authorities could reach their real or imagined Hungarian enemies.

All this resulted from a miss-judgement of the military situation by the Hungarian public on the morrow of the victory at Szentgotthárd. As had been explained above, that victory was to a large extent the result of a quirk of fate and left a strategic situation in which the continuation of the campaign against the Turks could have easily resulted in disaster for the Habsburg forces.

The repression that was unleashed on Hungary in the wake of the Wesselényi conspiracy resulted in discontent and the eventual outbreak, in the mid-1670s, of guerilla-type of warfare against the Habsburgs. In 1678 Count Imre Thököly assumed the leadership of the by then open rebellion against the Habsburgs. To achieve success against Vienna, Thököly allied himself with the Ottomans. The declining military strength of the Turks and the Habsburg-lead war for the liberation of Hungary from Turkish rule in the mid-1680s sealed the fate of Thököly's dream of freeing his country of both Austrian and Ottoman rule.

The defeat of the Turks by the Habsburgs by the end of the century forced Thököly into exile. At the same time the expelling of the Turks brought Habsburg rule to all of Hungary. The Viennese court treated the lands gained not so much as liberated territories but as conquered enemy lands whose economic output and commerce could be exploited by pro-Habsburg landowners and the imperial treasury.

The Thököly wars prompted new repression by the Viennese court in reunited Hungary. The new repression, along with Habsburg misrule in the recently "liberated" regions of Hungary, fuelled new resentment against the House of Habsburg. In 1703 a new Hungarian war of liberation broke out, lead this time by Prince Ferenc II Rákóczi, Thököly's stepson. This large-scale and protracted war (1703-1711) forced the Viennese court to divert many troops and precious resources from their struggle against the France of Louis XIV in the War of Spanish Succession. It was in this manner that the unintended consequences of the Battle of St. Gotthard resulted in the French king being repaid for having helped the Habsburgs in 1664. There can be no doubt that what Rákóczi's *kuruc* warriors did to benefit France during 1703-1711 was far more valuable than what the French had done to benefit Hungary in 1664.

The Rákóczi war began with remarkable Hungarian successes but became a protracted guerrilla-type conflict after it became evident that neither Louis (nor Peter the Great of Russia) could offer effective help to the Hungarians. In the end lack of foreign help and war-weariness prompted some of Rákóczi's followers to end the bloodshed, as well as the suffering of the people of Hungary, by suing for peace just when their leader went abroad to seek help. The resulting peace settlement, the Treaty of Szatmár of 1711, was a compromise which served as the basis for Habsburg rule in Hungary for the next century-and-a-half.

The Turkish war of the 1660s, the war for the liberation of Hungary from the Turks of the 1680s and 1690s, Thököly wars, and especially the bitter and protracted struggle under Rákóczi, constituted still more of those developments in the history of the Hungarian nation which witnessed much bloodletting, material destruction, the loss of life due to military action, as well as to the malnutrition and epidemics that usually accompanied military conflict in those days. Hungarian military casualties from 1703 to 1711 alone amounted to 80,000, a figure that is greater than Canada's losses in either the First or the Second World War. During these same eight years, over 400,000 Hungarians died in the epidemics brought on by the military hostilities.

France played no significant role in Hungary's evolution through much of the rest of the eighteenth century. As had been explained, from the time of the Seven Years War to the beginning of the French Revolutionary Wars of the same century, France was the ally of Austria. Thereafter the situation became more complicated. From the 1790s to the 1840s French revolutionaries were friends and inspirers of Hungarian liberals and reformers, while French conservatives became allies of conservative forces throughout much of Central Europe including Hungary. Next, Austria became a potential ally of France first against Prussia and then against a united Germany. Toward the end of the nineteenth century and the beginning of the twentieth, and especially during the First World War, most Frenchmen felt that their allies in Central and Eastern Europe were not the Germans of Austria, or even the Hungarians of the Dual Monarchy (after the 1867 Austro-Hungarian Compromise), but the Slavs and Rumanians. Thus it happened that at the after World War I France worked for the dismantling of the Habsburg Monarchy and within it, of the historic Kingdom of Hungary. History had come full circle since 1664: instead of fighting Hungary's enemies, in 1919 France became the most resolute supporter of them.

Almost a century later, fortunately, France is again a friend of Hungarians. In fact, today Frenchmen and Magyars are living in the same political unit, the European Union. Not even the Turks are enemies: they hope to join the same EU in the not too distant future.

The 1956 Revolution in Hungary: The Historical and International Context

One of the great themes of twentieth century history is the rise and subsequent decline of the world communist movement. In this story the Hungarian revolution in 1956 occupies a special place: the turning point that separated the ascending fortunes of this movement from the beginning of its gradual demise.

---

[*] This study was serialized in *Magyar Élet/ Hungarian Life* in the fall of 2006. I had written on the subject elsewhere as well, especially when I reviewed the documentary collection edited by Csaba Békés: *Az 1956-os magyar forradalom a világpolitikában: Tanulmány és válogatott dokumentumok* [The 1956 Hungarian Revolution in World Politics: A Study and Selected Documents] (Budapest: 1956-os Intézet, 1996), in *Tárogató: the Journal of the Hungarian Cultural Society of Vancouver*, 27, 4 (April 2000): 43-44. Békés's book is a useful collection with a detailed and lucid introduction. Other recent works related to the subject are László Borhi's *Hungary in the Cold War: 1945-1956* (Budapest: Central European University Press, 2004) and, especially, Charles Gáti, *Failed Illusions: Moscow, Washington, Budapest, and the 1956 Hungarian Revolt* (Stanford, Ca.: Stanford University Press, 2006); this book is available in other languages as well, including Hungarian. There are numerous articles on the subject also, many of them in the *Yearbook* [*Évkönyv*] of the 1956 Institute of Budapest. One of these is by the Institute's former senior scholar, the late György Litván, "Mítoszok és Legendák 1956-ról," in Kőrösi Zsuzsanna, Éva Standeisky, and János M. Rainer, eds., *Évkönyv*, VIII (Budapest: 1956 Institute, 2000): 205-18. The American scholar Johanna Granville has also written on the subject. One of her studies is "The Soviet-Yugoslav Detente, Belgrade-Budapest Relations, and the Hungarian Revolution (1955-56)," *Hungarian Studies Review*, 24, 1-2 (1997): 15-63. For a very recent bibliographical treatment of the subject see Julia Bock, "The Subject of the 1956 Hungarian Revolution in American Academic Libraries," *East European Quarterly*, 40, 4 (December 2006): 443-66. The article contains a selective list of recent books on 1956 (pp. 451-56) as well as other relevant material. A more extensive list has been compiled at the British Library: see http://www.bl.uk/collections/ easteuropean/hungary56/hun56bib/03.html .

It can be argued that the mid-1950s constituted the high-point in the history of world communism. It is interesting to note that those years seem to constitute the half-life of the movement, very much as certain elements, as well as medications, have a half-life, when they begin their journey toward inevitable decline. If we consider 1917 as the birth of the world communist movement and 1989 as the year of its demise, at least in Europe, 1956 is almost at the middle point.

The movement appeared on the world stage in the fall of 1917 when the Russian revolutionary Vladimir Lenin and a handful of his followers grabbed power in Petrograd and ousted the moderate left-wing revolutionary regime of Alexander Kerensky. And the movement disappeared as a major political force in the world when the Soviet Empire collapsed in Eastern Europe in 1989, followed by the U.S.S.R.'s implosion a short time later.

Of course communist ideology had been around for a long time before 1917. Karl Marx and other thinkers developed it during the 19th century, but it was not till 1917 that the ideology of Marxism, and its very different Leninist variety, triumphed in a major country, in Russia. Had Lenin and his Bolshevik followers not come to power in a country the size of Imperial Russia, our school textbooks would probably never mention Karl Marx.

Having come to power, the Bolsheviks were able to launch their movement for world domination. In this quest they were given a god-sent opportunity when in 1939 Nazi Germany embarked on the conquest of Europe and the Mediterranean and, by 1945, had collapsed in the process. The resulting political void, especially in Eastern and Central Europe, was filled by Russia's communists.

Antecedents in Hungary

At war's end the Soviet Union occupied Hungary. Unlike in Poland, Bulgaria and Rumania, the Soviet leaders did not impose a communist government on Hungary in 1945, yet they made preparations for its imposition later. During 1945-47, using the Red Army's presence in Hungary, the country was readied for a gradual communist takeover. By the end of the 1940s, the communists had eliminated the last of the opposition to their rule. They abolished the multi-party system and nationalized the economy. They introduced centrally planned production of all goods. They also began to persecute the churches and purged non-communists from the government and public institutions. Their aim was to replace the pluralistic society Hungary had had for centuries with a one-party government that exercised total control over every aspect of Hungarian life. Hungary was to become a miniature version of the Soviet Union where Stalinist totalitarianism had flourished since the late 1920s.

All this meant the rule of the secret police and the internment or deportation to concentration camps of all real and suspected opponents of the new order. There were purge trials for the more prominent of the Communist Party's opponents and many people were sentenced to long jail terms—or to death. The cult of personality intensified year after year. The Soviet leader Joseph Stalin and his Hungarian satrap Mátyás Rákosi were glorified and venerated an every possible occasion and everywhere.

Hungary was forced to focus on heavy industry while production of consumer goods was neglected. Peasants were forced into collective farms or had to work as labourers on factory farms owned and managed by the state. All this came with Hungary's total isolation from the West, and even from socialist, but not pro-Soviet, Yugoslavia. The Iron Curtain, that had been established already in 1945, was increasingly fortified and by about 1950 Hungary's border with Austria, and then also with Yugoslavia, had become guarded by special security forces, high barbed-wire fences, guard-dogs, and minefields. Ordinary citizens were forbidden from travelling to non-communist countries and they were ordered not to fraternize with the occasional visitor from the West.

After the death of Stalin in March 1953, a slow process of reversing the pace of the country's socialist transformation was started. In June of that year Moscow replaced as Prime Minister the unpopular Rákosi with another communist, Imre Nagy. Nagy implemented many reforms. His government allocated more funds for the production of consumer goods. It reduced taxes and deliveries paid in kind by peasants and peasant cooperatives to the state. In fact, Nagy even allowed peasants to leave the collectives—and many of them did.

Alas, reforms did little to improve the economic situation in Hungary and hard-liners such as Rákosi still retained much influence. Soon, Nagy's reform program was derailed and the Stalinists regained power. They were still in power early in 1956.

The International Background

On the international scene, the ten years leading up to the events of the fall 1956 in Hungary were times of the Cold War. There is general agreement among historians that the events that precipitated the Cold War included the following: Soviet insistence in 1945 to impose a Communist government on Rumania, Bulgaria and, especially, Poland. Added to this was Soviet help to communist insurgents in Greece, and Soviet attempt to starve West Berlin into submission (the Berlin Blockade). Then there was the communist *coup* in Czechoslovakia through which a western-style government was replaced by one dominated by local communists. At about the same time relations deteriorated between Stalin's Russia and Marshall Tito's Yugoslavia. The Soviets prepared to invade this "renegade" communist country but thought better of their plan when the United Nations, lead by the United States, intervened in the conflict between North Korea and South Korea. The years 1950-53, with their Korean conflict, constituted the height of the early Cold War.

Starting with the death of Stalin in 1953, East-West tensions were slowly relaxed. A high point in these new relations was the Austrian Treaty of 1955. Through it Austria was proclaimed a neutral (and disarmed) state and the Allied occupation forces left the country, including the Red Army from eastern Austria.

In February of 1956, Soviet leader Nikita Khrushchev denounced the crimes of the Stalin era at a closed session of the 20th Congress of the Communist Party of the Soviet Union. This speech further accelerated de-Stalinization in the Soviet Camp.

At the end of June, anti-communist disturbances took place in Poznan, Poland. They were put down rather ruthlessly by the Polish army. Nevertheless, Władysław Gomułka, who had spent much of the first half of the '50s in detention for the crime of "nationalist deviation", was re-admitted to the Communist Party and was soon named the party's First Secretary. Probably in order to prevent similar discontent and disturbances in Hungary, the Soviets removed the unpopular Rákosi—for the second time. Unfortunately for them, they replaced him with another seasoned Stalinist: Ernő Gerő. Not surprisingly, Hungary's public was not appeased.

In the meantime, disquiet in the country grew. The desire for further change, both in the country's leadership and in government policies, became openly voiced, even within the Hungarian Communist Party. The regime tried to make concessions. On October 6 took place the re-burial of László Rajk and his accomplices who had been the victims of a purge trial some half-dozen years earlier. The event turned into a mass demonstration against Hungary's existing leadership.

The Crises in Poland and Hungary

By this time a new crisis had developed in Poland. The reform-minded Gomułka demanded changes to the way his country was treated within the Soviet Camp. He insisted that Red Army officers in charge of the Polish Army be dismissed, that the policy of forceful collectivization of agriculture be relaxed, and that accommodation be reached with Poland's influential Catholic Church.

Anticipating a crisis Khrushchev and the other members of the Politburo (the supreme decision-making organ of the Soviet Communist Party) flew to Warsaw. At the same time the Red Army was put on alert. After arduous negotiations a compromise was worked out: Gomułka and his reforms were to stay but he promised that Poland would remain a loyal member of the Soviet Camp.

Meanwhile in Budapest university and college students were planning a demonstration to support of the reformers in Poland. The event took place on the 23rd. There were no clashes till the evening when a confrontation took place at the Radio Building. Soon, the panicked government of Gerő denounced the disturbances as a "counter-revolution" and called on the Soviet troops stationed in the vicinity of Budapest to disperse the demonstrators.

To gain control of the situation, on Khrushchev's orders, Imre Nagy was brought into the Hungarian cabinet, very much as Gomułka had been brought out from his enforced isolation in Poland. Next, the Central Committee of the Hungarian Communist Party appointed Nagy as Prime Minister. By this time a high-ranking Soviet delegation had arrived in Budapest but for the moment it saw no evidence of a dangerous crisis.

On the 25th a mass demonstration in front of the Parliament Building was dispersed by gunfire that resulted in many casualties. Following this Gerő was removed from his post on the order of the Soviet leaders and was replaced as Party Secretary by János Kádár, a former victim of the Stalinist purges.

The next day the revolution started spiralling out of control. Reports were reaching Moscow of the anti-Soviet overtones of the uprising. And, as the days passed, matters got worse for the Soviets. From the 28th on, Premier Nagy no longer called the uprising a counter-revolution. More importantly, he began appointing non-Communists to his government. Still another development came on the 29th:Israel attacked Egypt and with that act started what is known in history as the Suez Crisis. As it would have great importance for Hungary, we should examine it in some detail.

The Suez Crisis

The Suez Canal is a waterway that connects the Mediterranean Sea to the Red Sea. It makes the route from Europe to south Asia much shorter as ships do not have to circumnavigate Africa. There had been canals connecting these seas in ancient times but they had fallen into disrepair a few times, the last time in the 8th century a.d. In the late 1850s, almost hundred years before the Suez Crisis, the project was revived and a modern canal was built. Soon thereafter Britain acquired control of the company operating the canal. The canal was to be open to all shipping and Britain was to guarantee the neutrality of the canal. In 1936 a treaty was signed by the United Kingdom and Egypt that allowed British troops to remain in the Canal zone. After World War II the Egyptians began pressing for the withdrawal of these troops. In June of 1956 the British forces finally withdrew.

About this time Egypt became involved in plans to build the Aswan Dam on the Nile River. For some time it seemed that this project would be financed largely with American loans but in July of 1956 Washington cancelled these plans. In retaliation, Egypt's new leader Abdul Nasser established closer ties with the Soviet Union and nationalized the Suez Canal company. Soon thereafter he expelled some remaining British officials from Egypt. In the meantime the Egyptians continued to deny passage on the Suez Canal to Israeli ships.

These developments in the Middle East brought Britain, France and Israel together. Their governments began hatching a plot to wrest the Suez Canal away from Nasser. The plan was for Israel to attack Egypt, which would give and excuse for the British and the French to "intervene" and send troops to control the Canal. A crisis was about to erupt in the Middle East that would have consequences on the outcome of the revolution in Hungary.

The main players in this crisis would not be the British and the French, Western Europe's ex-great powers, but they would be the United States and the Soviet Union. To understand the roles each played, it is useful to examine their actions in the international relations of the 1950s.

American Attitudes and Policies

In 1945 the United States of America had emerged as of the world's most powerful economic and military power. With Germany and Japan in ruins, and Britain and France exhausted by war, America became a superpower. While throughout most of 1945 America's attention was focused on the defeat first of Nazi Germany and then of Imperial Japan, by the end of that year her diplomats and statesmen had turned their concern toward the emergence of the Soviet Empire in Eastern Europe and elsewhere. For many years Washington kept proclaiming the need to "liberate" Eastern Europe from Soviet rule while it also sought peaceful accommodation with Moscow. This two-faced policy became especially pronounced after the advent to power of the Eisenhower administration in January of 1953. Under Eisenhower, funds were made available to such establishment as Radio Free Europe, as well as anti-Soviet emigre organizations and their publications, all for the purpose of promoting the chances of the "liberation" of Eastern Europe from Soviet rule.

In reality, however, as the mid-1950s approached American diplomacy increasingly sought negotiated solutions to such East-West issues as the question of Germany and the status of Austria. When anti-Soviet demonstrations broke out in East Berlin in 1953, America was not able to do anything for the people of East Germany. In the eyes of many American politicians and defence experts this incident drove home the futility of the policy of roll-back. Yet, in American anti-Soviet propaganda the rhetoric of the "liberation" of what Americans called the "captive nations" continued.

While the United States never incited East European nations to rebel against Soviet rule and it never promised to aid any such rebellion, some Radio Free Europe broadcasts, made by Hungarian-language broadcasters, made statements that could easily be interpreted as promises of US intervention, or if not, the promise that Washington would, in case of a revolt in an East European country, put overwhelming pressure on Moscow to withdraw its forces from there.

Regarding American thinking during the period 1953 to the fall of 1956 we can say that Washington was not expecting any fundamental changes in Eastern Europe. The only change there that was seen as possible by a few American analysts, was the spread of the "Yugoslav model" of communism. Not surprisingly under the circumstances, when an anti-Soviet uprising broke out in Budapest on 23 October, the Eisenhower administration was taken by complete surprise. But there were other factors complicating the reaction of America to the events in Hungary. One was the fact that the United States was in the midst of a presidential election campaign. The other was the outbreak of the Suez crisis which caught Washington completely by surprise and disrupted the unity of the West.

Soviet Reactions

By far the most important factor in determining the fate of the Hungarian Revolution was the attitude of the Soviet leadership to the events in Hungary. The Soviet Union had, by the fall of 1956, become the other superpower of the world. It had emerged victorious in the Second World War and had occupied much of Eastern and Central Europe in 1944-45. There it created its new empire. In Asia it had extended its influence when China had gone communist, and it had gained the friendship of many Asian powers, including that of India. In 1956 the Soviet Armed Forces were numerically superior to any non-communist military in the world. The U.S.S.R. had developed atomic weapons and the capability to deliver them over hundreds of kilometres of distances. For the time being it lacked long and medium-range missile capabilities, a fact that probably made a difference in the minds of Soviet military leaders in the fall of 1956. The Soviet Armed forces could hit certain NATO bases, for example in northern Italy, only from Hungarian soil, a fact that made Hungary a more important strategic factor in Soviet military thinking than it could have been had the Russians had missiles with longer ranges. For the Soviets, the ability to counter the threat they perceived from NATO countries was a paramount consideration throughout the 1950s and in particular, during the fall of 1956.

While the Soviets feared "imperialist aggression" from the West, they did not feel it possible that there would be a local threat to their occupation forces in any of the satellite countries. Moscow was aware of discontent in countries such as Poland and Hungary, but it did not anticipate a major anti-Soviet, let alone anti-Communist outbreak there. So, Moscow was just as surprised by what took place in Hungary on the 23rd and 24th of October as was Washington.

When the news of these events reached Moscow, the first reaction there was one of caution. Some Soviet leaders, notably Politburo member Anastas Mikolyan, was unhappy about the fact that Soviet troops had been deployed against the demonstrators. Certainly, most of the Soviet leaders were anxious to resolve the crisis through negotiations rather than the use of force. Only the hard-liners insisted on harsh measures. Among these was V.M. Molotov in the Politburo and the Soviet ambassador to Hungary Juri Andropov in Budapest.

Elsewhere in the communist camp limited initial sympathies for the demonstrators in Budapest quickly evaporated when it increasingly became evident that the uprising in Hungary was not as much an anti-

Stalinist manifestation but an anti-communist movement. Especially important was the influence of the Chinese who after urging caution, in the end favoured the crushing of the revolution. Marshal Tito of Yugoslavia also had an input into the deliberations in Moscow. First he and his government sympathised with what they thought to be an anti-Rakosiite and anti-Gerő uprising, but changed their mind and advised harsh action when they realized that what was in danger in Hungary was not the influence of the Stalinists but the rule of the Communist Party itself.

Nevertheless, for some time, and especially on the 30th of October, the Soviet leadership came down on the side of caution and agreed to withdraw Soviet troops from Hungary—if by doing so it would make it easier for the Hungarian communists to restore order and preserve their rule. Even the hard-liners in Moscow acquiesced in this stand, but then events transpired that made the Soviet leaders change their mind within a day.

The End of October: The Time for Decision

During the closing days of the month of October matters came to a climax both in Hungary and the Middle East. In the former Prime Minister Imre Nagy came to the conclusion that he had to chose between the people of Hungary and those Hungarian communists who wished to preserve the "Socialist order" along with the Soviet alliance. He chose to side with the Hungarian people. Accordingly he endorsed the most important demands of the freedom fighters: the call for the withdrawal of Soviet forces from Hungary and the restoration of a multi-party democracy in the country.

Just about the same time in the Middle East, after the British and the French governments had sent an ultimatum to Israel and Egypt threatening to invade if the fighting didn't stop there, the British and the French air forces began their bombardment of Egyptian military airfields in preparation for the landing of Anglo-French forces in the Canal Zone. The news of these events reached Moscow about the same time that reports arrived from Hungary that anti-communist crowds had lynched members of the communist security establishment. This strongly suggested to the men in the Kremlin that the uprising was not aimed at a reform of the "socialist order" but at the abolition of communist rule.

It was under these circumstances that the Soviet leaders met again on the 31st of the month. Not surprisingly they reversed their decision of the day before about troop withdrawal from Hungary and a negotiated settlement of the crisis. They now agreed to crush the revolution. They also agreed to keep their intention secret for the time being so that the illusion would be created in Budapest that the Red Army is leaving the country. In their new decision the Soviet leaders had the support of the Chinese delegation that had been present in Moscow for some time.

Ever since this change in Soviet policy toward the events in Hungary has become known, historians have pondered over the question why, on the last day of October, the Soviet leaders abandoned the stand they taken only 24 hours earlier? Some commentators have pointed to the developments in the Near East as being the reason. After the British and French attack on Egypt, the Soviets realized that the Suez Crisis was a more serious threat to their interest than they had assumed it to be earlier. With Egypt under attack, it would be highly likely that Moscow would lose influence in the region and the dream of Egypt as a Soviet client state would crumble. Under these circumstances losing Hungary too would deal a double blow to Soviet prestige. And, as Khrushchev said at the time, withdrawing Soviet troops from Hungary would no doubt further embolden the "imperialists" in their quest to curb Soviet influence everywhere.

The Anglo-French attack on Egypt had further implications for the outcome of the events in Hungary. It put the Americans into a precarious position. With such Western democratic countries as Britain and France being involved in an invasion, it became more awkward for the United States to condemn Soviet aggression. More important was the fact that the Suez Crisis destroyed the unity of the West. At the United Nations America found itself voting with the Soviet Union in condemning French and British actions.

In any case, President Eisenhower feared that any military measures taken to oppose Soviet policy in Hungary could trigger a third world war that would probably be fought with nuclear weapons. Furthermore, military action was hardly a possibility with the Soviets having many divisions in Hungary while American forces were hundreds of miles away and would have had to cross neutral Austria just to approach the Hungarian border. In other words, neither the military nor the political situation made actual American aid to the freedom fighters in Budapest feasible.

In his most recent book about the Hungarian revolution, Professor Charles Gati has argued that Soviet withdrawal from Hungary would still have been possible, even without Western pressure, had the Hungarians not gone too far in demanding changes and in doing things that threatened with a loss of prestige for Moscow. He suggests that had the crowds in Hungary been more restrained and had they forgone the lynching of secret servicemen, and had Imre Nagy's government not started the restoration of a multi-party system, amounting to the abandonment of communist rule and even membership in the "socialist bloc", the Soviet leaders would not have reversed their decision of the 30th of October to pull Russian troops from Hungary. He is probably right, but such a "might-have-been" of history is quite unrealistic. The hatred of communism in Hungary was so deep-seeded that restraint could hardly be expected of the country's masses, even of its revolutionary leaders.

For the depths of that hatred the Soviet leadership was in large part responsible. True, Khrushchev cannot be blamed for most of the excesses of the Stalin era and of the Stalinist leadership in Hungary, but he and his colleagues could have been wiser in 1956. They should not have waited till the summer of 1956 with the replacement the much-reviled Rákosi. They made an even bigger mistake when they replaced him not with a reform communist but with another Stalinist in the person of Gerő.

The Soviet leaders made another mistake when, soon after the first pro-Polish demonstrations in Budapest, they allowed Gerő and Andropov to call into the city Soviet tanks from nearby Russian bases. Of course, had they been wiser, perhaps the discontent in Hungary would not have spilled over into an anti-communist uprising. Had the Soviets been wiser, and Ambassador Andropov been less alarming and more compromising, the course of events in Hungary could have followed the Polish example.

But this was not to be. The Hungarian people, angered by what they had seen as provocative measures dictated from Moscow, were not in the mood for compromise. And once concessions were made to them they demanded more, and ultimately they called for an end to communist rule and Russian domination of their country. But all that was too much for Moscow.

Letting Hungary leave the Soviet Camp and become a western-style country would have been too dangerous to the Soviet leadership. It would have resulted in a serious loss of face for Moscow. It would have meant a gap in the defensive ring surrounding the Soviet Union. It would have invited other members of the Socialist bloc to try quitting the alliance. For Khrushchev to support such a proposition would have undermined his leadership and would have left the door open for the Stalinists in Moscow to reclaim power. The Hungarian revolution had to be crushed.

The Aftermath

The Hungarian revolution had wide-spread international consequences. The fleeing of some 200,000 Hungarian citizens and their re-settlement in the countries of the Western world created a Magyar diaspora that in time would play an important role in keeping links between the Hungarian people and the nations and cultures of the Western world. Their largely indirect role in bringing communism to an end in Hungary has not been studied, but it will become obvious once it will be investigated by historians.

The crushing of the Revolution by the Soviets had an impact on American foreign policies. The event drove home to everyone in Washington the futility of the idea of the "roll back" of communism. After 1956 American rhetoric was adjusted to the policy of seeking peaceful coexistence with the Soviet bloc and finding accommodation and compromises.

The greatest impact of the defeat of the Hungarian Revolution was on Soviet history and the history of the world communist movement. For the Soviets, the sending into Hungary of thousands of Soviet tanks in early November was a costly affair. It led to the condemnation of Soviet actions in many parts of the world. It confirmed the suspicion of many people that communism as practiced in the Soviet camp was a tyrannical system backed by brute force alone.

More importantly, Soviet intervention in Hungary resulted in a great deal of disillusionment among communists everywhere regarding Soviet leadership of the world communist movement. This was especially true of communists in the West upon whose support Marxist parties depended. Only a decade earlier it seemed that some European countries, as for example France and Italy, might embrace communism through the electoral process. By 1956 the chance of this happening had diminished and, after November of that year, it decreased even further. Viewed from the distance of half a century, it seems that 1956 was the beginning of the end of the world communist revolution.

The demise of the Soviet Empire came 33 years later. By then the Soviets were ready to abandon their imperial ambitions. By the late 1980s they, especially new Soviet leaders such as Mikhail Gorbachev, saw in Eastern Europe a drain on Soviet resources. Furthermore, unlike in 1956 when the Soviet military regarded Hungary (and, in particular, her territory) as an invaluable military asset, by 1989 it felt that the country was not needed badly for the defence of the Soviet Union in the age of intercontinental missiles.

Not surprisingly that year Gorbachev let Hungary—as well as Poland, Czechoslovakia, and East Germany—go its own way, mainly by making it evident to the communist leaders in the country that the Red Army would no longer prop up their regimes. When Hungary's communist masters realized this, they did their utmost to assure that the transition to a non-communist society came about peacefully rather than through another bloody revolution.

The dreams of Hungarians about independence, democracy and association with the West started to be realized only in 1989. But the road to a Western-European style society and economy has not been an easy one. Forty years of communism had bequeathed the country a burdensome legacy. The most tangible part of this has been the national debt that had been amassed by the country's communist regime from the 1970s to the 1980s. Hungary of the times shouldered the heaviest per-capita national debt in Eastern Europe—and it still does. In the wake of 1989 Hungary had to reorient completely her external trade and replace Russia as her principal trading partner with Western Europe. She also had to phase out her uneconomical heavy industries and replace them with economic activities more in tune with European markets.

Another, somewhat less tangible unfortunate legacy of the Soviet era in Hungary had been the tradition of the dependence of the individual on the state that had been fostered in the communist era. Such attitudes will take at least a generation to eradicate. The country also has to learn, and this is a painful process for her people, that the cost of the cradle-to-grave social safety net that had been financed in János Kádár's Hungary with western loans is too great for an economy that has not yet made a full transition to the economic order that exists in much of Western Europe.

The stresses caused by the transforming of Hungary from a socialist state to one more in line with Western models and traditions are still with us today and has helped to foster much of the discontent that we witnessed in the country during the Revolution's 50th anniversary. We can only hope that by the time of the Revolution's centenary, all negative legacies of forty years of communist rule in the country will be eliminated.

Friends of Hungary
in the English-Speaking World*

Many Hungarians believe, somewhat erroneously, that throughout the ages their nation has had far more enemies than friends. They also hold the view that in a most critical period of our century, from 1914 to 1948, Hungary had very few influential sympathizers abroad and virtually none in any of the English-speaking countries of the world.

The existence of this latter belief among Hungarians should not surprise us in view of the fact that in the period indicated two all-out struggles were fought between the English-speaking world and the German one, and in both of these Hungary was associated with Germany. Furthermore, in this same period, two severely punitive peace treaties had been imposed on Hungary by peace conferences at which the two major "Anglo" powers, the United Kingdom and the United States, had played leading roles.

Notwithstanding these historical facts, it is not accurate to say that opinion among the elites of the English-speaking nations of the world was unanimously anti-Magyar from 1914 to 1948. It is the purpose of this study to remind Hungarians that, in this very period, there were influential individuals both in the U.K. and the U.S.—as well as in Canada—who were sympathetic to Hungary and Hungarians, and whose sympathies persisted even through the times when relations between Hungary's regimes and the governments of the Anglo-Saxon powers reached their lowest point. As limitations of space prevent us from

* My researches on this and related themes had been supported by grants from the Social Sciences and Humanities Council of Canada and from the Department of National Defence. For these I am grateful. Parts of this paper have been based on short articles I had prepared for *Tárogató*, the journal of the Hungarian House of Vancouver, in the mid-1990s. An earlier version of this paper also appeared under the title "Friends of Hungary in the English-Speaking World," in *Visszatekintés—Looking Back—Regard sur le passé*, ed. E. Puskas-Balogh (Montreal: Hungarian Literary Association, 1996), pp. 157-65.

examining a wide range of public attitudes to Hungary in the countries mentioned, we will have to be satisfied by looking at the activities and opinions of one such individual for each of the three nations in question.

Great Britain and Hungary

In any study of this nature it is appropriate to begin with Great Britain, the nation with which Hungary has had the longest-standing relationship. Though situated in different corners of the European continent, the citizens of these countries had maintained contact and kept informed about each others' national affairs since medieval times. In the nineteenth century, this relationship intensified. The 1848-49 War of Independence in Hungary had favourable echoes in England among the liberal and radical elements of that country's politically conscious public, though not among conservative government circles. The 1867 Compromise between Austria and Hungary, however, gained the approval of virtually everyone in Great Britain, and from that time on until the turn of the century, Hungary's image there was almost invariably favourable. Unfortunately for Hungarians, this state of affairs did not last forever and, by the end of the first decade of the twentieth century, Hungary's prestige had greatly declined in that most prosperous, advanced, and militarily still very powerful country.

The causes of this loss of English respect and sympathies were complex, but they had to do with the general re-alignment of the European international order and with the transformation of the British domestic political situation.[1] The overall effect of this change was the fact that by the time World War I had broken out, the English public no longer respected Hungarians as freedom loving peoples who were the driving force behind the modernization of the Habsburg Empire. Anti-Magyar propaganda in England had started in 1908, at the time when

---

[1] On this subject see Tibor Frank, *Picturing Austria-Hungary: The British Perception of the Habsburg Monarchy* (Wayne, N.J.: Center for Hungarian Studies and Publications, 2005; distributed by Columbia University Press, New York); also, Géza Jeszenszky, *Az elvesztett presztízs: Magyarország megítélésének megváltozása Nagy-Britanniában (1894-1918)* [The lost prestige: the Transformation of Hungary's Image in Great Britain (1894-1918)] (Budapest: Magvető, 1986); and the recent article on a related theme by Dany Deschênes, "French Intellectuals and the Image of Austria-Hungary in France: Prelude to the Break-up of Historic Hungary, 1918-20," *Hungarian Studies Review*, 33, 1-2 (2006): 93-120.

the United Kingdom sought to improve relations with Germany's enemies: France and Russia. The war of words began with the publication of the book of R.W. Seton-Watson, otherwise known as "Scotus Viator," *Racial Problems in Hungary*, which strove to demolish the "Kossuth myth" of a liberal Hungary and replace it with an image of Magyars as obstacles to progress and oppressors of minorities. This propaganda offensive intensified during the First World War, when other polemicists joined Seton-Watson's campaign aimed at defaming Hungary. This campaign reached its hight in 1917 when the goal of British (and Allied) diplomacy became the destruction of Austria-Hungary, and the Western public had to be prepared for this event.[2] Such negative images of the Magyars persisted throughout the 1920s and 1930s, and reached their lowest point at the end of the Second World War, when Hungary was referred to as Hitler's last ally, in spite of the fact that the majority of the country's population, and many members of the country's elite, made it obvious that they did not approve of Nazi ideas.

During the interwar period and the years of the Second World War, several groups of people in Great Britain strove to make sure that Hungary's reputation in the West remained negative. Foremost among these were the leaders of the revolutionary regimes of 1918-19. After going into emigration, these men spent much of their time and energies denouncing Hungary's ruling elite. In England, this task was carried out by such emigres as Count Michael Károlyi. There were also the spokesmen of the Little Entente countries who wanted to make sure that Hungary's reputation stayed negative while that of their own nations continued to be favourable. The most notable exception to this chorus of anti-Hungarian tirades, heard in Britain but also throughout the English-speaking world, was the voice of British historian Carlile Aylmer Macartney.

Macartney was born in 1895 in Kent, England, to Carlile and Louisa Macartney. He was educated in Britain's best schools, including Cambridge University's Trinity College. Later he earned a doctorate from Oxford University. During World War I he was wounded in action. Following the war he was the acting British vice-consul in Vienna. After returning to England from Vienna, Macartney first worked for the *Encyclopedia Britannica*, and then for the Intelligence Department of

---

2 László Marácz, "Western Images and Stereotypes of the Hungarians," in *Vampires Unstaked: National Images, Stereotypes and Myths in East Central Europe*, ed. André Gerrits and Nanci Adler (Amsterdam: Koninklijke Nederlandse Akademie van Wetenschappen, 1995), pp. 30-36.

the League of Nations Union of his country. In 1936 he was appointed a research fellow at Oxford University's All Souls College, a position which allowed him to continue his publishing activities and to have other employment. In fact, during the Second World War, he acted as the head of the Hungarian Section of the British Foreign Office's Research Department. In the meantime, he frequently made radio broadcasts to Hungary, an activity that he continued during the early years of the Cold War with Radio Free Europe. In 1949 he became Professor of International Relations at the University of Edinburgh.

What characterized Macartney's activities throughout these years was his publishing of one book after another on the subject of Central European history. The first of his monographs dealt with Austria while some of the later ones covered the nations of the Danube Valley in general; but most of his works were written on Hungarian subjects. He published two general histories of Hungary, and in 1957 he completed a monumental, two-volume history of Hungary from 1929 to 1944. These books projected an image of Hungary and Hungarians that went contrary to the stereotypes that had been and were still being presented by most contemporary Western authors. Limitations of space do not allow us to discuss this subject in detail, so a few representative examples shall have to suffice.

While most contemporary British and American commentators praised the settlement that had been imposed on Hungary through the Treaty of Trianon of 1920, in his *Hungary and Her Successors* Macartney pointed out that Magyar minorities in Czechoslovakia, Rumania and Yugoslavia had no protection as the terms of that treaty did not prevent the leaders of those countries from doing whatever they wanted to do with their Magyar subjects. Macartney in fact concluded that the policies of these states after 1920 amounted to "national imperialism." On the issue of Hungary's fatal involvement in the Second World War on Germany's side, Macartney, unlike many historians in the West—and, also, in Communist Hungary — refused to place the blame entirely or even predominantly on the shoulders of Hungary's leaders. In his opinion, Hungary's "doom" had been "dictated by forces far exceeding Hungary's own."[3]

It could be argued that Macartney was not the most influential British friend of Hungary during the interwar years. Indeed, there was Viscount Rothermere, the owner of the *Daily Mail* and other British

---

[3] C.A. Macartney, *Hungary: A Short History* (Chicago: Aldine, 1962), p. 226.

newspapers, who had far more money and more influential contacts than Macartney. Lord Rothermere, born as Harold S. Harmsworth in 1868, conducted a high-profile campaign during the late 1920s and throughout the 1930s aimed at the revision of the territorial clauses of the Treaty of Trianon that had dismembered the historic Kingdom of Hungary in 1920. Rothermere's efforts, however, were largely in vain and, in any case, he had lost his influence with the British public by 1940. He had argued that Adolf Hitler would cease asserting German power once Germany had regained the territories that had been unjustly taken from her in the Versailles peace settlement. Hitler's occupation of the rump Czech state in March of 1939 and his invasion of Poland six months later, left Rothermere a discredited man. Old, frail, and disappointed in life, Rothermere died soon thereafter. Macartney, on the other hand, continued to be active and would write additional important books on Hungarian history,[4] works that would have the potential of influencing the ideas of students of things Hungarian for generations to come.

The United States and Hungary

While Great Britain has been the most important English-speaking country for Hungary in the past, in recent decades that role has been increasingly usurped by the United States. Before the Second World War and even during the early phases of that conflict, however, the American republic played a distinctly secondary role in Hungarian affairs, but one that was becoming more and more important especially in view of America's growing influence in international affairs. How many, and what kind of sympathizers Hungarians had among America's elite, therefore was a matter of increasing importance of all Magyars.

During the first several decades of the existence of the United States of America, the vast majority of the Republic's population knew little or nothing about Hungary. That situation underwent a sudden change in the wake of the Hungarian War of Independence of 1848-49. Like in

---

4 Some of these books are: *October 15th* (Edinburgh: Edinburgh University Press, 1957, 2nd edition, 1963), published in the United States as *A History of Hungary, 1929-1944* (New York: Praeger, 1957); (with A. W. Palmer) *Independent Eastern Europe* (London: Macmillan, 1962); *The Hapsburg Empire* (London: Weidenfeld & Nicolson, 1969, 2nd edition. 1971). Macartney was also a regular contributor to prominent encyclopedias and to British and central European scholarly periodicals.

Europe, American opponents of absolute monarchical rule idolized the heroes of this war and their fiery leader, Louis Kossuth. It is a well-known fact that his visit to the United States in 1851-52 started a veritable Kossuth cult in North America which greatly enhanced Hungary's reputation there.

This situation lasted until the First World War. During that conflict English propaganda against Hungary reached the United States and was supplemented by local anti-Magyar propaganda after the US entered the war against the Central Powers in 1917. Anti-Hungarian sentiments persisted into the 1920s and 1930s. They were reinforced by the propaganda that was being spread by former members of the post-war revolutionary regime of Count Mihály Károlyi, as well as spokesmen of the Little Entente countries who wanted to make sure that Hungary's reputation in North America and elsewhere remained negative.

With the outbreak of the World War II in 1939, the situation further deteriorated, as the American public came to associate Hungary with the countries that had aligned their policies with those of Nazi Germany. In December of 1941 Hungary's reputation in North America reached its nadir when the American Republic became involved in the world conflict after the attack on Pearl Harbor by Japan, and after Hungary's government—imitating the example of Nazi Germany and fascist Italy—declared war on the United States.

During the three years that followed, Hungary was seen by Americans as Hitler's ally, and greater credibility was gained by those who wished to condemn Hungary or, at least, her ruling élite. The Hungarian emigre left went into high gear with its anti-Horthy propaganda, lead by such publicists as Oscar Jaszi and Rusztém Vámbéry.[5] These voices were echoed by Little Entente spokesmen, in particular by Eduard Beneš during his tour of the United States and Canada in 1943.

Fortunately for the people of Hungary and Hungarian immigrants in America, the leadership of the US was not uniformly anti-Hungarian in sentiment. In Washington in particular, some sympathy remained throughout the war, if not for the Hungarian government then for the people of Hungary and Hungarians in general. President Franklin Delano Roosevelt, despite his undeserved reputation among Hungarians as a Hungarophobe, was not antagonistic to the Hungarian nation. When

---

[5] N.F. Dreisziger, "Oscar Jaszi and the Hungarian Problem," in *Oscar Jaszi: Visionary, Reformer and Political Activist*, ed. N.F. Dreisziger and A. Ludanyi (Toronto: *HSR*, 1991): 59-79.

Hungary's government declared war on the United States in December of 1941, he was instrumental in delaying a US declaration of war on Hungary, saying that the people of that country had nothing to do with the government that allied itself with Nazi Germany. The US declaration of war was only issued half-a-year later. It should also be added that Roosevelt supported the idea of restoring the Austro-Hungarian empire in one form or another after the war.[6]

While the US President was not entirely unsympathetic to Hungary and Hungarians, many of his officials were. Among these were Sumner Welles, the Under-Secretary of State; Hamilton Fish Armstrong, the editor of the State Department's journal *Foreign Affairs*; and Alan Cranston who worked in the Foreign Newspapers section of the Office of Wartime Information for a better part of the war. One fairly influential American who was an exception in this respect, and was an avowed supporter of Hungary throughout these years, was J. F. Montgomery.

John Flournoy Montgomery was born in 1878 into an old-stock American family. He started his career in sales and business management and, for much of his early adult life, was an executive with various subsidiaries of what later became the giant Nestle Food Company. In fact, for some time, Montgomery was one of the directors of this firm, while he was owner of a smaller company, the International Milk Co. of Hillside, N.J. Throughout these years, he was a supporter of the Democratic Party. In fact, soon after the Democratic electoral victory in 1933, Montgomery resigned from most of his business directorships and accepted President Roosevelt's offer to become the American envoy to Hungary.[7]

From 1933 to 1941, when he was recalled from Budapest, Montgomery kept sending reports to Washington that revealed his sympathies for Hungary and most of her leaders. In fact, for Montgomery, the popular practice in English-speaking countries of labelling Hungary a "backward, feudal" land, was a convenient ex-post-facto justification for the ill-treatment which that country had received in the post-World War I peace settlement. And, he continued to express these views, both in newspaper articles and in State Department circles, after his departure from Budapest. On one occasion at least, Montgomery took on the task of defending Hungary's leaders against allegations made against

---

6 Ignác Romsics, ed., *Wartime American Plans for a New Hungary* (Highland Lakes, N.J.: ARP, 1992), pp. 6 and 33.

7 *The National Cyclopedia of American Biography*, Vol. 45 (New York: James T. White and Co., 1962), pp. 134f.

them by members of the Hungarian emigre left in the American English-language press. His most important act in support of Hungary and its pre-1944 regime, however, was the writing of the book: *Hungary, the Unwilling Satellite*. Unfortunately for Hungarians, the book did not appear in print until after the war's conclusion. Accordingly, it could not make an impact on American public opinion during the negotiations in 1945 concerning a post-war settlement in East Central Europe.[8]

In his book, Montgomery denied that Hungary was a "feudal" and "fascist" state, as her detractors would have had the American public believe. He argued that, for much of the time he had been in Budapest, the Hungarian regime strove to maintain a free hand in foreign policy. "Up to the time when Germany and Italy were pushed together by force of events, Hungary could and did balance between the two.... This policy... gave Hungary... considerable liberty of action...."[9] But Montgomery reserved most of his persuasive skills for a condemnation of the treatment that Hungary had received at the end of World War I. Excerpts from the book's preface might best illustrate his arguments and sentiments:

> [In 1919-1920] [w]e Americans were ordered to love Czechoslovakia, Rumania and Yugoslavia and to applaud the ill-treatment meted out to Hungarians and German-Austrians. We did. We bowed reverently to the fact that one [ethnically] mixed community, Austria-Hungary, was replaced and absorbed by a number of states, three of which,... were no less mixed than the dissected empire had been.... [W]e bowed to this settlement. To be quite exact, we did not care.... If it suited the British and French to put millions of German-Austrians and Hungarians under Czech rule, Hungarians under Rumanian, and Croats under Serbian domination, why should we be squeamish? But having helped our allies to win, we had our share of responsibility in the results of victory. We should not have washed our hands of all the injustice committed....
>
>   Even before Hitler shocked us into realizing our blunders, the truth had dawned upon some Americans... Businessmen, having visited first Croatia and then Serbia, or first Transylvania and then old Rumania, would ask... why advanced [peoples] had been put under the rule of... backward ones....

---

[8] John F. Montgomery, *Hungary, the Unwilling Satellite* (New York: The Devin-Adair Company, 1947); reprint edition by Vista Books, Morristown, N.J., 1993.

[9] *Ibid.*, (the 1947 edition), p. 18.

People deprived of their livelihood by their neighbors never even had a hearing. At the same time, those who profited by the victors' arbitrary discrimination showered us with an unceasing flow of propaganda.... the object of which was to keep what had been seized....

Having been American Minister to Hungary from 1933 to 1941, my regular post of observation... was Budapest. It was a unique post because the Magyars,... were always aware of being between the two fires of German and Russian imperialism. During those years, most of us saw only one fire, the German one. Hungary's vision was far ahead of ours. Had we listened to Hungarian statesmen, we should perhaps have been able to limit Stalin's triumph in the hour of Hitler's fall.

[B]etween the two wars,... from my watchtower on the Danube... what I witnessed was a tragic and insoluble conflict between fear and honor, in which fear was bound to win... Would it not have been better if we had opposed the arbitrary discrimination indulged in by the surgeons of 1919, who thereby afforded Hitler his most powerful arguments?...[10]

Alas, the sympathies of Montgomery and a few other Americans for Hungary were in vain, as Hungary became occupied by the Red Army at the end of the Second World War, which was followed in a few years by the gradual but inevitable imposition of totalitarian communism. The Hungarian nation would have to wait more than four decades for the development of an international situation in which it could enjoy the fruits of that limited American sympathy that did exist toward Hungary.

Canada and Hungary

Canada has never played a major role in the evolution of Hungary, and whatever little role it has played, has been hardly known to either Hungarians or to Canadians.[11] Nevertheless, Canadian attitudes to Hungary

---

[10] *Ibid.*, pp. 7-12 *in passim*. For a less flattering portrayal of Montgomery's views see Tibor Frank, ed., *Discussing Hitler: Advisers of U.S. Diplomacy in Central Europe, 1934-1941* (Budapest and New York: Central European University Press, 2003).

[11] The interaction of Canadian and Hungarian history has never been explored systematically although I and a few other Hungarian-Canadian historians have written about a few aspects of this subject. Most of these books deal with the Hungarian-Canadian experience in general, but some comment on the interactions of the new country with the old as well. See especially: N. F. Dreisziger, *Struggle and Hope: The Hungarian-Canadian Experience*

and things Hungarian were important, if for no other reason then for helping to shape the Canadian public's opinion of Magyar newcomers to the country.

Hungarian immigration to the Dominion of Canada in any appreciable numbers started at the end of the nineteenth century. In the eyes of certain Canadian politicians responsible for the shaping of immigration policy, Magyar peasants made good agricultural workers or even settlers, and were generally welcomed in the vast, largely empty lands of the Canadian prairies. This favourable view of Hungarians suffered a setback during the First World War when they became regarded as potential troublemakers for Canada's wartime authorities. Nevertheless, by the mid-1920s these concerns were put aside, as Canada once again encouraged the immigration of Hungarian agricultural labourers.

The Great Depression stemmed the tide of newcomers, but in the wake of World War II Canada's gates once again opened. The result was the influx of several thousand refugees or "displaced persons" from war-torn Hungary. Unlike the masses of agricultural workers who came from pre-1930 Hungary, the new arrivals were more often than not middle- or even upper-class elements, members of the professions or of the intelligentsia. They were followed in 1956-57 by over 37,000 refugees of the Hungarian Revolution, many of whom were also well-educated, professional people.

The influx of these newcomers was followed by the development in Canada of dynamic and sophisticated Hungarian cultural life. One consequence of this was that knowledge of Hungary and of things Hungarian became more wide-spread in Canada, mainly because of the existence of a large number of people here who spread that knowledge through their everyday activities. Another result was the increased com-

---

(Toronto: McClelland & Stewart, 1982) [which is available in French: *Lutte et espoir: L'expérience des Canadiens hongrois* (Ottawa: Multiculturalisme Canada, 1982)]; Martin Louis Kovacs, *Esterhazy and Early Hungarian Immigration to Canada* (Regina: Canadian Plains Research Center, 1974), and the same author's *Peace and Strife: Some Facets of the History of an Early Prairie Community* (Kipling, Sask.: Kipling District Historical Soc., 1980); John Kosa, *Land of Choice: Hungarians in Canada* (Toronto: University of Toronto Press, 1957); Carmela Patrias, *Patriots and Proletarians: Politicizing Hungarian Immigrants in Interwar Canada* (Kingston and Montreal: McGill Queen's U. P., 1994); Robert Keyserlingk ed., *Breaking Ground: The 1956 Hungarian Refugee Movement to Canada* (North York, Ont.: York Lane Press, York University, 1993).

plexity and frequency of interactions between Canada and Hungary.[12]

Long before this situation emerged in Canada, Hungary, Hungarian culture, and even Hungarian Canadians were hardly known to the vast majority of Canada's citizens. It was in this connection that one Canadian's work and opinions were of great importance. That Canadian was Watson Kirkconnell.

Kirkconnell was born in 1895 in Port Hope, Ontario, into a Scottish-Canadian family. He was an outstanding student who developed into a man of extraordinary academic achievement. He became familiar with fifty languages and published so much work in his lifetime, in various disciplines of learning, that his list of publications nearly fill a 371-page book.[13] One of the languages that he read and translated was Magyar, but in adult life his affinity for things Hungarian became reinforced by his discovery that he had more than an academic connection to things Hungarian: his researches into his family tree revealed that, on his mother's side, he may have been a descendant of St. Margaret, the late-eleventh century Scottish queen who was purportedly a granddaughter of St. Stephen, the founder of the Christian Kingdom of Hungary. The knowledge of this fact no doubt strengthened Kirkconnell's "great love for Hungary, its people, its language, [and] its culture..." to use the words of his biographer.[14]

There were no signs of Kirkconnell's interest in Hungary during the early phases of his life. What did become evident during his student days—first at Queen's University in Kingston, Ontario, and later at Oxford University—was his talent for and interest in verse translation. The latter increased substantially during Kirkconnell's stay in Winnipeg, Manitoba, during the 1920s and 1930s where he taught English and literatures at the college that later became the University of

---

[12] On this subject see N.F. Dreisziger, "The Hungarian Revolution of 1956: The Legacy of the Refugees," *Nationalities Papers, the journal of the Association for the Study of the Nationalities of the USSR and Eastern Europe*, 1, 2 (Fall 1985): 198-208; and by the same author, "The Impact of the Revolution on Hungarians Abroad," in *The First War Between Socialist States,* ed. Béla K. Király, *et al.* (New York: Brooklyn College Press, 1984), pp. 411-425.

[13] J.R.C. Perkin with James B. Snelson, *Morning in his Heart: The Life and Writings of Watson Kirkconnell* (Wolfville, Nova Scotia: Acadia University & Lancelot Press, 1986).

[14] Perkin, writing *ibid.*, p. 11. St. Margaret's Hungarian ancestry has since been questioned.

Winnipeg. During his first three years in this busy centre of Canadian immigrant life, the young university teacher did not develop close contacts with New Canadians. What led to Kirkconnell's life-long friendship with Canada's European immigrants was his serious involvement in verse translation.[15] He turned to this type of activity for solace when his wife died after giving birth to twin sons. In the lonely months that followed, Kirkconnell made plans for translating samples of Europe's best poetry into English as a memorial to his departed wife. His first volume of verse translation, *European Elegies*, appeared in 1928.

At first this activity served Kirkconnell only to reduce the pain of bereavement. Soon, however, the task assumed greater significance: it gained him new acquaintances, initially mainly among the academic and literary elites of several European countries, but later also among New Canadian intellectuals. Closer links with the world of immigrant ethnics wrought a change in Kirkconnell's approach to popularizing the European cultural achievement. His first work in the field of verse translation had a potential to serve the interests of Canadians of European background, but this had not been his original purpose. The young scholar's subsequent publications had different motives. In his next work, he deliberately set out to combat ignorance, the "mother of intolerance," as he put it in the volume's preface. He wrote further: "Saxon and Slav, Norseman and Celt, all have gifts that have been proved great in the annals of civilization; but sincere co-operation, whether in the New World or in the Old, becomes humanly possible only as men realize the worth of their fellow men."[16] This volume, some two hundred pages of appreciative comments about the cultural achievements of European nations, undoubtedly generated a warm

---

[15] Kirkconnell's first encounter with newcomers to Canada came before his Winnipeg stay. In 1922, on a return voyage from England he found himself surrounded by immigrants from many parts of Europe. Scattered throughout this large group, comprised mainly of agricultural workers, Kirkconnell found several well-educated refugees from Eastern Europe's civil wars and revolutions. He was apparently impressed and took an interest in them but alter arriving in Canada lost contact with them. See N.F. Dreisziger, "Watson Kirkconnell: Translator of Hungarian Poetry and Friend of Hungarian Canadians," in *Hungarian Poetry and the English-Speaking World: A Tribute to Watson Kirkconnell,* ed. N.F. Dreisziger, (Ottawa, Hungarian Readers Service, 1977), p. 125.

[16] Watson Kirkconnell, *The European Heritage: A Synopsis of European Cultural Achievement (London and Toronto: Dent and Sons, 1930), p. v.*

respect for European cultures in the hearts of its readers.

In addition to publishing translations of European poetry, Kirk-connell began publicising the works of New Canadian poets. His most substantial publication dealing with this poetry was *Canadian Overtones*, an anthology of verse translated from the "Canadian poetry" of Icelandic, Swedish, Norwegian, Hungarian, Italian, Greek and Ukrainian poets. The preface identified Kirkconnell's purpose: to "reveal to English-speaking Canadians a transient but intensely significant phase" of Canada's national literature. Then he stunned his readers by stating that, "in Western Canada... this unknown poetry has surpassed that of Anglo-Canadians both in quantity and in quality."[17] Kirkconnell also observed that Canadian attitudes toward immigrants had passed through two "ignorant and discreditable phases." At first many Canadians considered immigrants as "European coolies," who were good only for back-breaking work that no one else wanted to perform. Later, Canadians showed a patronizing interest in the newcomers' folk-costumes and folk-dances, aspects of their culture which were no more than "picturesque incidentals which have about as much vital share in their lives as the kilt and the highland fling have in that of the average Scotch-Canadian." Kirkconnell hoped that by getting to know New Canadian poetry, native-born Canadians would develop a "third and much truer attitude" towards immigrants.[18]

In the preface to this volume Kirkconnell revealed his concept of a Canadian multi-ethnic identity. New Canadian poetry would help to develop in future generations of Canadians a "Canadianism nourished by pride in the individual's racial past." A person with an awareness of his ancestry and pride in his forebears' achievements was a better citizen of his country. "As a Canadian, he is not poorer but richer because he realizes his place in a notable stream of human relationship down through the centuries." Kirkconnell had only contempt for the person who denied his ancestry. He who claimed to be "one hundred per cent" Canadian is commonly one "who has deliberately suppressed an alien origin in order to keep the material benefits of a well-advertised loyalty." There was no chance of "noble spiritual issues from such a prostituted patriotism." It was regrettable that this type of behaviour was encouraged by the "ignorant assumption" of many English-Canadians

---

[17] *Canadian Overtones* (Winnipeg: Columbia Press, 1935), p. 3.

[18] *Ibid.*, p. 4.

that an alien origin was the "mark of inferiority." "He who thinks thus," Kirkconnell continued, "is a mental hooligan." He argued further that the development of a general Canadian multi-ethnic awareness could only come through a change in public attitudes to immigrant minority cultures. This change could be achieved only with the help of civic and educational institutions. He also believed that the state had a responsibility in preserving the "full potentialities of our several peoples."[20] In expressing these views, Kirkconnell anticipated by some four decades the concept of government supported multicultural programmes.

By the time Kirkconnell developed these ideas about a multicultural Canadian identity, he was in increasing contact with the Hungarian community in Canada, particularly with the growing Magyar colony of Winnipeg which, during the 1920's, had become one of the most influential in the country. Indeed, it was Kirkconnell's activities in the field of verse translation that attracted the attention of Béla Báchkai Payerle, the publisher of the *Kanadai Magyar Újság* (Canadian Hungarian News) of Winnipeg, Canada's largest Magyar-language newspaper. Having read Kirkconnell's translations from Magyar, Payerle encouraged him to publish a separate volume of verse translation from Hungarian. In 1930 this venture resulted in the completion of a manuscript. Alas, the Depression brought many publishers to near ruin or bankruptcy and the volume's publication became impossible for the time being, but instalments from it were printed in the *News* and, later, in Payerle's English-language magazine, the *Young Magyar-American*. Then in 1932 Lord Rothermere visited Winnipeg and contributed $200 to the cost of printing the collection. The Hungarian government advanced a further $500. Payerle did the typesetting, gratis, and early in 1933 *The Magyar Muse* at last became available.[21]

Later more translations from Magyar poetry followed: from the work of János Arany, but also of the poetry of emigre Hungarian poets, including the Premonstratensian canon László Mécs, Tibor Tollas and others. In 1967, after his retirement from the Presidency of Acadia

---

[19] *Ibid.*, pp. 5f.

[20] *Ibid.*, p. 6. On this subject see also my paper, "Watson Kirkconnell and the Cultural Credibility Gap Between Immigrants and the Native-Born in Canada," in *Ethnic Canadians: Culture and Education*, ed. M.L. Kovacs (Regina: Canadian Plains Research Center, 1978), pp. 87-96.

[21] Dreisziger, "Watson Kirkconnell," pp. 129f.

University, Kirkconnell completed one of his old projects, a translation of Arany's *Toldi*. Next followed translations from other, more recent Hungarian poets, such as Dezső Kosztolányi, Lajos Kassák, Milán Füst, József Erdélyi, Lőrinc Szabó, Gyula Illyés, and many others. Finally, in 1985 followed the posthumous volume *Hungarian Helicon*, a nearly 800- page anthology of Hungarian verse translations by this Canadian friend of Hungarians.[22]

Kirckonnell's significance went beyond gaining respect for Hungarians, both in Hungary and elsewhere, by making their poetry available to the public of English-speaking countries. His pro-immigrant writings during the 1930s, and especially, during the early phases of the Second World War, probably contributed to the fact that during this conflict, European "enemy aliens" in Canada were better treated than they had been during the First World War. Hungarians, in fact, were almost completely free of the restrictions that were imposed during the war on newcomers from enemy countries. Kirckonnell was also an intellectual father of a new government agency that was set up during the war, the Nationalities Branch of the Department of national War Services, a bureau that was the precursor of the Canadian government's Multiculturalism Directorate of the 1970s and 1980s.[23]

Conclusions

Watson Kirkconnell was not the only Canadian that had a favourable view of Hungary and Hungarians. Several of his contemporaries shared his opinions, though perhaps none of them had done so much work for them as Kirkconnell. And there were members of the generation that

---

[22] This massive anthology had been completed in 1973. Its printing and marketing by the University of Toronto Press at the time would have cost $28,000, which made publication commercially unfeasible. A request for a grant from the multicultural programme of the Department of the Secretary of State in Ottawa had been supported by a number of Hungarian cultural organisations, but was turned down. Finally, after Kirkconnell's death in 1977, the Széchenyi Society of Calgary came to the project's rescue, and made the volume's publication a reality.

[23] On the beginnings of this agency see N.F. Dreisziger, "The Rise of a Bureaucracy for Multiculturalism: The Origins of the Nationalities Branch, 1939-41," in *On Guard for Thee: War, Ethnicity, and the Canadian State, 1939-1945*, ed. Norman Hillmer *et al.* (Ottawa: Canadian Committee for the History of the Second World War, 1988), pp. 1-29.

followed Kirkconnell's whose attitudes were similar. In fact, after the Hungarian Revolution of 1956 public opinion in general had turned in favour of Hungary and Hungarians in Canada, and in the other English-speaking countries as well. The admission to Canada of over 37,000 refugees in the wake of that event, after the suspension of many of the usual immigration procedures, is a testimony to this changed attitude to Hungarians. While the reputation of Hungary and Magyars in general have remained fairly favourable since 1956, Hungarians ought to remind themselves that the preservation of a certain degree of national prestige is not automatic. Hungary had lost its prestige in the past, and could do so again in the future. Although the rise and decline of national reputations is the result of complex factors, sometimes having little to do with the behaviour of the people or country in question, a nation does have to be on its guard to do its utmost to preserve and enhance its good reputation. In other words, Hungarians should never take for granted the friends they have in the international community.

Part IV

Hungarian Communities

in the New World

Essays about:

Hungarians in North America

Hungarians in Brazil

and

The Historiography

of these Communities

Canada's Hungarian
Communities a Century Ago*

1905 was an important year in the evolution of Canada. It was in that year that the provinces of Alberta and Saskatchewan came into being; they were carved out from the Northwest Territories that had been administered until then from Ottawa. Although there had not been a similarly dramatic event in the history of Canada's Hungarian community that year, we can say that 1905, or at least the middle of the first decade of the twentieth century, also saw important developments in the evolution of this country's Magyar ethnic group. This article will describe the state of the Canadian West's Hungarian colonies a century ago.

The first groups of Hungarian immigrants came to settle in Canada in the mid-1880s. Before then only individual or small parties of Hungarians strayed to Canada's shores. These pre-1880 arrivals were either visitors or were sojourners who did not intend to settle permanently in what before 1763 used to be known as New France, and after that year as British North America.

The Magyar newcomers who came in 1885 and 1886 were directed by Canadian authorities to the newly-opened Canadian West. We should remember that the Canadian Pacific Railway, Canada's first trans-continental transportation link, was completed just at that time. The Hungarians who came then were originally peasants or agricultural labourers and arrived from the United States where they had gone to work a few years earlier to the coal-mining regions of Pennsylvania and Ohio. They had been promised that on the Canadian Prairies they could get free land and could return to their original lifestyle of cultivating the soil.

The pioneer farming communities these early Hungarian arrivals founded did not prosper for long. It was only about a decade later, when

---

* This study was based on the research I had done for a long article: "The Quest for Spiritual Fulfilment among Immigrants: The Rise of Organized Religious Life in Pioneer Hungarian-Canadian Communities, 1885-1939," *Magyar Egyháztörténeti Vázlatok–Essays in Church History in Hungary*, 16, 3-4 (fall-winter 2004): 95-124.

peasant immigrants began arriving in Canada directly from Hungary's villages, that the first viable Hungarian farming colonies became established in this country. By 1905 a few of them had even begun prospering.

The Dominion of Canada, as Canada became known in 1867 when some of Britain's North American colonies joined in a confederation of their own, was still a young country in 1905. Until that year it consisted of only seven provinces. A mere generation earlier the Canadian West, that vast stretch of land from Lake Superior to the Pacific Coast, had been mostly devoid of population, in particular of agricultural settlers. While the more fertile regions of the prairies had started filling up by the end of the century, urban development was still lagging behind. At the time of the fourth Canadian population census in 1901, no urban centre between Winnipeg (population 42,340) and Vancouver (population 29,432) was inhabited by over 5,000 people. Edmonton and Calgary came close, Regina had a population of only 2,249, and Saskatoon, a mere 113.

What agricultural population there was on the Canadian Prairies was scattered on isolated homesteads. These were usually situated kilometres from each other. In this world of isolated farmsteads there was a patchwork of "ethnic islands" as immigrants from various parts of Europe (and, to a lesser extent from Eastern Canada and the United States) tried to settle in proximity to each other. The result was the emergence of colonies of European immigrants with distinct ethnic characteristics. By 1905 there would be districts in which Ukrainian homesteaders predominated, while in others Scandinavians, Germans, French-Canadians, Slovaks, Rumanians, just to name a few. By 1905 there were a handful of such Hungarian districts as well, but in comparison with the Ukrainians for example, these were almost negligible in number.

One important reason for the slow development of Hungarian colonies on the Canadian prairies was the fact that Hungarians were rather late in coming to Canada in large numbers. Before 1900 Hungarians who wanted to try their luck in the New World were far more likely to do so in the United States, where economic progress was more robust, or in some of the more prosperous Latin American countries such as Argentina or Brazil. Annual immigration of Hungarians to Canada before 1900, and for a few years even thereafter, amounted to a few hundred newcomers only, as opposed to the thousands or even tens of thousands who were going to the United States.

Precise statistics on this migration are difficult to find partly because of the practice of Canadian authorities to label everyone coming from the Dual Monarchy of Austria-Hungary as an "Austrian," and partly because some of the people who came from the Hungarian half of the Monarchy were not Hungarians but were Slovaks, Ruthenians, Germans, etc. Contemporary Canadian census statistics are also useless for estimating the size of Canada's Hungarian community at the turn of the century, even after census takers abandoned the practice of listing every immigrant from Austria-Hungary as an "Austrian," because then they started to lump Hungarians together with other East Europeans such as the Lithuanians. Because of these problems with the demographic data, our best estimate of the Canadian West's Hungarian population in 1905 can only be a guess: two, perhaps three thousand. When we keep in mind that Hungarian settlements were scattered over an area the Canadian West that was many times the size of Hungary, we can imagine the difficulty of communications, let alone meaningful social interaction, among the people of these scattered colonies.

Another reason for the delayed development of pioneer homesteading by Hungarian peasant immigrants was above all the fact that newcomers from Hungary, like newcomers from many other places of the world, found life on the Canadian prairies difficult. The hardships they encountered were numerous: the long, cold winters; the enormous distances; the lack of vegetation familiar to them; the unpredictability of weather and climate; the frequent infestations of harmful insects: black flies, mosquitoes and in some years, locusts.

Piled on top of these physical hardships were the social and spiritual ones. Homesickness, social isolation and profound loneliness, were the hallmarks of life on the Canadian Prairies where European immigrants had to make the difficult adjustment from lives lived in a closely-knit and geographically compact villages, to ones in the physical isolation of a prairie homestead. Not surprisingly under the circumstances, the rates of failed attempts at pioneer homesteading were very high, not only among newcomers from continental Europe but also among homesteaders from other parts of Canada, or from the British Isles, or the United States. Failure rates for attempts at pioneer homesteading were 45% in Alberta and 57% in Saskatchewan.

No statistics exist as to what percentage of Hungarian pioneers sooner or later abandoned prairie farming, but the anecdotal evidence suggests that the ratio was very high. While leaving the prairie farm— whether for urban centres in the Canadian West, or the cities of Central Canada—alleviated some of the physical hardships of Hungarian newcomers, it often did not solve the problems of social isolation and spiritual malaise. Hungarian immigrants who exchanged pioneer existence for life in more established regions of the country were often left just as lonely and homesick as they had been on the prairie farm.

Perhaps the most important cause of the loneliness and social isolation of Hungarian immigrants to early twentieth century Canada was their inability to learn English and therefore to communicate with their non-Hungarian neighbours. The vast majority of Magyar newcomers at the time were peasants with little or no education. Learning another language was very difficult for them, especially since they worked on isolated farms or among other immigrants who spoke rudimentary English at best.

To overcome this problem of social isolation, Canada's Hungarian immigrants were left to their own devices. It was up to them to establish their Hungarian social circles and organizations. What Hungarian immigrants to Canada often missed most, both on the prairie farms and in their little immigrant colonies elsewhere in the country, was organized religious life. Not surprisingly, soon after their settlement in a Hungarian "ethnic island" on the Canadian Prairies they often tried to establish at least the rudiments of formal religious life for themselves. This meant that they strove to create parishes or congregations of their own or, at least, tried to arrange for the visits of priests or ministers to their little communities.

These efforts were a part of the larger aspirations of early Hungarian-Canadian society to re-establish in their new country at least some of the institutions that they had been accustomed to in their native land. In this quest, Hungarian immigrants, more often than not, were faced by myriad obstacles, some of which would prove insurmountable, at least for the first years of their stay in Canada. In this quest they were faced with many difficulties, both the kind that were external to their communities and those that were internal to them.

Factors external to the Hungarian immigrant community that hindered in the building of religious organizations included the great distances between Hungarian colonies. There was also the aloofness and at times even hostility that East European newcomers to the country encountered among Canadians. Among the internal factors that played a role in impeding the emergence of organised religious life among Hungarian immigrants were such circumstances as the small size of most early Hungarian-Canadian colonies, the scarcity of effective community leaders, the social divisions within these colonies, and last but not least, the deep-rooted denominational fragmentation of Hungarian society both in the mother country and in the new one. Despite these difficulties, in the two decades after the mid-1890s, a small number of the "old" Hungarian-Canadian communities made considerable progress in organizing their religious and social life.

It should be emphasized that the organizations that emerged in the communities of Hungarian immigrants in the Canadian West were a pale shadow of those that these people had been familiar with in their native land. This statement is especially true of the religious ones. In Hungary the churches, and especially the Catholic Church, was a prosperous and hierarchical institution that played a dominant role not only in the religious life of the country but also in education, cultural and even in economic affairs. What emerged in Canada's Hungarian communities had, in the beginning, little to do with the centres of church influence. Later, the Canadian churches, and especially the country's Catholic Church, would take note of developments at the grassroots level and would try to influence and even control them. Before that happened, the Hungarian pioneers were on their own in most cases when they strove to establish religious life in their communities.

The establishment of Hungarian ethnic institutions, and among them the ethnic churches, was already taking place in a handful of Hungarian colonies at the turn of the century. For reasons that would be too complex to explain we will take only three of these colonies and trace the history of the institutions they built to 1905. It so happens that one of these colonies was predominantly a Protestant one, the second was Roman Catholic, and the third a mixed one, but unlike the other two that were colonies of homesteaders, this one was an urban one. In the next few paragraphs we will examine the Hungarian colonies of Békevár, of Eszterház-Kaposvár and of Winnipeg as they existed in and around the year 1905.

Békevár, Hungarian-Canada's earliest Protestant pioneer settlement

The colony of Bekevar (originally Békevár), in Saskatchewan (near the present town of Kipling), was one of the most prosperous settlements of the Magyar immigrants to Canada at the turn of the nineteenth century. It is also the best known one to historians as a result of the researches that the late Professor Martin L. Kovacs (1918-2000) of the University of Regina had done during the 1970s and 1980s.

The majority of the Hungarian pioneers of the Bekevar area came from the village of Botrágy (in what then was Bereg County in eastern Hungary, today's Northwestern Rumania); from Tornyospálca as well as a few other villages in Szabolcs County (still a part of eastern

Hungary); with a sprinkling of newcomers from elsewhere, from the villages of Karcag and Kisújszállás of the region of Kunság (east-central Hungary); and from Csetény (Veszprém County, in Transdanubia, west-central Hungary). Although from Tornyospálca came several Greek Catholic settlers and from elsewhere a few Roman Catholics, the vast majority of the Hungarian inhabitants in the Bekevar region belonged to the Reformed (Calvinist) Church. In fact, the Bekevar colony, a Magyar ethnocultural island on the Canadian Prairies, was as much an ethnic island as it was a religious one. Its earliest pioneers were Calvinists who made strenuous efforts to recruit their co-religionists as settlers. Among the recruits they invited was Kálmán Kovácsi, a Reformed church missionary from the Debrecen, the city Hungarians regard as the "Calvinist Rome." He arrived in 1901 and served as the Bekevar community's religious leader for almost a decade.

In Bekevar religion, religious teachings and practices, and especially the study of the Bible, were taken very seriously. Every family had a copy of the bible that was consulted and read regularly. Some people memorized large parts of it. These bibles were handed down from generation to generation. Almost equal attention was paid to the singing and memorization of hymns. The more dedicated members of this scriptural community coalesced in a lay fraternity called the Christian Spiritists' Society. More a cultic group than a congregation, this organization and its cultural equivalent, the Self-Training Circle, were instrumental in establishing the Bekavar colony as a leading Hungarian culture centre in Saskatchewan.

Before the construction of schools in the area (which could accommodate religious services on Sundays) and, especially, before the building of a church to house the congregation, the residents of Bekevar took turns hosting Sunday services. Minister Kovácsi boarded with one then another of the families in his congregation.

These rudimentary beginnings of organized institutional life in Bekevar lasted for a few years only. By about 1905 the community had received its first (one-room) school building, which they named the "Kossuth School." The township next door, which also had a fairly large Hungarian settler population, opened another school that was known for some time as the "Magyar School." These buildings, but especially the former, would serve for many years as the locale of the Bekevar Calvinist congregation's Sunday services. The construction of a substantial church building was also put on the agenda. It was meant to be the crowning achievement of Bekevar's Hungarian community's work.

The evolution of organized ethnic life in Bekevar from the rudimentary and informal arrangements to the establishment of orderly social and religious routine set the pattern of development of community life in the more prosperous of the Protestant Hungarian settlements of the Canadian Prairies. The evolution of predominantly Catholic communities of Magyar pioneers showed a somewhat different pattern.

The Roman Catholic Community of Esterhaz-Kaposvar

Since Catholic immigrants from Hungary outnumbered Protestants about two to one in the pioneer Hungarian-Canadian settlements of the Canadian West, it is not surprising that one of the first Magyar colonies established there happened to be a predominantly Catholic one. It was the colony known as Esterhaz-Kaposvar (originally Eszterház-Kaposvár) in eastern Saskatchewan, about 20 km east of the present-day town of Esterhazy.

The roots of this colony go back to the second half of the 1880s when Count Paul Oscar Esterhazy (1831-1912), a Hungarian settlement agent operating from the United States, brought a group of immigrants to the Canadian prairies from the mining and smelting town of the American mid-west. Esterhazy, a veteran of the Hungarian War of Independence of 1848-49, was probably neither an aristocrat nor a legitimate member of Hungary's princely family of the Esterházys, but he must have been an excellent salesman. He managed to get several dozen immigrants from Northern Hungary (today's Slovakia) sold on the idea of starting life anew as Canadian farmers, and also succeeded in convincing Canadian immigration officials that he could get a large number of settlers for the virgin prairies of Saskatchewan.

Unfortunately for Esterhazy, his plans for a viable, prosperous and populous Hungarian colony were not realized until about a decade later when Hungarian peasant newcomers began arriving in the colony (as well as nearby places) directly from Hungary. Despite of his partial success in his colonization venture, Esterhazy was honoured by Canada when a small settlement (with hardly any Magyar settlers) was named after him in the early 1900s. It eventually developed into the town of Esterhazy, Saskatchewan.

One of the first "ethnic" institutions that appeared in this colony of Esterhaz-Kaposvar was a Catholic parish. At first the Hungarian pioneers of this little community were served by non-Hungarian speaking priests assigned to them by the bishop of St. Boniface. The parishioners had little influence over the affairs of their parish as the bishop expected his priests to handle their flock in a patriarchal manner. Still, the community of Esterhaz-Kaposvar was much better off than most of the Catholic Hungarian parishes that came into existence later: it had a priest of its own. Furthermore, some of the priests that served the parish managed to advance the colony's development. Perhaps the most remarkable of these was the Belgian priest Father Jules Pirot. Pirot arrived in 1904 and soon undertook two ambitious projects. He began to learn Hungarian and he breathed new life into a campaign to have a church constructed for the parish.

The Hungarian Colony of Winnipeg

The first urban centre in the Canadian West that had a little Hungarian colony was Lethbridge, Alberta. Hungarian immigrants, mainly trans-migrants from the United States, began working in that community's coal-mines as early as the mid-1880s. In the late 1890s more Hungarians arrived, newcomers who came directly from Hungary. By 1901 there were enough of them to establish the First Hungarian Sick-Benefit Society of Lethbridge. The association collected regular fees from its members and paid modest support to those who lost their income because of illness. When the Reverend Peter A. Vay, a Hungarian priest on a tour of the Magyar communities of North America, visited Lethbridge a few years later, he reported meeting hundreds of Hungarian residents in the town.

By then Lethbridge had begun to be surpassed as the home of the largest Hungarian colony in the Canadian West by Winnipeg, capital of the Province of Manitoba and the fastest-growing commercial centre in Canada west of Toronto. It was the place where most Hungarian newcomers passed through on their way to the virgin lands of the Canadian prairies. Eventually a few of them began settling in the city. Soon after 1900 a small Hungarian colony came into existence. Oral tradition among these early Winnipeg residents had it that the first Hungarian to settle in the region was Péter Nagy, a refugee of the 1848-49 Hungarian Revolution against the Habsburgs. Nagy built his farmhouse near what in the 1850s was called Fort Garry, in the lands that had been administered in those days by the Hudson's Bay Company. By 1900 this farm had become a part of the urban development of the city of Winnipeg. One of Nagy's descendants was still living there at the time.

Only a few years later, the city had a Hungarian colony numbering into the few hundreds. The First Hungarian Sick-Benefit Association of

Winnipeg was already functioning and plans were being made for the establishment of a Calvinist congregation. It would be led by the newcomer Lajos Kovácsi, the brother of Kálmán, the already-mentioned minister in Bekevar.

Progress and then Setbacks, 1906 to 1918

The half-dozen years that followed 1905 constituted the most promising period in the early evolution of Canada's Hungarian community. Immigration from Hungary grew by leaps and bounds, reflecting the rapid development of the Canadian West until almost the eve of the First World War when economic expansion slowed down. The general prosperity allowed for the rapid development especially in the well-established Hungarian colonies. Signs of progress could be seen everywhere. In the colony of Esterhaz-Kaposvar the stone church Father Pirot had envisaged after his arrival there in 1904 became a reality two years later. In the colony of Bekevar a church was constructed later, in 1912. It was a fine, distinguished building.In Winnipeg the above-mentioned Calvinist congregation became a reality in 1906. The following year the city's Hungarian Catholics established a sick-benefit association of their own.

More important perhaps than the construction of churches and the establishment of still more Hungarian organizations was the fact that in Winnipeg for example a small group of educated, middle-class Hungarians had gathered. Under their leadership came the first attempts at publishing Hungarian-language newspapers. These attempts coincided with the first try in Hungarian-Canadian history to create a nation-wide (or, at least, Canada West-wide) umbrella organization of Hungarian parishes and organizations. These efforts were accompanied by a campaign to get Hungarian-speaking teachers for the schools of Canada's Hungarian colonies.

The campaign for a Hungarian federation and especially for Hungarian schools was unsuccessful. Serious disagreement developed between the largely Protestant advocates of "Hungarian schools" and the Hungarian Catholic colonies of the Canadian West or, more precisely, the Canadian West's Francophone Roman Catholic hierarchy that was adamant to retain control over the education of Roman Catholic immigrants. Even when the disagreement had subsided, the "importation" of Hungarian speaking teachers became a problem because there were few volunteers for such work and those who came found their pay inadequate and rarely stayed for longer than one school-year.

Finally, when war broke out in the summer of 1914, all progress in Canada's Hungarian communities ground to a halt. Immigration from Hungary was halted. Austria-Hungary being an ally of Germany meant that most Hungarian newcomers to Canada became "enemy aliens." This made many of them subject to police measures: among other things there were restrictions placed on their movements. Not surprisingly under the circumstances a few Hungarian-Canadian leaders left Canada during the early part of the war for the still neutral United States. Later a few Hungarian organizations ceased functioning. And, after the war, laws were passed in the Canadian West that made the setting up of "ethnic schools" illegal. This development put an end to the idea of "Hungarian schools" even if Magyar-speaking teachers could have been found to teach in the schools of Hungarian settlements.

Though most Hungarian pioneer farmers felt discriminated against during the First World War, many of them managed to prosper because the price of wheat and other produce kept rising between 1914 and 1918. But general prosperity and progress did not return to the Hungarian-Canadian communities of the prairie provinces until the mid-1920s when immigration resumed from Hungary and economic growth recommenced in the country. But that is another story that best be told some other time.

Hungarians in Brazil

Are there Hungarians in all parts of the world? Some time ago, I had a chance to see the Brazilian film *Central Station*. It is the story of a boy who lives with his mother in one of Brazil's big cities. When his mother is killed in a traffic accident, the young child goes in search for his father who works on the frontiers of this huge country. The film portrays a world so strange and alien to us accustomed to the "civilized" life of Europe and North America, that I could not imagine that any of my countrymen could be found in those end-of-the-world parts of Brazil. Yet, when my mother-in-law's great-grandson visited us that summer, I realized that he comes precisely from such a region of Brazil, from Petrolina in the state of Pernambuco. What surprised me even more, he told me that there is a small colony of Hungarians there. Most of them are what the Germans call *Gastarbeiter:* contract workers with technical expertise that is hard to find in Brazil.

I always knew that there have been sizable colonies of Hungarians in that vast country ever since the late nineteenth century. I had assumed, however, that most Hungarians there lived in the big cities, two of which indeed have had, and still have, large colonies of Magyars. Very little is known outside of Latin America about these islands of the Magyar diaspora. My own considerable library offers next to nothing on the subject.[1] Yet, not long ago I came across material that gives evidence of a vibrant Magyar cultural life in the Brazil of the not too distant past. The most important of these is the *Évkönyv* [Yearbook] of the

---

[1] In this respect Gyula Borbándi's book, *A magyar emigráció élatrajza, 1945-1985* [The Biography of the Hungarian Emigration, 1945-1985] (Munich: published by the author, 1985) contains only brief references to Hungarians in Brazil, see for example pages 75-76 and 331-32. Even less informative is Miklós Szántó's little book, *Magyarok Amerikában* [Hungarians in America] (Budapest: Gondolat, 1984). For the story of early Magyar adventurers, soldiers of fortune, and Jesuits in pre-1900 Latin America, see László Szabó, *Magyar múlt Dél-Amerikában (1519-1900)* [Hungarian Past in South America] (Budapest: Európa, 1982). Finally, for the story of Hungarian filmmakers in Brazil, see the study of Szilágyi, Ágnes Judit, "The One Who Could Photograph the Soul: Rudolph Icsey and Hungarian Filmmakers in Brazil," *Hungarian Studies Review,* 21, 1-2 (1994): 77-90.

Délamerikai Magyar Hirlap–Gazeta Húngara [Hungarian Gazette of South America] for the year 1961. The *Yearbook* is a publication of impressive bulk: over 400 pages, and it speaks of a long history: it is volume 13, indicating that the *Year-book*'s roots go back to the late 1940s. Its editors are Imre Gácser and Lajos Kutasi Kovács. The former is a Benedictine father of high education, the latter is the one of the better-known writers of the post-World War II Hungarian emigration. Kovács is also one of the volume's contributors, along with many other exiles from communist Hungary. There are the works of other authors as well, most of them re-printed for the readers' convenience. The volume's contents is a melange of poetry, short stories, political commentary, community reports, and the inevitable advertisements.

The part of this book that is of interest to the historian of the Hungarian diaspora is the very end. Here, three reports throw valuable light on the social and cultural activities of the contemporary Hungarian community of Brazil. The first traces the first ten years of the activities of the Könyves Kálmán Free University (*Könyves Kálmán Szabadegyetem*). The second tells the story of the St. Stephen Parish of São Paulo, and the third reports on the history and activities of the Hungarian Beneficial Association of Brazil (*A Braziliai Magyar Segélyegylet*).

The article on the Könyves Kálmán Free University (KKFU) testifies to the active cultural life of the Hungarian community of São Paulo. It lists many of the speakers that the leaders of this organization had invited to give guest-lectures in the program of the "university". Though the KKFU had its administration styled after a college (a *dékanátus*), it did not offer courses and a program of studies.

The report on the St. Stephen's Parish (Comuniade Rom. Católica do Rei Santo Estevão) reveals not so much the story and organizational structure of this religious organization but the general religious life of Catholic Hungarian immigrants to Brazil and, especially, its two great cities, São Paulo and Rio de Janeiro. Interestingly enough, it indicates that much of this activity took place not so much in the parish church but in other churches of São Paulo and Rio. In the latter city, for example, in the church of the local Polish community where "mass was said in Hungarian on the third Sunday of each month." From the description of these activities we get the impression that São Paulo did not have a Hungarian community, but each of the city's major districts had one and these functioned more-or-less separate from each other.[2]

---

[2] This is exactly the picture we get of the Hungarians of the late 19th and early

The report also tells the story of the celebrations of the Hungarian communities of São Paulo and Rio. We learn, for example, that one of the participants of the high mass held to celebrate Hungary's national holiday (March 15)—held in one of the non-ethnic churches of the city—was the local Hungarian community's Ferenc Liszt Choir. And, we also learn about the celebration of such events by the Hungarian lay community, both in São Paulo and in Rio. The article also contains reports about pilgrimages undertaken by Hungarians, the activities of the Hungarian School and of the Hungarian Scouts. A detailed report about the parish's financial affairs for the year 1960 is also included. There is also a men tion of the Saint Emeric of Hungary College of São Paulo, a school established in 1951 by Benedictine fathers from Hungary.[3]

Indicating the fact that in 1960 Hungarians lived elsewhere in Brazil as well, this article mentions the visits that São Paulo's Hungarian priests made that year to Hungarian colonies in the hinterlands: in such places as Matto Grosso, Árpádfalva, Londrina, Jacutinga, Ceboleiro, Arapongas, Rolandia, Apucarana, Marialva and Maringa.

From the article on the *Braziliai Magyar Segélyegylet* (Associação Beneficente "30 de Setembro" or Hungarian Beneficial Association of Brazil—to give a translation of the Hungarian name only) we learn about other aspects of Hungarian life in Brazil. First of all we find that the organization was founded back in 1926. Nevertheless, the report on it speaks of great difficulties in the year 1960: the old, thirty-odd-years-old building of the Association was ordered demolished and the organization had to find new—this time rented rather than owned—headquarters. This situation prompts the article's author to review the highlights of the Association's work since 1926, a fact which makes this brief article very valuable for the historian of Brazil's Hungarian community.

The old building, described as "kicsi házikó" (little hut), with its

---

20th centuries in Chicago when we read Zoltán Fejős's work: *A chikagói magyarok két nemzedéke, 1890-1940: Az etnikai örökség megőrzése és változása* [Two generations of the Hungarians of Chicago, 1890-1940: The preservation and transformation of the ethnic heritage] (Budapest: Közép-Európa Intézet, 1993).

3 For more information on this school, which functioned both at the elementary and junior-high level, see the article of Engelbert Sarlós, "A levágott törzs újra sarjad: Szent Imre Kollegium São Puloban" [The Severed Branch is Reborn: the Sait Emeric College in São Paulo], in *Kárpát* (Buenos Aires) 1, 1 (1958): 7-9.

courtyard, had served as a Hungarian island for the Hungarians of this rapidly growing city ever since the 1920s. It was this modest home that provided headquarters for São Paulo's numerous Hungarian schools, as well as to an active Scout movement. The building was also the birthplace of the committee for the revision of the Treaty of Trianon (*reviziós bizottság*), and of the *"magyar a magyarért"* (Hungarians for Hungarians) movement.[4] It also hosted the Hungarian community's celebrations and its drama productions. The author tells how other local Hungarian organizations—sport clubs, newspapers, etc.—ceased to function one by one, while the Beneficial Association, along with the Hungarian churches, managed to survive.

In 1947 the Association's home received the first refugees of the Second World War (known to us as Displaced Persons), and it was from here that the newcomers spread out to try to rebuild their lives in Brazilian emigration. In the meantime, the old emigration began to experience its decline. Fewer and fewer students attended its six schools, until 1951 when even the last of these places, those of Anastacion and Moóca, had to close their Hungarian schools.

To generate some revenue, the Association opened an eatery at about this time, which attracted Hungarians longing for home-style food. Next came the building of a nursing home, about whose functioning the author regrettably says nothing.

We next learn that the abandonment of the Association's old home meant that the dining hall had to be closed, though the occasional community dinners remained a possibility at the new rented premises. Also, there was room for the Ferenc Liszt Choir (already mentioned above) to continue its practice sessions, and there was space for the establishment of a library. Further, the Association's bureau continued its role as advisor to the membership in matters related to employment, as well as financial, legal and even personal affairs. The report concludes by detailing the Association's financial affairs for the year 1960.

What has happened to the above institutions since 1961, and in fact, to the *Yearbook* as well as the *Délamerikai Magyar Hirlap–Gazeta Húngara*? The books and journals in my library offer only fragmentary

---

[4] The lobbying for the revision of the territorial clauses of the Treaty of Trianon, which had shorn Hungary of two-thirds of its territory in 1921, extended to all corners of the Hungarian diaspora in the interwar years. The Hungarians for Hungarians movement aimed to help the Hungarian victims of the Second World War, especially in what is now the Voyvodina, northern Serbia.

answers to this query. From a paper published in 1990 by Lajos Kutasi Kovacs in *Nyelvünk és Kultúránk* (Our tongue and culture), we learn that São Paulo's Hungarian "Free University" continued to function throughout the 1970s and 1980s, mainly as a forum for guest-lectures, but the author concludes his report by wondering aloud if it would survive for another decade.[5] From the same article we get indirect assurances that both the Saint Emeric School and the Beneficial Association continued to function long after 1961—or even in 1990—as they are reported as hosting the lectures organized by the Free University. As to the *Yearbook*'s fate, I have no direct information. From Gyula Borbándi's work we know however, that its publisher, the *Délamerikai Magyar Hirlap,* transferred its operations to Argentina where it merged with the *Délamerikai Magyarság* under the new name *Magyar Hirlap.* This publication, described by Borbándi as South America's only substantial Hungarian newspaper, was still appearing in Buenos Aires in the early 1980s, at the time of Borbándi's writing.[6]

Right now (and this was written in 1999), the World Federation of Hungarians is in the midst of publishing the histories of all countries where significant Hungarian presence exists or had existed.[7] When the volume on Brazil will be out, we might get more answers to our questions, in fact we might get a comprehensive picture of the story of Brazil's Hungarian communities. Until then we have to rely on fragmentary evidence in the printed record. Or perhaps on the recollections of those who have lived there much of their lives.

---

[5] Lajos Kutasi Kovacs, "A São Paulo-i Könyves Kálmán Szabadegyetem negyven éve" [Forty Years of the Könyves Kálmán Free University of São Paulo], *Nyelvünk és Kultúránk* [Our tongue and culture] (Budapest), 79 (Sept. 1990): 31-33.

[6] Borbándi, *op. cit.,* p. 140.

[7] The first of these volumes deals with the Hungarians of the United States: Elemér Bakó, *Magyarok az Amerikai Egyesült Államokban* [Hungarians in the United States of America], complied and introduced by László Papp (Budapest: World Federation of Hungarians, 1998). Rather than being a historical or even a journalistic survey, this volume is a haphazard collection of previously published stories and documents, most of them written or edited by publicist and librarian Elemér Bakó. The fact that a substantial body of scholarly literature exists on the subject (see above note 1) is not even mentioned in this book.

Appendix 1. *

I sent drafts of this article to a number of people about whom I know that they have a good knowledge of the Hungarian diaspora and/or that they had been to Brazil. One of these was Miklós (Nicholas) Mattyasovsky-Zsolnay who for decades had been involved in the life of the Hungarian-Canadian community, especially in Montreal, as well as in the Hungarian scout movement of the New World. His reply to my letter included a brief paragraph about Brazil: "I [and my wife] visited the Hungarians of Brazil — mainly those of São Paulo — once, in 1980. At the time [Benedictine friars] Imre Gácsér and István Taubinger (Majláth) were still alive. A few years before us His Holiness Pope John Paul also visited there. He did not stay with the [local] Cardinal, but with the Magyar Benedictine fathers. What these fathers had accomplished is remarkable." From Dr. Zsolnay we learn that while in São Paulo, he gave a lecture at the Könyves Kálmán Free University.

Appendix 2.

The other person I sent a copy of my article to was Tibor Cseh, the editor of the periodical *Transylvania* and co-editor of two other Hungarian journals. I came across his name in my readings about Brazil and, indeed, I found out that he had lived in that country for many years. Here is a part of his reply to me that I "adopted" (i.e. very loosely translated) into English:

Tibor Cseh on the Hungarians of São Paulo and Elsewhere:

The great-grandson of your mother-in-law is a member of a truly rare segment of the Hungarian diaspora. Few Hungarians from São Paulo would accept work in Petrolina, not only because of the hot climate, but because of the primitive social and cultural conditions. In this huge part of Brazil, the *Nordeste*, a large part of the population lives in poverty. Many of them are cowboys (*vanqueiros*) herding cattle on huge ranches. Others are agricultural workers on estates (*fazendas*) producing

---

* An earlier version of this study appeared in two installemts in the journal *Kaleidoscope* (Toronto), vol. II, no. 12 (Dec. 1999), and in vol. III, no. 1 (Jan. 2000): 13-15. Both Miklós Mattyasovsky-Zsolnay and Tibor Cseh have died since 1999.

sugar-cane, cotton and tobacco. Most of these estates had been established during the age of slavery and the lot of their workers today is not much better than that of their slave ancestors. The people's misery is compounded by the semi-arid conditions which bring drought on a cyclical basis. In time of prolonged drought, masses of people migrate to the south to escape starvation. It is these refugees that have made the cities of the south huge in size and it is they who fill up the ghettos of the impoverished, the *flavelas*. [....]

During the 1970s the government of Brazil started a campaign of industrialization in order to curb the migration of the masses from the Northeast to the south. They built a network of roads there, provided electricity, and established tax-free zones in order to attract investment. This campaign was partially successful. The newly established industrial centres required trained workers by the thousands. Most of these were brought in from abroad with multi-year contracts. As Hungarian workers are just as good as those in developed countries but are willing to work for lower wages. They came by the hundreds and dispersed in Northeastern Brazil, just as many of them had gone to other exotic places a such as Indonesia, Saudi Arabia, Nigeria, etc.

At one time most urban-dwelling Hungarians in Brazil lived in Rio de Janeiro and São Paulo. In recent decades the Hungarian colony of the former has declined. When Rio ceased be Brazil's capital, its significance as a manufacturing centre declined. Its hot and humid climate was another factor. Eventually most of Rio's Hungarians moved to São Paulo or emigrated to the United States. São Paulo not only had a more moderate climate but had better economic opportunities. The city underwent unprecedented growth. Form 1950 to 1990 its population grew from 4 to 13 million. It is a grim, heartless, polluted place. Hundreds of thousands of its residents escape during the weekends to the resorts of the seacoast 100 to 150 kilometres away.

As far as I know—and accurate statistics do not exist in part because Hungarians who had come from the regions detached from Hungary do not show up in the census statistics as Hungarians—there are probably 50,000 to 70,000 Hungarians in Brazil. At least two-thirds of these live in the state of São Paulo, and 80-90% of these in the city of São Paulo itself. Among the cities of the south, Hungarian colonies exist in Campinas, Curitiba, Porto Algere and in Belo Horizonte, in the state of Minas Gerais. The city of Londrina, in the state of São Paulo, was the place where the managers and most of the engineers of the Hungarian firm Nitrogénművek settled after World War II and established a chemical factory that later produced shells, explosives and pesticides. The city still has a small Hungarian colony.

The yearbooks of the *Délamerikai Magyar Hírlap*, along with the issues of this newspaper, and many other publications are to be found in the library of the Benedictine Abbey of São Paulo. This library is the most important archival depository of the Hungarians of Brazil.

The most important institution of São Paulo's Hungarians was probably the Abbey of the Hungarian Benedictine fathers. The very first of these was sent out from the Pannonhalma Abbey of Hungary in the 1930s, to take care of the religious life of Brazil's Hungarians. It was at this time that the Saint Stephen church was built in Anastacio, a suburb of São Paulo, through the efforts of Hungarian worker and peasant immigrants. The post-World War II wave of Hungarian newcomers, made up mainly of middle-class elements, settled in the city of São Paulo itself, where the Benedictine fathers held Sunday masses for them in rented facilities. The Benedictine monks established their Saint Emerick College and rented offices in the city's centre. It was here that the Hungarian colony of São Paulo held its gatherings: celebrations, banquets, lectures, the meetings of the scouts, of the choir, and the folk-dance group, as well as the classes of the Hungarian school.

The members of the Reformed Church had a church building of their own in the suburb of Lapa. This building, reminiscent of the "provincial gothic" churches of Kalotaszeg in Hungary, was also a cen-tre of active cultural life. São Paulo still has four functioning Hungarian scout troops, two each sponsored by the Catholic Parish and the Protestant congregations respectively. The Beneficial Association has built—with the help of public funds — a nursing home for single, elder-ly members of the Hungarian colony. This home is maintained with the help of donations raised from the community and with the revenue derived from an annual grand Hungarian ball. This year the Könyves Kálmán Free University celebrates the 50th anniversary of its establish-ment. It is presently under the leadership of Father Veremund Toth.

In the 1960s the Fathers purchased a very large lot in what years later became one of the exclusive districts of the growing metropolis. There they built Brazil's Benedictine Abbey—Pope John Paul II stayed there during his visit to São Paulo—the Church of Saint Gellért, and the ultramodern Saint Emerick College, with its sports facilities and parks. Since that time this school has become the most sought-after educa-tional institution of its kind in South America. All this was the dedicat-ed and persevering work of the Benedictine monks from Hungary. However, with the establishment of their new centre, the Fathers had given up their rented facilities in the city's centre and the Hungarian colony's cultural and social life had come to an end there. To a certain degree, this loss was compensated for by the establishment in the 1980s of the Hungarian House. The scope of the colony's social and cultural activities however, have declined greatly in recent years. This is the result of the ever dwindling numbers of the immigrant generation—due to out-migration, ageing and death—and the ever increasing assimilation of the members of the subsequent generations.

The Erosion of the Hungarian Linguistic Presence in Canada*

Hungarians have been arriving in Canada in substantial numbers since the end of the nineteenth century and their numbers have climbed in Canadian census figures throughout most of the twentieth. These figures — whether identified as "Canadian residents born in Hungary," or "Canadians of Hungarian descent," or "Canadians with Magyar as their mother-tongue," or "Canadians speaking Hungarian in the home" — have tended to grow, though not necessarily in a steady, even manner. There have been periods of slow increases as well as dramatic jumps, such as between the censuses of 1951 and 1961, when the arrival of thousands of the Hungarians who had been displaced by World War II during the early 1950s was compounded by the coming of nearly forty thousand refugees after the Soviets suppressed the Hungarian Revolution in the fall of 1956. One figure that has kept climbing and increased even in recent times is the number of Hungarians who claim Hungarian as their ancestry. People who designated "Hungarian" as one of their ethnic backgrounds, that is persons of mixed ancestry that includes Hungarian, have increased in number from ca. 210,000 in the partial census of 1986 to nearly 270,000 in the (full) census of 2001.[1]

Other recent census figures, however, suggest a decline of the Hungarian-Canadian community; more precisely, an erosion of its cultural identity and distinctiveness. There has been a decline even in the numbers of those who reported Hungarian as their only ancestry, from over 100,000 in 1986 to fewer than 92,000 in the latest census. Of course, neither the figures with people with multiple ancestries which

---

* An earlier version of this paper had appeared in the *Yearbook of the Hungarian Community of Friends*, ed. A. Ludanyi (Portland, OR, 2004), pp. 58-62.

[1] There has also been a slight increase in this same period in the number of people reporting Hungarian as their mother tongue: from ca. 73,000 to over 75,000. Census data relating to Hungarians can be found on the website of the Hungarian-Canadian Cultural Centre: www.hccc.org.

includes Hungarian, nor those for persons with Hungarian as the only ethnic background indicate the vitality of Hungarian community life in Canada. These figures include second, third, and fourth (and even some fifth) generation Hungarian-Canadians, most of whom have little knowledge of, or affinity with, things Hungarian. A much better indicator of an ethnic community's cultural strength and vigour are the data regarding language use. Most of these data, unfortunately, suggest an unmistakable trend toward cultural decline in most parts of Canada where Hungarians have settled over the last one hundred years.

Magyar Language Use in Canadian Census Statistics

Canada's linguistic make-up is constantly evolving. The 2001 census data, for example, reveal that the proportion of both English- and French-speaking Canadians has declined somewhat between 1996 and 2001. Speakers of English, for example, decreased from 59.8 percent to 59.1 percent of the total population. At the same time, the proportion of people reporting neither of Canada's official languages as their mother tongue has increased. For example, the number of people listing Chinese as their language has grown almost by 18 percent. In fact, the Chinese have become the third largest linguistic group in Canada. In the past, that "honour" had usually gone to the Germans or the Italians.[2]

Hungarians have never constituted a major linguistic group in Canada, though they had been such a group at times in the past in municipalities such as Welland, Ontario and Kipling, Saskatchewan. As far as provincial distribution is concerned, in the 2001 census by far the most Canadian citizens who claimed Hungarian as their mother tongue resided in Ontario, 45,275 to be precise. In the second place was British Columbia with 10,775; and in the third was Quebec with 7,315. Alberta was a not too distant fourth, with 6,980. Saskatchewan, which used to

---

2 The numbers speak for themselves. In the 2001 census, 17,352,315 Canadians reported English as their mother tongue; 6,703,325 reported French, and over half a million listed other, non-official languages as "mother tongue." Among the latter were close to 200,000 people who designated one or another of the aboriginal tongues spoken in Canada as their first language. The census statistics on "mother tongue" revealed a continued Hungarian presence in Canada as well. The 2001 census listed 75,555 persons who declared Hungarian as their mother tongue. Individuals who listed more than one "mother tongue" were not included in this figure by the staff of Statistics Canada.

be the centre of Hungarian life in Canada three generations ago, reported only 2,700 people with Hungarian as their mother tongue.[3]

These figures might well be compared with the data that had been obtained in the partial census of Canada of 1996. The following table illustrates the evolution of Canada's "Hungarian by mother tongue (single responses)" population from 1996 to 2001 (some jurisdictions with very small numbers are omitted):

Province:	1996	2001
Nova Scotia	310	325
New Brunswick	150	140
Quebec	8,655	7,315
Ontario	44,060	45,275
Manitoba	1,975	1,840
Saskatchewan	3,045	2,700
Alberta	7,575	6,980
British Columbia	11,225	10,775

The above data demonstrate conclusively that Hungarian linguistic presence in almost all regions of Canada is in decline. The exception is the Province of Ontario which had experienced a modest increase in the half-decade under review.[4]

The 2001 census results also tell how many people in Canada and its various provinces speak Hungarian. The numbers given are larger than those found under mother tongue (single responses). These statistics, along with the relevant data from the 1996 census, are revealed in the following table (from which provinces and territories with fewer than 100 Hungarian speakers are omitted):

---

[3] Information on how to purchase the results of the 2001 census can be obtained at the website of Statistics Canada: www.statcan.ca. I had been able to access some of the results of the census through the University of Toronto, whose libraries subscribe to the electronic information services provided by Statistics Canada.

[4] Some people have given multiple responses to the census takers, that is they had designated more than one language as their mother tongues. No doubt many people of Hungarian background had done so. If these people would have been counted, the data on Hungarians would show somewhat larger numbers.

Province	1996	2001	change
Nova Scotia	350	390	+40
New Brunswick	190	170	-20
Quebec	11,465	9,810	-1,655
Ontario	53,910	53,275	-635
Manitoba	2,435	2,035	-400
Saskatchewan	3,295	2,990	-305
Alberta	8,895	8,125	-770
British Columbia	12,885	12,205	-680

The decline from 1996 to 2001 in the number of people who speak Hungarian is especially remarkable in the Province of Quebec which lost 1,655 such individuals in half a decade. The prairie provinces collectively, experienced a similar decline (1,475 persons).

Hungarian as a Language of the Home

One of the best indicators of language maintenance by a linguistic cultural group is the category known as "language spoken at home." In fact, this category is a better measure of cultural persistence than "language spoken," or "mother tongue," because language spoken at home indicates a long-term commitment to culture maintenance. Further, it is a predictor of language transmission to the next generation. The 2001 census has valuable information on the use of Hungarian in the home by members of Canada's Hungarian community.

The census reveals that in 2001, 44,590 people in Canada used Hungarian as a language of the home. Out of this number, 11,575 used Hungarian as the only language of communication at home, while the rest used it in combination with another language or languages. 17,265 people used it "regularly" but not exclusively.

The distribution of the individuals who in 2001 used Hungarian as the only language of the home is as follows: Quebec 1,225; Ontario 7,885; Alberta 760; and British Columbia 1,375. Elsewhere the numbers were negligible. Only five years earlier, the situation had been somewhat better. In 1996 Ontario still had 15,710 people who reported that they used Hungarian only as the language of the home.

The sad data revealed by the 2001 census, might well be compared with the data from the 1771 census which probably represents the time when the Hungarian community in Canada was at the zenith of its cultural vitality. The following table compares the relevant data regarding the category "Hungarian by mother tongue":

Province:	1971	2001
Newfoundland	75	55
Nova Scotia	315	325
New Brunswick	235	140
Quebec	12,605	7,315
Ontario	46,370	45,275
Manitoba	3,035	1,840
Saskatchewan	6,270	2,700
Alberta	8,890	6,980
British Columbia	8,885	10,775

As we can see, these statistics show meaningful increase only for British Columbia, steep declines for Quebec, Manitoba and Saskatchewan, and smaller shrinkage for Alberta and Ontario.

For the "language spoken at home" category, the greatest decreases came in the Western provinces, as the following table illustrates:

Province	1971	1981	2001
Manitoba	1,765	835	150
Sack.	1,945	830	120
Alberta	4,545	3,130	760
B.C.	4,320	3,100	1,375

Remarkable in this story is the decline of the Hungarian linguistic presence in Saskatchewan. From 1,945 in 1971, we witness a decline to 830 in 1981, to 360 by the time of the 1991 census, and to 120 in 2001.[5] Should this trend continue, the census of 2011 might find only a handful of people, or perhaps even no one, who uses Hungarian as the only language of the home in that province. Elsewhere in the country, in

---

[5] The decline shown is probably accentuated by the varying definitions of the term "language spoken at home" used in the four censuses. The figures for 2001 indicate the number of people who use Hungarian as the "only language of the home" whereas figures for previous censuses may include people who used Hungarian as well as other languages in the home.

Ontario, British Columbia and Alberta, the Hungarian linguistic presence might persist for a few more decades.

Only a new large influx of Hungarian newcomers could avert the eventual decline of Hungarian language use in Canada to complete insignificance. In the past, there had been a number of such mass arrivals. Alas, these mass arrivals were invariably the result of calamities in Hungary—economic and social crises, wars and foreign occupations—and we can not wish that our mother country should experience one of these again.

The Historiography of the Hungarian Communities of the New World

The publication of two books dealing with the Hungarian-American experience in recent years is certainly an event that ought to be celebrated. One of these books is Steven Béla Várdy's *Magyarok az Újvilágban* [Hungarians in the New World]. The other is Julianna Puskás, *Ties that Bind, Ties that Divide: One Hundred Years of Hungarian Experience in the United States.*[1] The appearance of these works should be cherished not only because never before in the centuries-old history of Hungarian presence in the United States have such substantial historical studies seen the light of day in the course of a single year, but also because monographs of this kind had not really appeared before, at any time.

This is not to say that there had not been many books, as well as shorter studies, written on the subject of Hungarian immigration to—and Hungarian life in—"*Amerika,*" as Hungarians have traditionally referred to the United States and, at times, the whole of the New World. The primary purpose of this historiographical essay is to survey this literature and to place the two works referred to above into the wider context of a century of Hungarian-American (as well as Hungarian-Canadian, etc.) historical writing.

Because the history of the Hungarian-American experience is to a large degree inseparable from the phenomena of Hungarian emigration to and settlement in other parts of the Americas, and also because Várdy's book is, in fact, entitled *Hungarians in the New World*, this survey will look at the wider historiographical context and will examine literature dealing with the Hungarian experience not only in the United States but also in other countries of the Western hemisphere.

In a somewhat arbitrary fashion, I will begin my survey with a book that has the same title as Várdy's book. This is László Juhász's

---

* This paper is a revised version of a study that appeared in the 2005 volume of the *Hungrian Studies Review*, 32, 1-2 (spring-fall, 2005): 97-112.

[1] Translated by Zora Ludwig (New York and London: Holmes & Meier, Ellis Island series, 2000), xix + 444 pages, illustrations.

Magyarok az Újvilágban [Hungarians in the New World] (Munich: Nemzetőr, 1979). Although a pioneering work at the time of its writing, Juhász's book has two major shortcomings. Like Várdy's book, it concentrates mainly on Hungarians in the United States, but unlike Várdy's volume, it is a very cursory treatment of its subject—in fact, it hardly deals with the developments and personalities of the twentieth century.

If there had been no satisfactory overviews of the Hungarians of the New World that present-day historical researchers could use as an introduction to their subject, we might wonder if there have been such studies of the entire Hungarian diaspora. Unfortunately, there are no surveys of this kind either. Several books have been published in Hungary, especially during the early decades of the country's "communist era," but most of these are polemical and have only marginal scholarly value. Not even Miklós Szántó's book, *Magyarok a nagyvilágban* [Hungarians in the wide world] (Budapest: Kossuth, 1970) constitutes much of an exception to this generalization, nor does Samu Imre's similarly entitled essay in *Tanulmányok Magyarországról, magyarokról* [Studies about Hungary, Hungarians] ed. László Jablonszky (Budapest: Magyarok Világszövetsége, n.d. [1989 ?]), pp. 239-80. There is at least one useful work however. It was written in the West by one of the Hungarian emigration's preeminent scholars, Gyula Borbándi: *A magyar emigráció életrajza, 1945-1985* [The biography of the Hungarian emigration, 1945-1985] (Munich: published by the author, 1985). Unfortunately, as the title suggests, that work deals only with the post-1945 decades.

Literature on Hungarians in Latin America

Reliable and substantial works on the history of the Hungarian communities in Latin America are few. Evidently very little research has been done in this large field by either social scientists or journalists, either in Hungarian or in Spanish or Portuguese. Alternately, if there has been such research done, its results have not come to the attention of North American historians who have an interest in the subject. Nevertheless, there are a handful of relevant works. One of these is László Szabó, *A magyar mult Dél-Amerikaban* [Hungarian past in South America] (Budapest: Európa, 1982), and another is Tivadar Ács, *Magyarok Latin Amerikában* [Hungarians in Latin-America] (Budapest, 1944). On the subject of Hungarians in Argentina we have the good fortune of having a recent monograph available in Judit Kesserű Némethy, *Az argentínai magyar emigráció, 1948-1968* [The Hungarian emigre community of Argentina, 1948-1968], based on a doctoral dissertation, completed in

1999. An expanded version of this work is now available in book form.[2] On the Hungarians of Brazil, there is Szeverin J. Kögl, *Magyarok Braziliában* (São Paulo: Könyves Kálmán Szabadegyetem, 1992). The periodical literature on this subject is somewhat meagre. Agnes J. Szilágyi has published on the subject, including an article: "The One Who Could Photograph the Soul: Hungarian Film-makers in Brazil," *Hungarian Studies Review*, 21, 1-2 (1994): 77-90. Agnes Kaczur-Bató's study, "Magyarok Braziliában [Hungarians in Brazil]," *Világtörténet* 1, 3-4 (1990): 64-75, covers its subject only to the 1930s, but does offer a useful bibliographic note (which refers to a few more articles dealing with Hungarians in Brazil before 1939) as well as some information on the research going on regarding Hungarians in Latin America at Szeged University (formerly József Attila University) in Hungary.[3]

Studies on the Hungarians of Canada

While Professor Várdy might be excused for not exploring the subject of Hungarians in Latin America in his book, on the grounds that too little information is available on the subject to write of a work of synthesis, he can be absolved for not covering the Hungarians of Canada because that subject has been explored in fair amount of detail in books that are readily available to the reading public. I have in mind first and foremost my own book, *Struggle and Hope: The Hungarian-Canadian Experience* (Toronto: McClelland and Stewart, 1982), produced in collaboration with three other scholars.[4]

---

[2] Judit Kesserű Némethy, *Az argentínai magyar emigráció, 1948-1968* [The Hungarian emigre community of Argentina, 1948-1968], doctoral dissertation, József Attila University, Szeged, 1999. Published under the title: *"Szabadságom lett börtönöm". Az argentínai magyar emigráció története, 1948-1968* ["My freedom became my prison." The history of Hungarian émigrés to Argentina] (Budapest: A Magyar Nyelv és Kultúra Nemzetközi Társasága, 2003).

[3] A fair amount of information on the Hungarian community of Brazil can be found in Ágnes Judit Szilágyi and János Sáringer, *Ifj. Horthy Miklós, a Kormányzó kisebbik fia* [Mikós Horthy jr., the younger son of the Regent] (Budapest: Holnap, 2002). My own modest contribution to the subject is "Hungarians in Brazil," serialized in *Kaleidoscope* (Toronto), starting with 3, 1 (Jan. 2000), 13-15.

[4] My collaborators in the writing of this book were Professors Paul Bódy, Martin Kovács and Bennett Kovrig, each whom had written an introductory chapter to the main body of the book.

Like Várdy's book, this work too, is in part based on already existing historical literature, which is outlined in detail in the book's bibliographical essay (pp. 232-39). A shorter and more recent synthesis, based mainly on my own writings, can be found in the entry "Hungarians" in the *Encyclopedia of Canadian Ethnic Groups* (Toronto: University of Toronto Press, 1999), pp. 660-674.[5] Still another such overview is Carmela Patrias, *The Hungarians in Canada* (Ottawa: the Canadian Historical Association, 1999). This booklet, designed mainly for secondary school students, also has a useful bibliography (see pages 31-33). The history of some of the early Hungarian settlements of the Canadian West is told in detail mainly in the works of Martin L. Kovacs,[6] while the interwar immigration and settlement have been dealt with by John Kosa,[7] Professor Patrias,[8] and myself.[9]

---

[5] There is an even shorter version, also by myself, "Peoples of Canada: Hungarians in Canada," in *Horizon Canada*, 10, no. 110 (June 1987): 2630-35.

[6] Martin (Márton) L. Kovacs, was born in Budapest in 1918 and died in Regina, Saskatchewan in 2000. In 1956 he left Hungary and settled in Australia, from where he immigrated to Canada to teach at the University of Regina. His most important book on early Hungarian settlement in the Canadian West is *Peace and Strife: Some Facets of the History of an Early Prairie Community* (Kipling. Saskatchewan: Kipling District Historical Society, 1980). He also published articles relating to the subject. Some of these are "The Hungarian School Question," in *Ethnic Canadians: Culture and Education*, ed. M.L. Kovacs (Regina: Canadian Plains Research Center, 1978), 333-58; "Searching for Land: The First Hungarian Influx into Canada," *Canadian-American Review of Hungarian Studies*, 7, 1 (Spring, 1980): 37-43; "From Industries to Farming" *Hungarian Studies Review*, 8, 1 (Spring, 1981): 45-60; as well as chapter three of *Struggle and Hope*.

[7] John Kosa, *Land of Choice: Hungarians in Canada* (Toronto: University of Toronto Press, 1957). At the time of his death in the mid-1970s, Professor Kosa was member of the faculty at Harvard University.

[8] Especially in her article "Hungarian Immigration to Canada Before the Second World War," in *Hungarians in Ontario,* ed. Susan M. Papp (Toronto: Multicultural History Society of Ontario, 1980), a special double issue of *Polyphony*, 2, 2-3 (1979-80): 17-21; as well as in her monograph, *Patriots and Proletarians: Politicizing Hungarian Immigrants in Interwar Canada* (Kingston and Montreal: McGill Queen's University Press, 1994), *in passim*. Professor Patrias teaches in the Department of History of Brock University, in St. Catharines, Ontario.

[9] In chapters four and five (entitled "Years of Growth and Change, 1919--

Earlier Histories of the Hungarians in the United States

If we were to say that much has been written on the history of Magyars in the United States even before the year 2000, we would be making an accurate statement. If we were to argue that the history of Hungarians has not been adequately covered before the two major works that were published in 2000, we would also be truthful. The fact is that the history of the Hungarian ethnic group in the USA is such a large subject that it cannot be considered adequately explored even though scores of publications have tried to cover it—or at least, have claimed to do so. This is not to say that some specific aspects of this story have not been researched in a systematic and competent manner.

In the introduction to his book, Béla Várdy himself refers to four major works of synthesis that had been published prior to the year 2000 on the history of Hungarians in the United States. One of these is Várdy's own earlier English-language study: *The Hungarian Americans* (Boston: Twayne Publishers, 1985). The second one is Géza Kende's *Magyarok Amerikában* (Cleveland, 1927, 2 vols.), and the third is Emil Lengyel's *Americans from Hungary* (Philadelphia and New York: Lippincott, 1948). It might be added that Lengyel's book is a quite

---

1929," and "A Decade of Setbacks: The 1930's" respectively) of the volume *Struggle and Hope*, as well as elsewhere: "In Search of a Hungarian-Canadian Lobby: 1927-1951," *Canadian Ethnic Studies*, 12, 3 (Fall 1980): 81-96; "Aspects of Hungarian Settlement in Central Canada," in *Hungarian-Canadian Perspectives: Selected Papers*, ed. M.L. Kovacs (Ottawa: Hungarian Readers Service, 1980), 121-21; "Immigrant Lives and Lifestyles in Canada, 1924-1939," *Hungarian Studies Review*, 8, 1 (Spring 1981): 61-83; "Immigration and Re-Migration: The Changing Urban-Rural Distribution of Hungarian Canadians, 1986-1986," in *The Tree of Life: Essays Honouring a Hungarian-Canadian Centenary*, ed. M.L. Kovacs and N.F. Dreisziger (Toronto: HSR, 1986); "The 'Justice for Hungary' Ocean Flight: The Trianon Syndrome in Immigrant Hungarian Society," in *Triumph in Adversity: Studies in Hungarian Civilization*, ed. S. B. Várdy (Boulder, Co.: East European Monographs, 1988), 573-89; "Immigrant Fortunes and Misfortunes in Canada in the 1920s," a documentary article in the *Hungarian Studies Review*, 17, (Spring 1990): 29-59; "Sub-ethnic Identities: Religion, Class, Ideology, etc. as Centrifugal Forces in Hungarian-Canadian Society," *Hungarian Studies* (Budapest), 7 (1992): 123-138; and,"Jövőépítés Kanadában, az első magyar bevandorlástól 1948-ig," [Building a future in Canada from the time of the first Hungarian immigration to Canada to 1948], in *Itt-Ott* [Here and there, the journal of the Hungarian Society of Friends, USA] 33 (2000): 21-23.

informative and highly readable work, but evidently it is now quite dated.

The fourth and last book mentioned by Várdy is Julianna Puskás' *Kivádorló magyarok az Egyeslüt Államokban, 1880-1940* [Emigrant Hungarians in the United States] (Budapest: Akadémiai kiadó, 1982) which is a scholarly work based on a great deal of painstaking research and represents the culmination of its author's decades-long work on Hungarian emigration to and settlement in the United States. Puskás has published other, shorter works on the subject as well, including a volume in English. Most of these deal with the pre-1914 period, although in some of them (in particular in *Kivádorló magyarok*) she adds some information on the fate of the communities of the pre-1914 immigrants in the post-World War I decades.[10]

Of course, there have been many other attempts to offer a comprehensive or a partial overview of the history of the Hungarian-American ethnic group. In breadth of coverage or in the quality of research, however, these are not on par with the above-listed works. Not surprisingly, they do not earn a mention in Várdy's introduction in his *Magyarok az Újvilágban*, though they are listed in the book's biblio graphy. One of these is the above-mentioned book by Miklós Szántó. Another is Leslie Könnyü's *Hungarians in the U.S.A.: An Immigration Study* (St. Louis, MO: *American Hungarian Review*, 1967), and there is also the recently-published (more exactly, re-issued in a different incarnation) Elemér Bakó's *Magyarok az Amerikai Egyesült Államokban* [Hungarians in the United States of America], ed. László Papp (Budapest: Magyarok Világszövetsége, 1998). A more scholarly but shorter overview is offered in Paula Benkart, "Hungarians" in the *Harvard Encyclopedia of American Ethnic Groups*, 462-471. An excellent demographical and sociological survey of Hungarian-American society in the 1980s is offered in Zoltán Féjős, "Magyarok az Egyesült Államokban az 1980-as években: Demográfia, társadalmi adatok, fogalmi problémák" [Hungarians in the United States in the 1980s: Demography, social characteristics, and problems of definitions], in *Magyarságkutatás*, (the yearbook of the Magyarságkutató Intézet) (Budapest: Magyarságkutató Intézet, 1988), 177-216.

---

10 Dr. Puskás's other Hungarian-language studies include "Kivándorlás Magyarországról az Egyesült Államokba 1914 elött" [Emigration from Hungary to the United States before 1914], *Történelmi Szemle*, 27, 1-2 (1974): 32-68; her English-language monograph is *From Hungary to the United States (1880-1914)* (Budapest: Akadémiai Kiadó, 1982).

There are also other relevant works, some of which are difficult to categorize either as popular or scholarly literature. One that belongs to the former category is Aladár Komjáthy, *A kitántorgott egyház* [The Church that staggered out (i.e. overseas)] (Budapest: Református Zsinati Iroda, 1984). Additionally, there are collections of very informative and interesting documents. Perhaps the most remarkable and useful of such works is Albert Tezla (with K. E. Tezla), eds., *"Valahol túl, meseországban..." Az amerikás magyarok, 1895-1920* ["Somewhere beyond, in Fairy-tale Land...": American Hungarians, 1895-1920], 2 vols. (Budapest: Európa könyvkiadó, 1987), which has been published in English as well: *The Hazardous Quest. Hungarian Immigrants in the United States, 1895-1920* (Budapest: Corvina, 1993), in one massive volume.

There have also been a handful of "local histories" written about particular Hungarian-American communities. Perhaps the most scholarly and best-researched of these is Zoltán Fejős, *A chikagói magyarok két nemzedéke, 1890-1940: Az etnikai örökség megőrzése és változása* [Two generations of the Hungarians of Chicago, 1890-1940: The preservation and transformation of the ethnic heritage] (Budapest: Közép-Európa Intézet, 1993).[11] There are also excellent case studies of particular aspects of Hungarian-American society, or a specific development in Magyar-American history, some by Fejős, others by Professors Béla Vassady, Béla Várdy, Stephen Beszedits, and myself.[12]

---

[11] There are also studies of other localities, but these tend to be written for popular rather than academic consumption. See for example Malvina Hauk Abonyi and James A. Anderson, *Hungarians of Detroit* (Detroit: Ethnic Studies Division, Wayne State University [ca. 1975]), Susan M. Papp, *Hungarian Americans and their Communities of Cleveland* (Cleveland: Cleveland Ethnic Heritage Studies, Cleveland State University, 1981); Paul Bődy and Mary Boros-Kazai, *Hungarian Immigrants in Greater Pittsburgh, 1880-1980* (Pittsburgh, PA: Hungarian Ethic Heritage Study Group, 1981); Magdalene Havadtoy, *Down in Villa Park: Hungarians in Fairfield* (by the author, 1976); and Leslie Konnyu, *Acacias: Hungarians in the Mississippi Valley* (Ligonier, PA.: Bethlen Press, 1976).

[12] Zoltán Fejős's specialized studies include his "'Magyar ruha', 'szüreti bál' és az amerikai-magyar etnikus kultúra néhány kérdése" ['The Hungarian dress', 'the grape harvest festival' and some questions of American-Hungarian ethnic culture], *Magyarságkutatás* (Budapest: Magyarságkutató Csoport, 1987); and "Harc a háború ellen és az új Magyarországért" [Struggle against the war and for the new Hungary], *Medvetánc* [Bear-dance]

On a few subjects then, the author of a synthesis on Hungarian-American history is confronted by an abundance of literature, not all of which is reliably researched. However, on most other aspects of this large subject the writer of a general overview is plagued by the scarcity of information. The most praiseworthy feature of Dr. Várdy's new book

---

(Jan. 1988): 282-332, a work that deals mainly with the left-wing Hungarian-American periodical *Harc* [Struggle]). A more recent artilce by Dr. Fejős is "Education in the Mother Tongue: The Perpetuation of Ethnic Consciousness among Hungarian-Americans, 1890–1920," *Hungarian Studies Review*, 33, 1-2 (spring-fall, 2006): 17-38. Still other such publications by Fejős are listed in the bibliography of S. B. Várdy's latest book, pp. 665f.

Still another valuable specialized study is Béla Vassady, "Kossuth and Újházi on Establishing a Colony of Hungarian 48-ers in America," *Hungarian Studies Review* 6, 1 (Spring 1979): 21-46; and the same author's "Hungarian-American Mutual Aid Associations and their 'Official' Newspapers: A Symbiotic Relationship," *Hungarian Studies Review* 19 (1992): 7-27. Dr. Vassady teaches in the Department of History of Elizabethtown College, in Elizabethtown, Pennsylvania.

Most of Béla Várdy's relevant publications are listed in the bibliography of his *Magyarok az Újvilágban*, pp. 701-711. Stephen Beszedits' publications on Hungarians in the American Civil War are reproduced on the website of the Hungarian American Foundation, Inc.: www.hungarianamerica.com/ harc/papers.asp. My relevant studies include the articles: "The 'Justice for Hungary' Ocean Flight: The Trianon Syndrome in Immigrant Hungarian Society," in *Triumph in Adversity: Studies in Hungarian Civilization in Honor of Professor Ferenc Somogyi*, ed. S. B. Várdy and A. H. Várdy (Boulder: East European Monographs, 1988), 573-89; "Emigre Artists and Wartime Politics: The Hungarian-American Council for Democracy, 1943-45," in *Hungarian Artists in the Americas*, ed. Oliver Botar (Toronto: HSR, 1994), 43-75; "The Atlantic Democracies and the Movements for a 'Free Hungary' during World War II," in *20th Century Hungary and the Great Powers*, ed. Ignac Romsics (Boulder, Co.: Social Science Monographs /Columbia University Press, 1995), 185-205; which has also appeared in Hungarian translation: "Az atlanti demokraciák és a 'Szabad Magyarországért' mozgalmak a II. világháboru alatt" [The Atlantic Democracies and the movements for a "Free Hungary" during World War II], in *Magyarország és a nagyhatalmak a 20. szádadban* [Hungary and the Great Powers], ed. Ignác Romsics (Budapest: Teleki László Alapítvány, 1995), 149-62; and "Oscar Jaszi and the 'Hungarian Problem:' Activities and Writings during World War II," *Hungarian Studies Review*, 18, 1-2 (1991): 59-91; reprinted in *Hungary in the Age of Total War, 1938-1948*, ed. N. F. Dreisziger (New York: East European Monographs/Columbia University Press, 1998), 267-86.

is his attempt to gather and integrate in one comprehensive volume all the disparate parts of this large and many-faceted story. Inevitably, such work has to be selective and even eclectic (*rendhagyó* as we would say in Magyar) in the treatment of its subject.

Béla Várdy's Synthesis

But first, we should introduce the author, even though for most readers of our journal, he needs no introduction. Professor S. B. Várdy is a pro-lific Hungarian-American historian who has devoted himself to writing on subjects such as the historiography of Hungary and the history of Hungarians in the United States. This is what he says about himself in his book: "... Steven Bela Várdy (known in Hungary as Béla Várdy), is McAnulty Distinguished Professor of European History at Duquesne University (Pittsburgh, Pennsylvania), and a member of the International P.E.N. as well as of the Hungarian Writers' Federation. He is the recipient of Hungary's "Berzsenyi-Prize", the Árpád Academy's Gold Medal, and of his University's "Distinguished Presidential Award for Excellence in Scholarship." He is likewise the author or co-author of sixteen books and about four-hundred-fifty chapters, articles, essays, and reviews."[13]

Béla Várdy's *Magyarok az Újvilágban* is actually a history of the Hungarians of the United States of America. Most of the book focuses on the twentieth century, the time of substantial Magyar presence in that country. The book is the most extensive and exhaustive treatment of the history of Magyar-America in the Hungarian language and, as a matter of fact, in any language. It is an unusual work, as the author himself acknowledges in the book's subtitle. It dispenses with certain academic conventions, a fact that detracts little from a work that is intended primarily for the Hungarian general reading public. Professional historians might quarrel with, for example, the discussions of speculative aspects

---

[13] Várdy, *Magyarok az Újvilágban*, p. 765. One of the books that he has published is the more than 800-page *Historical Dictionary of Hungary* (Lanham, Md., and London: The Scarecrow Press, 1997). For a complete list of his publications (to the year 2000), see *Hungary's Historical Legacies: Studies in Honor of Professor Steven Béla Várdy*, ed. Dennis P. Hupchick and R. William Weisberger (Boulder, Colorado and New York: East European Monographs/ Columbia University Press, 2000), pp. xiv-xli. This list was compiled by his wife and occasional co-author, Ágnes Huszár Várdy of Robert Morris University.

of ancient Hungarian-American connections, but it is probably these parts of the book that the non-academic Hungarian reader will find the most interesting.[14]

Várdy explores such themes, for example, as Captain John Smith's (of Jamestown fame) sometimes disputed Hungarian patent of nobility, and George Washington's rather doubtful claim to Hungarian ancestry.[15]

---

[14] A case in point is the very first "Hungarian" visitor to the New World whom Várdy introduces to his readers, the man called Tyrker. Apparently he accompanied the Viking explorer Leif Ericsson on his trip to the shores of North America around the year 1000 A. D. As Várdy points out, the ethnic identity of Tyrker has been the subject of much historiographical debate. Those that endorse the hypothesis that he was a Hungarian adventurer attached to the Vikings of Greenland list a number of factors that support their contention. One of these is the story, told in one of the sagas of the Greenlanders, that when Leif and his companions came upon the land they called Vinland, Tyrker left camp for some time, ate "grapes" he had found, returned drunk and babbled in a language incomprehensible to his companions. A drunkard speaking a strange tongue—not exactly irrefutable evidence of a Hungarian identity. Of course there are problems with this evidence, most of which Várdy admits. One is the fact that it is hard to get drunk from eating grapes, the other is the circumstance that Vinland was probably not named after the "grapes" the Vikings were supposed to have found there, but more likely the vines they harvested for use as fasteners. In any case, the sagas of the Greenlanders are fantastic stories, which were probably embellished by each generation that handed them down orally, until they were finally written down centuries after the events they described.

[15] Many people who claim a "Hungarian ancestry" in the English-speaking world are descendants — or putative descendants—of St. Margaret, the 11th century Queen of Scotland, whose mother, Agatha, was supposed to have been a Hungarian princess, possibly a "daughter of King St. Stephen". The myth of Agatha's Hungarian background has been debunked by Gabriel Ronay of the London *The Times* who has argued that she was the daughter of Liudolf, the Prince of West Freisland, and that she wasn't even born in Hungary but in Kiev, the capital of Kievan Rus. Gabriel Ronay, *The Lost King of England: The East European Adventures of Edward the Exile* (Wolfeboro, N.H.: Boydell Press, 1989). As a small child, Margaret did live in Hungary, with her parents, at the court of Andrew I (ruled 1046-1060). The "Hungarian royal ancestry" of Margaret has been endorsed by none other than Watson Kirkconnell (the late President of Acadia University) who identified her as "dau. of (Saint) STEPHEN, King of Hungary, and his wife GISELA." Watson Kirkconnell, *Medieval Mosaic: A Geneological Supplement...* (Wolfville, N.S.: by the author, 1976), 18 (also, 14).

More appropriate from the scholarly point of view is Várdy's discussion of the work, travels and various exploits of Hungarian priests, military officers, and travellers in the North America of the 18th and early 19th centuries.

Next, Várdy discusses the coming of the refugees of the abortive 1848-1849 Hungarian War of Independence against the House of Habsburg. The central theme in this connection is the visit of Louis Kossuth to the American Republic in 1851-52, as well as the attempts by some of Kossuth's followers to establish colonies of Hungarian 48-ers in America. As is well known, Kossuth's visit started as a triumph for the Hungarian statesman, but ended as a disaster as it contributed nothing to the dream of Hungary's liberation from Habsburg rule. The colonies Kossuth's followers established, fared hardly any better. Still, the American adventures of the Hungarian 48-ers, especially those who took part in the Civil War, make interesting reading.

After describing the fate of the 19th century Hungarian political emigration, Várdy turns to the story of the economic migrants of the last decades of the century. In fact, the next 250 pages of his book describe the origins and history of the immigrant ethnic communities that these migrants had created from the 1880s to the 1920s, when immigration of Hungarians to the US was reduced to a trickle by the so-called "quota laws" of the post-World War I period.

The scale of this "new immigration" dwarfed that which had existed before. By the turn of the century, the previously existing Hungarian-American community, was swamped by the newcomers. There was another change as well. The pre-1880 arrivals had been ex-officers, gentlemen adventurers, and people looking for commercial opportunities. The post-1880 newcomers were predominantly agricultural labourers. With their arrival, the American public's image of Hungarian immigrants would start to change to the detriment of the latter.

What drove people from Hungary, according to Várdy, was poverty in their homeland and the hopelessness associated with it. In this connection the reader might wish that Várdy had explained why mass emigration from Hungary took place exactly at a time when the country was making rapid progress toward modernization and industrialization. Perhaps emigration took place not so much because of poverty throughout the country, but because economic progress by-passed many regions and many social groups. Emigrants were "pushed" not so much by "country-wide poverty" but by dislocations caused by rapid economic change. Added to these economic factors, as Várdy observes, were the sociological and psychological ones, such as the existence of an outdated social order in Hungary which denigrated the labouring classes to the bottom ranks of the social ladder.

Among the "pull factors" that played a role in attracting Hungarian to the US was the American Republic's rapidly expanding economy as well as an image of the US in Hungary as a "land of plenty." For many newcomers, these inflated expectations were often quickly deflated. Still, in the new country they were more likely to be able to save some money and be treated with more respect than they had been used to in the old. Responding to the claim that the members of many of Hungary's nationalities left their land of birth because of the "oppression of the minorities," Várdy cites trends, as well as data on re-migration to minority-inhabited areas of Hungary, that suggest other, mainly economic reasons for the emigration of Hungary's non-Magyar ethnic groups.

The chapters describing the pre-1914 influx of Hungarians to the US are followed by the stories of the myriad economic, social and religious institutions that they established. Although it is possible to categorize these immigrant organizations along these lines, most of them served several purposes. This is especially the case with ethnic churches as they catered not only to the spiritual requirements of the immigrants but also to their social and cultural needs. The churches also reinforced the newcomers' ethnic identities, while at the same time they facilitated their adjustment to American society.

Next Várdy describes the political activities of the Hungarian American immigrants, as well as those of more recent "professional emigres" of the World War II years. He then devotes chapters to subjects such as Hungarian-American literature and theatre. There is even an account of the swindlers and con-men who inhabited America's Magyar colonies and preyed upon inexperienced and vulnerable fellow ethnics—especially, women. In the following chapters Várdy describes the post-World War II wave of immigrants and the impact of their arrival on Hungarian-American community life. This part of the book is mainly political history, although here too, we find chapters devoted to such cultural activities as publishing ventures, the arts and the fine arts, the ethnic theatre, folk-dancing, and so on. Among the concluding chapters we find one dealing with Hungarian-American reactions to the 1989 regime change in Hungary, and another devoted to outstanding Hungarian Americans. The book is supplemented by an extensive bibliography (pp. 651-715), a chronology of important events (pp. 716-729) as well as an English-language summary (pp. 733-765). There is also a detailed index.

Stephen Béla Várdy's *Magyarok az Újvilágban* is a work of synthesis in that it uses information gathered by previous students of Hungarian-American history, as well as his (and Ágnes Huszár Várdy's) pervious publications on the subject. The volume he produced is a massive storehouse of anecdotal and scholarly knowledge about the Hungarian-American past. Although it is extensively documented and provides a massive bibliography, it dispenses with some academic paraphernalia such as a theoretical framework and substantive conclusions. It might have been titled "Forty-four Essays on Hungarian Americans." It is probably for these reasons that Várdy calls his work an "irregular" or "eclectic" [*rendhagyó*] history.[16]

Julianna Puskás's Monograph

As has been mentioned in the first paragraph of this paper, the publication of Várdy's volume coincided with the appearance on the book market of another work on Hungarian-American history: Julianna Puskás, *Ties that Bind, Ties that Divide*. This is a different work from Várdy's. It is published in English and is intended for North American scholarly audiences. It comprises one of the volumes in the "Ellis Island series" of American immigration and ethnic histories, published by Holmes & Meier Company of New York.

Hungarians who came to the United States from the late nineteenth to the mid-twentieth centuries brought with them their customs, culture, traditions—along with their religious, linguistic, class, occupational and ideological ties. Their immigrant experiences reinforced some of these and weakened others. Still other bonds were developed by the newcomers after their arrival in America. These bonds gave rise to what we might call sub-ethnic identities which, according to Puskás, were particularly abundant and marked among the people who came to the US from Hungary. All in all, these ties served both to bind and to divide—

---

16 Várdy's book can be regarded as "eclectic," "irregular" or "unorthodox" also because it deals in great detail with aspects of Hungarian-American past that are known, and leaves out those that have not been recorded or researched by previous commentators, or by Várdy and/or his wife. This shortcoming, however, is hardly unusual: most histories of ethnic groups suffer from it. This is so because the evidence (most importantly, the old-timers who could tell the story) is no longer there for historians to reconstruct certain aspects of the past. Inevitably, any discussion of an eclectic book is also eclectic, in the case of my examination of it, perhaps even more so than scholarly conventions would warrant.

in a complex and ever changing manner—the communities that immigrants from Hungary established here. Puskás tells the story of their interplay in an effective and readable manner.

More than most other historians of the American immigrant experience, Puskás emphasizes the transitory nature of the stay of the pre-World War 1 arrivals. Their "emigration" from Hungary was a "temporary emergency solution to a problem at home."[17] Such migration resulted in a lot of cris-crossing of the Atlantic by "immigrants" until the war and the subsequent social, economic and political upheavals in East Central Europe put an end to such travelling.

Puskás is ready to go out on a limb and reinforce unexpected findings of other scholars who have examined patters of European emigration, or to debunk widely-held theories that are not supported by evidence. In the former category, Puskás emphasizes the fact that emigration from Hungary to the United States peaked in years when there was considerable prosperity and economic progress in Hungary. The explanation lies partly in the fact that advances in economic development caused dislocations for a large number of peoples—including craftsmen who suffered as a result of the expansion of factories.

One of the often voiced myths Puskás questions is the allegation that political discrimination was an important factor contributing to the decision by members of Hungary's ethnic minorities to emigrate.[18] She points out the fact that a great many Germans left Hungary before 1914, just at a time when in the Dual Monarchy of Austria-Hungary there was no political discrimination against German-speaking citizens. Another myth that Puskás dismisses is the one that holds that the old economic migrants discovered their ethnic nationalism after their arrival in America. This was, at most, partially true in the case of the early Hungarian immigrants and certainly does not hold water for later groups.

Staring with the 1920s came the transformation of America's immigrant Hungarian communities into ethnic ones. At first, immigrant culture flourished, but then came times of accelerated assimilation and inter-generational conflicts, all against the backdrop of the hardships caused by the Great Depression and World War II. The coming of new waves of Hungarian immigrants (with very different social and ideological backgrounds) after the war did little to retard the "waning of the Hungarian identity in the United States."[19]

---

[17] Julianna Puskás, *Ties that Bind, Ties that Divide,* p. 304.

[18] *Ibid.,* pp. 33f.

[19] *Ibid.,* p. 302.

In this connection it should be mentioned that, aside from comments such as this one, neither Puskás nor Várdy explored in detail the theme of the prospects of the Hungarian ethnic group in the U.S. Puskás emphasizes instead the great changes that America's Hungarian communities had undergone in the past—and are undergoing even in our days. She points out that we can hardly talk of an ethnic identity among the pre-1914 Hungarian immigrants to the US because these people were not members of an American ethnic community — they considered themselves sojourners. Only the post-war period saw the transformation of America's transient Hungarian communities into ethnic ones.

In two sentences devoted to the subject of the future of the Hungarian-American communities,[20] Várdy basically agrees with Puskás's conclusions. Actually, he had covered this subject in a separate study, in an article that appeared in Hungary. He was quite pessimistic. He felt that the preservation of Hungarian identity and culture in America succeeded for three generations at best—in the case of the refugees of the 1956 Hungarian revolution, and in the case of the more recent arrivals—not even that long.[21]

While we can celebrate the appearance in recent years of not one but two major syntheses of the history of America's Hungarian communities, we must not be under the impression that the task of uncovering the Hungarian-American past has been accomplished. While both of these books are the results of monumental labour, they both have their shortcomings. Scholars will probably bemoan the fact that Várdy is not more analytical, that he does not try to develop overarching themes, or at least, to offer substantial conclusions—a chapter instead of two paragraphs.

Admittedly, Puskás's *Ties that Bind* tries to do all this. It is a comprehensive, scholarly study, filled with refreshing arguments. It offers an all-encompassing, original theme. It is most authoritative in discussing the pre-1920s immigration of Hungarians to the United States and the evolution of their communities. Alas, the post-1940 decades and the tumultuous world of wartime and post-war emigre politics are not covered by it in the same knowledgeable manner. In fact Puskás admits that some aspects of this age await examination by historians in the future.

---

[20] Várdy, *Magyarok az Újviágban*, p. 632.

[21] Béla Várdy, "A magyar öntudat és a magyar megmaradás kérdése" [The question of Hungarian identity and survival], *Nyelvünk és Kultúránk*, 110 (April–June, 2000): 74–76.

204   *Hungarians: from Ancient Times to 1956*

Indeed, much new research will have to be done before a truly comprehensive and scholarly synthesis of the history of America's Hungarian communities can be written. Above all, more specialized studies will have to be undertaken, ones based on painstaking research in archival and/or oral history sources, the kind of work that had been presented in the past in Puskás's earlier books, and in the works of Fejős and Vassady to name the most obvious.

Appendix

A Bibliography of Nándor Dreisziger's Publications

A. Papers published in journals (also, chapters in books, on-line articles):

"New Twist to an Old Riddle: The Bombing of Kassa (Kosice), June 26, 1941," *Journal of Modern History*, 44, 2 (June 1972): 232-42.

"The Great Lakes in United States-Canadian Relations: The First Stock-Taking," *Inland Seas, The Quarterly Journal of the Great Lakes Historical Society*, 28, 4 (Winter 1972): 259-71.

"The Campaign to Save Niagara Falls and the Settlement of United States-Canadian Differences, 1906-1911," *New York History*, 45, 4 (Oct. 1974): 437-58.

"Count Istvan Bethlen's Secret Plan for the Restoration of the Empire of Transylvania," *East European Quarterly*, 8, 4 (Winter 1974): 413-23.

"The Canadian-American Irrigation Frontier Revisited: The International Origins of Irrigation in Southern Alberta, 1985-1909," Canadian Historical Association *Historical Papers*, (1975): 211-29.

"A Surveyor Advises the Government: J. S. Dennis Jr., and Canadian-American Negotiations, 1895-1910," *Canadian Surveyor*, 29, 1 (Mar 1975): 141-44.

"Civil-Military Relations in Nazi Germany's Shadow: The Case of Hungary, 1939-1941," in *Swords and Covenants: Essays in Honour of the Centennial of the Royal Military College of Canada*, ed. Adrian Preston and Peter Dennis (London: Croom Helm, 1976): 216-47.

"The Hungarian General Staff and Diplomacy, 1939-1941," in *Proceedings of the First Banff Conference on Central and East European Studies*, ed. T.M.S. Priestly (Edmonton, 1977): 247-67.

"Watson Kirkconnell: Translator of Hungarian Poetry and Friend of Hungarian Canadians," in *Hungarian Poetry and the English-Speaking World: A Tribute to Watson Kirkconnell*, ed. N. F. Dreisziger (Ottawa, 1977): 117-43.

"Official Nationalism in Hungary Since 1964," commentary in *Nationalism in the USSR and Eastern Europe in the Era of Brezhnev and Kosygin*, ed. G.W. Simmonds, (Detroit: University of Detroit Press, 1977): 441-43.

"Contradictory Evidence Concerning Hungary's Declaration of War on the USSR in June, 1941," *Canadian Slavonic Papers*, 19, 4 (Dec. 1977): 480-88.

"Watson Kirkconnell and the Cultural Credibility Gap Between Immigrants and the Native-Born in Canada," in *Ethnic Canadians: Culture and Education*, ed. M.L. Kovacs (Regina, 1978): 87-96.

"The Role of War Planning in Canadian-American Relations, 1867-1939," a review article in *The Canadian Review of American Studies*, 10, 3 (Winter 1979): 100-06.

"Wrangling Over the St. Mary and the Milk," *Alberta History*, 19, 2 (Spring 1980): 6-15.

"In Search of a Hungarian-Canadian Lobby: 1927-1951," *Canadian Ethnic Studies*, 12, 3 (Fall 1980): 81-96.

"Aspects of Hungarian Settlement in Central Canada," in *Hungarian-Canadian Perspectives: Selected Papers*, ed. M.L. Kovacs (Ottawa: 1980): 121-21.

"National Hungarian-Canadian Organizations," in *Hungarians in Ontario*, ed. Susan Papp (Toronto: Multicultural History Society, 1980): 50-54.

"Immigrant Lives and Lifestyles in Canada, 1924-1939," *Hungarian Studies Review*, 8, 1 (Spring 1981): 61-83.

"Dreams and Disappointments," in *The International Joint Commission Seventy Years On*, ed. Robert Spencer, *et al.* (Toronto: Centre for International Studies, 1981): 8-23.

"Hungarian History in North American Perspective," review article in the *Historical Journal*, 25, 3 (1982): 765-73.

"The Critical Visitor: Alexander Boloni Farkas' Tour of Canada in 1931," *Quarterly of Canadian Studies*, 5, 3 and 4 (1982): 147-52.

"The Kassa Bombing: The Riddle of Adam Krudy," in *Hungary and the Second World War*, ed. N.F. Dreisziger (Toronto: 1983): 79-98.

"Central European Federalism in the Thought of Oszkar Jaszi and His Successors," in *Society in Change: Studies in Honor of Béla K. Kiraly*, ed. S. B. Vardy and A. H. Vardy (Boulder, CO: East Eur. Monographs, 1983): 539-56.

"International Water Management in Canadian-American Relations, 1894-1907," *Canadian Water Resources Journal*, 8, 3 (Summer 1983): 58-76.

"The Impact of the Revolution on Hungarians Abroad," in *The First War Between Socialist States*, ed. B. K. Kiraly, *et al.* (New York: Brooklyn College Press, 1984): 411-425.

"Minorities and Minority Politics in Hungary, 1935-1975", an introductory essay, *Hungarian Studies Review*, 11, 1 (Spring 1984): 5-12.

"The Hungarian Revolution of 1956: The Legacy of the Refugees," *Nationalities Papers, the journal of the Association for the Study of the Nationalities of the USSR and Eastern Europe*, 13, 2 (Fall 1985): 198-208.

"Hungarians in the Canadian West," *Prairie Forum, the Journal of the Canadian Plains Research Center*, 10, 2 (Fall 1985): 435-53.

"Bering Sea Dispute," *Canadian Encyclopedia* (Edmonton: Hurtig, 1985), Vol. I, p. 64. "Boundary Waters Treaty," *ibid.*, p. 209. "Cadets," (co-author), *ibid.*, p. 254. "Hungarians," *ibid.*, Vol. II: 848-49. "International Joint

Commission," *ibid.*, Vol. II, p. 892. "Lend-Lease," *ibid.*, Vol. II, p. 998.

"The Dimensions of Total War in East Central Europe, 1914-18," in *East Central European Society in World War I*, ed. B. K. Kiraly *et al.* (Boulder & Highland Lakes: Social Science Monographs, Columbia U. P., 1985): 1-23.

"Peoples of Canada: Hungarians in Canada," *Horizon Canada,* Vol. 10, no. 110: 2630-35.

"Immigration and Re-Migration: The Changing Urban-Rural Distribution of Hungarian Canadians, 1986-1986," in *The Tree of Life: Essays Honouring a Hungarian-Canadian Centenary,* ed. M. L. Kovacs and N. F. Dreisziger (Toronto, 1986): 20-41.

"The 'Justice for Hungary' Ocean Flight: The Trianon Syndrome in Immigrant Hungarian Society," in *Triumph in Adversity: Studies in Hungarian Civilization,* ed. S. B. Vardy (Boulder, Co.: East Eur. Monographs, 1988): 573-89.

"The Rise of a Bureaucracy for Multiculturalism: The Origins of the Nationalities Branch, 1939-41," in *On Guard for Thee: War, Ethnicity, and the Canadian State, 1939-1945*, ed. Norman Hillmer *et al.* (Ottawa, 1988): 1-29.

"Mission Impossible: Secret Plans for a Hungarian Government-in-Exile in Canada During World War II," *Canadian Slavonic Papers,* 30, 2 (June 1988): 245-62.

"Canadian Studies on Hungarian Canadians," review article in the *Journal of Canadian Studies,* 24, 2 (summer 1989): 153-56.

"'Bridges to the West': The Horthy Regime's Reinsurance Policies in 1941," *War and Society*, 7, 1 (May 1989): 1-23.

"Hungarian Minorities in East Central Europe: An Introduction," with Andrew Ludanyi, in *Forgotten Minorities: The Hungarians of East Central Europe,* ed. N. F. Dreisziger and A. Ludanyi (Toronto, 1989): 5-18.

"L'Evoluzione dello *Status* degli italiani 'stranieri nemici' in Canada durante la Seconda Guerra Mondiale" [The Evolving Status of Italian 'Enemy aliens' in Canada during World War II] in *Il Canada e la Guerra dei Trent'anni* ed. Luigi Bruti Liberati (Milan, Guerini Studio, 1989): 229-39.

"Polyethnicity and Armed Forces: An Introduction," with Richard A. Preston, in *Ethnic Armies: Polyethnic Armed Forces from the Time of the Habsburgs to the Age of the Superpowers,* ed. N. F. Dreisziger (Waterloo: Wilfrid Laurier University Press, 1990): 1-20.

"Immigrant Fortunes and Misfortunes in Canada in the 1920s," a documentary article, *Hungarian Studies Review,* 17, 1 (Spring 1990): 29-59.

"Tracy Philipps and the Achievement of Ukrainian-Canadian Unity," *Canada's Ukrainians: Negotiating an Identity,* ed. L. Luciuk and S. Hryniuk (Toronto: U. of Toronto Press, 1991): 326-41 and 477-83.

Oscar Jaszi and the Hungarian Problem: Activities and Writings during World

War II," in *Oscar Jaszi: Visionary, Reformer and Political Activist*, ed. N.F. Dreisziger and A. Ludanyi (Toronto and Budapest, 1991): 59-79.

"The Evolution of Oscar Jaszi's Political Ideas during the First World War," in *Király Béla emlékkönyv* [Bela Kiraly *Festschrift*], ed. Paul Jonas, Peter Pastor, and Peter P. Toth (Budapest, 1992): 1159-67.

"Sub-ethnic Identities: Religion, Class, Ideology, etc. as Centrifugal Forces in Hungarian-Canadian Society," *Hungarian Studies* (Budapest), 7, 1-2 (1992): 123-138.

"Between Nationalism and Internationalism: Oscar Jaszi's Path to Danubian Federalism, 1905-1918." *Canadian Review of Studies in Nationalism*, 19, 1-2 (1993): 19-29.

"The 1956 Hungarian Student Movement in Exile," introd. to a documentary article, *Hungarian Studies Review*, 20, 1-2 (1993): 103-116.

"The Refugee Experience in Canada and the Evolution of the Hungarian-Canadian Community," in *Breaking Ground: The 1956 Hungarian Refugee Movement to Canada*, ed. Robert H. Keyserlingk, (North York, Ont.: York Lane Press, York University, 1993): 65-86.

"Canada seen through Hungarian Eyes in 1831," *Krónika* (Toronto) 20, 3 (May-June 1994): 18-19.

"Emigre Artists and Wartime Politics, 1939-45," in *Hungarian Artists in the Americas*, Oliver Botar, ed. (Budapest and Toronto: HSR, 1994): 43-75.

"Az atlanti demokraciák és a 'Szabad Magyarországért' mozgalmak a II. világháború alatt" [The Atlantic Democracies and the Movements for a "Free Hungary" during World War II], in *Magyarország és a nagyhatalmak a 20. században*, ed. Ignác Romsics (Budapest: Teleki László Alapítvány, 1995): 149-62.

"A Dove? A Hawk? Perhaps a Sparrow: Bárdossy Defends his Wartime Record before the Americans, July 1945," in *Hungary Fifty Years Ago*, ed. N. F. Dreisziger (Toronto and Budapest, 1995): 71-90.

"The Atlantic Democracies and the Movements for a "Free Hungary" during World War II," in *20th Century Hungary and the Great Powers*, ed. Ignác Romsics (Boulder, Colorado: Social Science Monographs, 1995): 185-205.

"Hungary in 1945: An Introduction," in *Hungary Fifty Years Ago* (Toronto and Budapest: HSR, 1995): 5-12. Based on comments made at a session, entitled "Hungary in 1945 Reconsidered," given at the annual meeting of the American Historical Association, Chicago, January, 1995.

"John F. Montgomery and the Image of Hungarians in Wartime North America," in *Tárogató: the Journal of the Hungarian Cultural Society of Vancouver*, 23, 5 (May 1996): 39-40.

"Friends of Hungary in the English-Speaking World," in *Visszatekintés–Looking Back–Regard sur le passé*, ed. E. Puskas-Balogh (Montreal: Hungarian Literary Association, 1996): 157-65.

"Prime Minister László Bárdossy was Executed 50 Years Age as a 'War Criminal'," in *Tárogató*, 23, 11 (November 1996): 56-57.

"Miklós Horthy and the Second World War: Some Historiographical Perspectives," in *Regent Miklós Horthy, István Horthy and the Second World War* (Toronto and Budapest: special volume of the *Hungarian Studies Review*, 23, 1-2, 1996): 5-16.

"Edmund Veesenmayer on Horthy and Hungary: An American Intelligence Report," in *Regent Miklós Horthy, István Horthy and the Second World War*, (Toronto and Budapest, 1996): 43-66.

"Mutual Images and Stereotypes: The United States and Hungary," a review article in *Hungarian Studies Review*, 23, 2 (fall, 1996): 109-116.

"7 December 1941: A Turning Point in Canadian Wartime Policy Toward Enemy Ethnic Groups?" *Journal of Canadian Studies*, 32, 1 (Spring 1997): 93-111.

"The Tragic Story of Prime Minister (General) Géza Lakatos," in *Habsburg*, an Electronic Bulletin, Aug. 1997.

"Miklós Horthy in North American Perspectives," *Tárogató*, 24, 12 (Dec. 1997): 46-47.

"Hungary and the Second World War," an introduction to *Hungary in the Age of Total War, 1938-1948*, ed. N. F. Dreisziger, (New York: East European Monographs/Columbia University Press, 1998): 3-24; "Hungary Enters the War: March-December, 1941," *ibid.*: 61-72; "Miklós Horthy and World War II: New Historiographical Perspectives," *ibid.*: 239-252; "Oscar Jaszi: Activities and Writings during World War II," *ibid.*: 267-286; "Was László Bárdossy a War Criminal? Further Reflections," *ibid.*: 311-320.

"Jews and Gentiles, Soldiers and Civilians: Hungary during World War II," in *Habsburg*, an Electronic Bulletin, 1998.

"Theodore Roosevelt, Albert Apponyi, and the Fate of Hungary after World War I," *Tárogató*, 25, 12 (Dec. 1998), p. 39. Also: "Some Thoughts on István Horthy's Tragic Death in 1942," *ibid.*, 26, 3 (March 1999): 31-32. "Francis S. Wagner, 1911-1999," *ibid.*, 26, 10 (Oct 1999), p. 37 (an obituary).

"Transylvania in the Grips of Hitler," *Carpathian Observer* 20, 1 (Fall, 1999): 1-3.

"I Primi 25 Anni della Hungarian Studies Review," in *Rivista di Studi Ungheresi* (Rome), 24 (1999): 121-145 (including an index).

"Péter Gosztonyi, 1931-1999: A Prolific Historian," *Kaleidoscope* (Toronto), 2, 11-12 (Nov.-Dec. 1999): 12-14.

"The Hungarian Studies Review," *Hungarian Studies Newsletter* (New Brunswick, N.J.), nos. 55-57 (1999): 10-11. A similar report appeared in Hungarian: "A *Hungarian Studies Review* első negyed évszázada" [The First Quarter Century of the *Hungarian Studies Review*], in *Itt-Ott* (the journal of the Hungarian community of friends, USA), 32, 2 (1999), p. 48.

"Francis S. Wagner (1911-1999) and Peter Gostony (1931-1999): Obituaries," *Hungarian Studies Review* 26, 1-2 (1999): 171-174.

"The Hungarians," the *Encyclopedia of Canadian Ethnic Groups* (Toronto: University of Toronto Press, 1999): 660-74.

"The Year 2000 and the End of History: Especially for Hungarians," in *Tárogató*, 26, 12 (December 1999): 45-48. An abbreviated version of this appeared under the title "The Decline of Hungarian Historical Studies in Canada," *News in Hungarian Studies* (the newsletter of the Hungarian Studies Assoc. of Canada), no. 53 (Dec. 2000): 6-7.

"Hungarians in Brazil," *Kaleidoscope* 2, 12 (Dec. 1999); continued in 3, 1 (Jan. 2000): 13-15

"Bárdossy, László (1890-1946)," and several other entries, in the *Encyclopedia of Eastern Europe,* ed. Richard Frucht (New York and London: Garland Publishing, 2000): 56, 237, etc.

"Time of Troubles for the Multicultural History Society of Ontario," in the bulletin of the Finno-Ugric Studies Assoc. of Canada, 2000.

"The Great Powers and the 1956 Revolution in Hungary," in *Tárogató*, 27, 4 (April 2000): 43-44. (A review article)."Social Progress and Ethnic Solidarity: Ambrosius Czakó's *Tárogató,*" *ibid.*, 27, 9 (Sept. 2000): 55-56.

"Jövőépítés Kanadában, az első magyar bevándorlastól 1948-ig," [Building a future in Canada from the time of the first Hungarian immigration to Canada to 1948], in *Itt-Ott [Here and there,* the journal of the Hungarian Community of Friends, USA], 33, (2000): 21-23.

"Stalin's Wartime Plans for Transylvania, 1939-1945," in *Hungary's Historical Legacies: Studies in Honor of Professor Steven Béla Várdy,* ed. Dennis P. Hupchick and R. William Weisberger (Boulder and New York: East European Monographs/Columbia University Press, 2000): 146-54.

"Rose-gardens on Ice-floes: A Century of the Hungarian Diaspora in Canada," *Hungarian Journal of English and American Studies*, 6, 2 (Fall, 2000): 239-58.

"How French Troops Helped to Save Hungary from the Turks in 1664," in *Tárogató. the Journal of the Hungarian Cultural Society of Vancouver*, 28, 5 (May 2001): 45-46. "How French Troops Saved Canada from the Iroquois in 1665-66," *ibid.*, 28, 8 (Aug. 2001): 47-49.

"Towards a History of the Hungarian Ethnic Group of the United States," an online paper posted on the website of the Hungarian American Resource Center: http://www.hungarianamerica.com/harc/ (2001).

"Thousand Years of Hungarian Survival," an introduction to *Hungary, 1001-2001: A Millennial Retrospection*, the selected proceedings of a University of Toronto conference on "1000 Years of Hungarian History" (Budapest and Toronto, 2001): 1-72; "Hungarian Survival—in Hungary and beyond the Borders," a postscript to the same volume: 211-39.

"From Ethnic Cleansing to Apologies: The Canadian Experience in Dealing with Minorities in Wartime," in *Canadian Military History since the 17th Century*, ed. Yves Tremblay (Ottawa, 2001): 533-542.

"Rallying Canada's Immigrants behind the War Effort, 1939-1945," in *Forging a Nation: Perspectives on the Canadian Military Experience*, ed. Bernd Horn (St. Catherines, ON: Vanvell, 2002): 177-94..

"Raimondo Montecuccoli, Prince" (Field-Marshall & military theorist, 1611-80); "Louis-Joseph Montcalm, Marquis de (1712-1759);" "Office of Strate gic Services (OSS)," entries in *Ground Warfare,* a volume in the new *ABC-Clio Encyclopedia of World Military History* (Santa Barbara, CA: ABC-CLIO, 2002): 586-88 and 643-44.

"The Long Shadow of Trianon: Hungarian Alliance Policies during World War II," *Hungarian Studies* (Budapest), 17, 1 (2003): 33-56.

"The United States and Hungary, Hungary and the United States," a preface to the volume *The United States and Hungary in the Twentieth Century* (Toronto and Budapest: HSR, 2003): v-x; "Keeping an Eye on Hungarians in Wartime America: The Spencer Taggart Memorandum (Part 1)," a documentary article in the above volume: 63-112.

"Redrawing the Ethnic Map in North America: The Experience of France, Britain and Canada, 1536-1946," in *Ethnic Cleansing in Twentieth-Century Europe* ed. Steven Béla Várdy and T. Hunt Tooley (New York: East European Monographs/Columbia University Press, 2003): 45-62.

"From Heroes to Enemies: Finns in Canada, 1937-1947," *Scandinavian-Canadian Studies* 14 (2002-03): 142-44. A Review article.

"The Erosion of the Hungarian Linguistic Presence in Canada," in the *Yearbook of the Hungarian Community of Friends*, ed. Andrew Ludanyi (Portland, OR, 2004): 58-62.

"The Quest for Spiritual Fulfilment among Immigrants: The Rise of Organized Religious Life in Pioneer Hungarian-Canadian Communities, 1885-1939," *Magyar Egyháztörténeti Vázlatok–Essays in Church History in Hungary*, 16, 3-4 (fall-winter 2005): 95-124.

"Towards a History of the Hungarian Communities of America," *Hungarian Studies Review*, 32, 1 (2005): 97-114.

"Spying on 'Mr. Bartok' in Wartime America," *Hungarian Quarterly*, 46, 3 (Autumn, 2005): 116-24.

"A Hungarian Liberal in American Exile: The Life of Oscar Jaszi," *Hungarian Studies Review*, 32, 2 (2005): 127-36. A review article.

"A Hungarian Patriot in American Exile: Béla Bartók and Émigré Politics," *Journal of the Royal Musical Association* (Oxford University Press), 130, 2 (Dec. 2005): 283-301.

"Oscar Jászi: Prophet and Danubian Federalist," *Hungarian Quarterly* (Budapest), 47, 1 (Spring, 2006): 159-63. A review article.

B. Books, edited volumes (including special volumes of journals):

Hungary's Way to World War II (Toronto: Helicon, 1968), 240 pages. Paperback edition in the "Problems Behind the Iron Curtain" series, (Astor Park, Fa.: Danubian Press, 1968). Reviewed in the *American Historical Review* (Dec. 1969), p. 545.

The Hungarian Revolution Twenty Years After: Selected Papers and Perspectives (Ottawa: Hungarian Readers' Service, 1976), 144 pages. An edited volume, reviewed in American, British and West German journals.

Mobilization for Total War: The Canadian, American and British Experience, 1914-1945 (Waterloo, Ont.: Wilfrid Laurier University Press, 1981), xvi + 115 pages. (Proceedings of the 1980 RMC Military History Symposium). Reviewed in Canadian, American and British journals.

Hungarian Cultural Presence in North America, co-edited with George Bisztray (Toronto: *Hungarian Studies Review,* 1981), 2 parts, 208 pages.

Struggle and Hope: The Hungarian-Canadian Experience (Toronto: McClelland and Stewart, 1982), vii, 247 pages. With introductory chapters by B. Kovrig, P. Body and M.L. Kovacs. In the *History of Canada's People's* series. Reviewed in the *Canadian Historical Review* (Dec. 1983): 446-50, and other (Canadian, Australian and Hungarian) journals.

Lutte et espoir: L'expérience des Canadiens hongrois (Ottawa: Multicultur alism Canada, 1982), x + 264 pages. (A French edition of the above book.)

Hungary and the Second World War, editor and contributor (Toronto: *HSR,* 1983), 196 pages.

Minorities and Minority Politics in Hungary, editor (Toronto: *HSR,* 1984), 64 pages.

The First War Between Socialist States: The Hungarian Revolution of 1956 and its Impact (New York: Social Science Monographs & Brooklyn College Press, 1984), 608 pages. Co-edited with Bela K. Kiraly and B. Lotze. Distributed by Columbia University Press.

The Hungarian Experience in Ontario. Author, a special issue of *HSR,* 12, 2 (Fall, 1985), 88 pages.

East Central European Society in World War I, (New York: Social Science Monographs, 1986). Co-edited with B.K. Kiraly. 628 pages. Distributed by Columbia University Press.

The Tree of Life: Essays Honouring a Hungarian-Canadian Centenary (Toronto: Hungarian Studies Review, 1986), co-edited with M.L. Kovacs. A special issue of *HSR,* 13, 2 (Fall, 1986), 91 pages.

Forgotten Minorities: The Hungarians of East Central Europe, co-edited with A. Ludanyi (Toronto: *HSR,* 1989). The Proceedings of a 1986 conference held at Oberlin College, 152 pages.

Ethnic Armies: Polyethnic Armed Forces From the Time of the Habsburgs To the Age of the Superpowers (Waterloo, ON: Wilfrid Laurier U. P., 1990), vi + 202 pages. Proceedings of an R.M.C. Military History Symposium.

Oscar Jaszi: Visionary, Reformer, Political Activist, co-editor and contributor (Toronto and Budapest: *HSR*, 1991), 104 pages.

Hungary Fifty Years Ago, editor and contributor (Toronto and Budapest: *HSR*, 1995), 127 pages.

Regent Miklós Horthy, István Horthy and the Second World War, editor and contributor (Toronto and Budapest: *HSR*, 1996), 127 pages.

Hungary in the Age of Total War 1938-1948 (Bradenton: East European Monographs, distr.: Columbia U. Press, 1999), editor and contributor. 384 pages.

The Wartime Origins of Ethnic Tolerance in Canada (Toronto: Robert F. Harney Program in Ethnic, Immigration and Pluralism Studies, University of Toronto, 1999) Lectures and Papers in Ethnicity no. 29; ii + 25 pages.

Hungary, 1001-2001: A Millennial Retrospection, the selected proceedings of a U. of Toronto conference on "1000 Years of Hungarian History," a special volume of the *Hungarian Studies Review*, 28, 1-2 (2001), vi + 242 pages.

The United States and Hungary in the Twentieth Century (Part I), a special vol. of the *Hungarian Studies Review*, 30, 1-2 (2003), viii + 155 pages.

The United States and Hungary in the Twentieth Century (Part II), a special vol. of the *Hungarian Studies Review*, 32, 1-2 (2005), vi + 148 pages.

The Image of Hungary and Hungarians a special vol. of the *Hungarian Studies Review*, 33, 1-2 (2006), v + 206 pages.

C. Papers delivered at meetings of Learned Societies:

Canadian Historical Association, 1972, 1975; American Historical Assoc., 1995; Atlantic Canada Studies Conference, 1976; Central and East European Studies Assoc. of Canada, 1977, etc.; The Historical Society of Alberta, 1979; Canadian Ethnic Studies Assoc., 1979, 1985 and 1989; Hungarian Studies Assoc. of Canada, since the 1980s; Hungarian-American Educator's Assoc., 1988, 1993, 1999 and 2006; The American Association for the Advancement of Slavic Studies, 1982, 1988, 1992, 1996, 1999 and 2005; The Canadian Committee for the Study of World War II, 1986; World Congress for Soviet and East European Studies, 1990; The Finno-Ugric Studies Assoc. of Canada, 1995; Canadian Assoc. of Slavists, 2002; Canadian University Teachers of Music Society, 2002; etc.

D. Lectures given at universities or university-sponsored conferences:

University of Toronto (several times from 1974 to 2006); Bishop's University, 1974, 1999; Queen's University, 1975, 1986; Carleton University, 1975; University of Detroit, 1975; University of Winnipeg, 1975; University of New

Brunswick, 1976; University of Regina, 1976; New College of the U. of South Florida, (several times in the 1980s and 1990s); Brooklyn College of the City U. of New York, 1981; Trent U., 1982; Royal Roads Military College, 1984; University of Victoria, 1984; Dawson College (Montreal) 1986; York University (Toronto), 1986; University of Calgary, 1989; University of Ottawa, 1990, 2006; University of Waterloo, 1991; Siena College, 1991; University of Maryland, 1993; Indiana University, 1994, 2003, 2006; John Carroll University, 1999; Dusquesne University, 2000; Concordia University, 2003; College of Charleston, 2004.

E. Papers given at international conferences:

Conference on War and Society in East Central Europe, 1914-19; participant and co-editor of the meeting's proceedings. Rockefeller Conference Center, Bellagio, Italy, 1983. Conference on the Hungarian diaspora, Budapest, Hungary, 1984. Conference on Canada and Italy in Two World Wars. Sponsored by Italy's Center for the Study of Canada, and its Center for Historical-Military Studies. University of Pisa, Italy. February, 1988. World Congress of Soviet and East European Studies, Harrogate, England, 1990. Etc.

F. Book reviews published in the following journals:

Canadian Historical Review, Canadian Journal of History, The Historian, Slavic Review, Agricultural History, The (Cambridge) Historical Journal, Canadian Ethnic Studies, Canadian Slavonic Papers, Humanities Association Review, Queen's Quarterly, Canadian-American Slavic Studies, Szivárvány (Chicago), *Journal of American History, Social History, Canadian Review of American Studies, Journal of Canadian Studies, Hungarian Studies Review, Hungarian Studies* (Budapest), *Austrian History Yearbook, International History Review, Holocaust and Genocide Studies, Hungarian Studies Newsletter, Scandinavian-Canadian Studies, Canadian Review of Studies in Nationalism, Eurasian Studies Yearbook* (formerly the *Ural-Alaische Yahrbuch*), *The Hungarian Quarterly*, etc.

G. Research grants received:

Canada Council Leave Fellowship 1977-78. Social Science and Humanities Research Council of Canada Leave Fellowship, 1984-85. A research and publication grant from the Ministry of Culture and Citizenship of Ontario. Senior Fellowship in Canadian Ethnic Studies 1986-87 (the first such grant awarded by the Secretary of State for Multiculturalism of Canada). Social Sciences and Humanities Research Council of Canada Research Grant 1990-91. Social Sciences and Humanities Research Council of Canada Research Grant (multi-year) 1992-1995. Several one-year and multi-year research grants from the Department of National Defence of Canada and R.M.C.

MARQUIS

Marquis Book Printing Inc.

Québec, Canada

2007